DIALOGUES ON MORALITY AND RELIGION

JAKOB FRIEDRICH FRIES

Dialogues on Morality and Religion

Edited by D. Z. Phillips
Translated by David Walford
Introduction by Rush Rhees

BARNES & NOBLE BOOKS
TOTOWA, NEW JERSEY

BJ
1107
.F74
1982

English translation © Basil Blackwell 1982

Selections from *Julius und Evagoras*, second edition, 1822
(2 volumes, C. F. Winter, Heidelberg)

English translation first published in USA 1982 by
Barnes & Noble Books
81 Adams Drive
Totowa, New Jersey 07512

All rights reserved. No part of this publication may be reproduced, stored in a retrieval system, or transmitted, in any form or by any means, electronic, mechanical, photocopying, recording or otherwise, without the prior permission of the publisher.

Library of Congress Cataloging in Publication Data

Fries, Jakob Friedrich, 1775-1843.
  Dialogues on morality and religion.

  (Values and philosophical inquiry)
  Includes index.
  1. Ethics.   2. Religion   3. Philosophy.   I. Phillips, D. Z. (Dewi Zephaniah)   II. Title.   III. Series.
  BJ1107.F74 1982   100   82-13787
  ISBN 0-389-20326-2

Printed in Great Britain

Contents

	Preface *by D. Z. Phillips*	vii
	Introduction *by Rush Rhees*	ix
	Translator's Note	xv
I	Peace of Soul	2
II	Beauty of Soul	14
III	Moral Development of the Spirit	33
IV	Julius and Evagoras	46
V	Julius to Eugene	74
VI	Providence	83
VII	Religious Practice	98
VIII	Eternal Truth	125
IX	Knowing and Knowledge	157
X	Of Faith and the World of the Good and Beautiful	178
XI	Man's Sense of Guilt	198
XII	Intuitive Awareness	209
XIII	Beauty	220
	Index	245

Preface

The importance of the work of J.F. Fries for philosophy of religion was first drawn to my attention by Rush Rhees who has kindly provided an Introduction to the present work. The work chosen is the second edition of *Julius und Evagoras* which Fries published in 1822. The title would not have been informative to the present day reader and so I decided to re-name it *Dialogues on Morality and Religion*. The new title reflects the main emphases in those sections of the original which have been translated by David Walford. Initially it was the whole work that was translated, but on reflection it became obvious that the philosophical public would be served best by a concentration on specifically philosophical material. This decision was not made lightly, since it meant cutting out almost half of the original text. Having made the cuts, I consulted Rush Rhees and David Walford. Their judgement concurred with mine, more or less, but the responsibility for the cuts made remains mine alone.

I have no doubt that the *Dialogues* repay serious study by the student of the philosophy of religion, having a major contribution to make to issues concerning relations between morality and religion and, more importantly, to questions concerning how ideas of the reality and will of God enter human life. In these contexts Fries raises questions which should be central in the philosophy of religion.

I am extremely pleased to have Fries' work in the series. I am glad our publishers, Basil Blackwell, were interested in publishing the work. They, along with myself, are glad to have this opportunity of acknowledging with gratitude the generous help and support of the Society for the Furtherance of the Critical Philosophy in the publication of this work.

D.Z. PHILLIPS

Introduction

These dialogues are the central parts of what Fries called "a philosophical novel", which he published first at the end of 1813, with the title *Julius und Evagoras, ein philosophischer Roman*. He was professor of philosophy at Heidelberg at the time, and he had already published what is perhaps his best known book, *Wissen, Glaube und Ahndung*, a short exposition of his philosophical position, and his two most important works, *Neue Kritik der Vernunft*, in 1807, and *System der Logik* in 1811.

He had begun sketching various scenes for the 'novel' in 1811, and published it anonymously. He hoped it would be read by students in the various movements for a new society. These were the offspring partly of ideas which came from the French Revolution and reactions to them in the "Wars of Liberation", but the excitement had increased especially with the news of Napoleon's defeat in Russia. (See Bousset's Introduction to his edition of *Julius und Evagoras* in 1910.) Fries was sympathetic with the hopes. But he was depressed because the student politicians gave so little thought to the phrases and slogans on which they acted. In a letter he wrote at the time (quoted in Henke's biography of Fries, and quoted again in the introduction by Lutz Geldsetzer and Gert König to their new edition of Fries's *Handbuch der praktischen Philosophie*, 1970) Fries remarked,

I could not understand a general tone of peevishness and dissatisfaction towards whatever is already established, among these politicians, who were confident they could bring in better times very quickly. This tone spread in the way they talked of how bad it was and how it must be changed for something better, without being able to say what it was about it that was so bad and in what way that which ought to be would be better.

Evidently the students read the book, and in a year or two it was out of print.

Consideration of questions like those — *"wherein* is it so bad?", "wherein would that be better?" — would lead to the central questions of philosophy. To discussions which surround a question regarding the point or 'why?' of a human being's existence, and the different question of the point or 'why?' of the world (the existence of anything at all): showing that it lies deep in the soul or character of a human being to ask this of the world, but that if he tries to answer he has misunderstood. This would probably start with discussions of morality and of religion. Fries wanted to show, I suppose, that the questions which come up may be discussed in ordinary language, with objections and questions which anyone might ask who had not spent time on philosophy. — This must have been one of his reasons for writing the book as a 'novel'.

Those parts of the 'novel' which tell what the characters do in the Wars of Liberation may have helped to show how these philosophical questions had a place in that fighting. But they do not help much now, and the editor has left them out. He has kept the dialogues in philosophy. Fries wrote the book so that these might be read, I imagine. — Roughly half were added in a second edition, which he published in 1822.

Fries had lost his professorship then. He had become more involved in the student movements. In 1817 the National Association of Students (*die deutsche Burschenschaft*) met in Wartburg to celebrate the anniversary of Luther's nailing his theses to the door, and there were scenes with the police as the conference ended. Fries attended the conference and made a short speech, but he was not in the scenes which followed. He wrote in defence of the students against the public outcry. Conflicts of students and police went on in other cities, and the police accused Fries. He was deprived of his professorship in 1820. — When he published the second edition of *Julius und Evagoras* he omitted the subtitle "Or the New Republic" which the first edition had had; and the publication was not meant primarily to influence the thinking of political movements. It was an account in ordinary language of his views on the principal questions of philosophy.

In 1824 he was made professor of mathematics and physics. He published in these fields, but his principal work was still in philosophy.

Fries always called himself a pupil of Kant in philosophy. In moral philosophy and in the philosophy of religion he made important developments or changes from Kant. Kant had said that the only duty was to act out of respect for 'the *form* of the moral law alone'. So that if I asked, "What is my duty?", the answer should be: "It is to do your duty." In his philosophical writings Schiller had criticised this, and had said that the development of character and the expression of character in one's action are as important for the morality of it as the regard for a general law or principle. Schiller used the expression "Schönheit der Seele". There might have been better expressions for what he meant. In English "beauty of soul" seems affected and probably stultifies discussion. Fries used the same expression, and he connected this with saying that my sense of the perfection of character for which I ought to strive is an aesthetic one, judging what I do, not as 'means to an end', but rather in analogy with the relation of one part to others in a work of art.

He said that a religious view of 'the world' was an aesthetic one too. And he thought that the perception of natural beauty (if 'perception' is the right word: I perceive the mountains, but I do not perceive the beauty of the scene in this sense) — he thought that this 'awareness' of natural beauty was a *religious* awareness of the reality before me. This is a development which is not in Kant nor in Schiller either.

His use of the term "feeling" is almost bound to bring misunderstanding, although he does his best to prevent this.

When Fries speaks of a feeling or a sense of the world as a whole or as one, he compares this with a sense of aesthetic unity in a poem or in a drama or in the beauty of a natural scene. But also — even more — in our feeling for what we meet in the lives of saints, in the unrecognised heroism of someone hardly known, or in the common life of some community or a man and wife. (Think of Goethe's portrayal of Baucis and Philemon.)

This is not Spinoza's 'third kind of knowledge' of everything *sub specie aeternitatis*. Fries speaks of our sense of the world as a whole — or simply: of a *world* — as a sense of everything as coming from a single source or creator. This is not a feeling we can explain in general terms or concepts. We can find its expression in certain religious poetry. (I think especially of Donne's religious sonnets, where it would have no sense to ask for an explanation of his images or 'symbols'.) People say in religion, as Fries's Philanthes does (p.200), "we believe in God, the holy Creator of all things." When I think of creation, my image — and the image of Genesis — is of creation in time; starting with this and finishing with that; and of using materials, making something *out of* something; etc. This is an image in which I think of material and living things in relation to God. But if I treat the image as an historical account of how it took place — then I am taking "creator" in a sense which it does not have in that religious statement. The phrase "creator of *all* things" would be just a set of incongruities, if we tried to read it so. Whereas for centuries it has meant something in the lives of religious people. And we show a misunderstanding if we ask "Well, what *does* it mean there?" and want a phrase we could substitute for it. This does not mean that there could be no answer at all.

We could answer, perhaps, by mentioning other remarks Fries makes in connection with it. I have not the space here; but I would point to what he says (in Dialogue XI: Man's Sense of Guilt) of "a human being's sense of inadequacy" or "a human being's feeling of responsibility for the imperfection of human life" or "responsibility for the inadequacy of human existence — for that degraded form of existence which is life on earth".

In his *Religionsphilosophie* (published in 1832, ten years later than *Julius und Evagoras* and including a number of passages from it) Fries distinguishes different ways in which a man may think of the morality or the good and evil of his life. In the feeling I have for my life there is my conviction — obscure or more pronounced — that I am answerable or responsible. But here we must distinguish between (1) my ethical judgement that in my life so far my character has been deplorable and weak, and that I must try step by step and persistently to improve it — "This aims at the sort of freedom which the Stoics ascribed to their 'philosophers' ('those who are wise'), that power of the will over emotions and passions which cannot be presupposed in everyone, and has to be acquired (by training and education). This is the task of the natural development of the will [i.e., development by methods which have been proved in practice]". It will depend on natural conditions for its success or failure. And I cannot be held morally responsible for it at any given moment. — We must distinguish between this and (2) what Fries calls a responsibility which belongs to a religious view of human life. I can see that there is nothing admirable about the life I have led, and I can see its defects more clearly if I compare it with a life which I admire. But Fries would say that this conviction itself does not have any sure foundation. One reason why I ought never to condemn outright the life and character of another human being, is that I cannot have insight into what has gone on in his mind at those times when I want to say he has behaved foully, what his difficulties have been, what other course he may have been trying to take, or what his motives have been — whether he was thinking *only* of himself — in those actions about which I feel indignant; but even more plainly, I cannot see very deeply into my *own* motives, when I may think I have acted out of a sense of duty or from consideration for someone else. ("You don't want to help him, you want your neighbour to think well of you", or — more likely — ". . . you want to think well of yourself".) But also the other way, so to speak: the apostles ask Jesus, "When did we do this, Lord?" — I cannot help feeling that I have failed to come up to any halfway decent moral standard; and I may pray for help. But this does not have the fundamental importance for the philosophy of religion which Fries sees in the conviction — mine or anyone's — that there is something imperfect and degraded about human life on earth altogether. — I say "life on earth" where Fries says "life in the world of appearance in space and time". — And where I say "degraded", perhaps it would be in Fries's sense to add: 'religiously, rather than morally, degraded'.

Fries does not quote the Gospel words, "Be ye perfect . . ." here, but he does speak of the idea or ideal of a perfect or divine or holy will (we have to keep from asking what "will" could mean there). And he says that a holy or perfect will *could* not exist or appear in space and time. To exist in space and time is to be subject to the conditions of bodily existence, of physical forces and of physiological dependence on them, and to live so that one's will has constantly to contend with these influences: so that "strength of will" is often measured by them. Fries says that in nature there is no force so strong that it cannot be overcome by a stronger. And he applies this phraseology in speaking of the human will. — A life in space and time — a life on earth — cannot be a perfect life. And *this* is not because it lacks something which it might have had and which we may find in the life of someone else.

If someone says that the life a man has led is his own doing, his own fault or his own achievement, this seems a familiar way of speaking, whether we agree with it or not. But Fries speaks here of freedom of the will and of the spirituality of the soul (which is much the same) as 'timeless' or as eternal. They are not *conjectures*, but neither has their reality been shown by science. Our certainty that they are real is something we know in a feeling which plays a part in our lives and actions, akin to the feeling which is our conviction of the reality of the world and of God. — In speaking of this Fries uses analysis and forms of what he calls 'deduction' which I will not describe. If I believe I have a will that is free, in his sense, then I believe it has a reality which is not just that of phenomena in space and time. If my will exists in space and time, then it *acts* in space and time (in other words, I *act*): this is something it has chosen or chooses, for which it is responsible. In the speech of Otto, pp. 201–2 here:

We believe in the freedom of the will and as a consequence we must regard ourselves as the authors of our temporal existence. The moral inadequacy of our lives is, therefore, of eternal significance. If the spirit of man did not bear this lack within itself, it would not manifest itself in such an imperfect temporal existence.

This is like the myth in Plato's *Republic*, Book X. Fries does not emphasise its character as an image or a metaphor as strongly as when he speaks of religious symbolism elsewhere. If we take it as a subject to be discussed, we see incongruities. If it is a picture — and myths are often pictures from which something has been left out — it is an expression of what Fries called 'the religious way of looking at the world'. He distinguished between, for example, the way of looking at the world as material nature, explaining what happens in terms of theoretical physics; the morphological view of the world which is interested in classification — as in the earlier stages of botany and geology; the ethical and political view of the world; the aesthetic and religious view of the world. We are guided by different criteria, and draw conclusions in different ways, by different principles, in one such view of the world and in another. Or we might say, "true" and "false" mean something different in one such way of considering things, and in another. We cannot look for some one system in which they are all brought together.

RUSH RHEES

Translator's Note

It has not always proved possible consistently to adopt a single translation for certain key terms employed by Fries. This is, in part, due to a curious feature of the German language. An important part of its vocabulary has to perform a dual function: a single word may have both an ordinary, straightforward, everyday meaning and also a more specialised or more limited meaning. In English, these two functions tend to be divided between the Anglo-Saxon and the Graeco-Roman elements of the language. The following is a list of the words, in the case of which I have found myself constrained to adopt two different English equivalents, depending on the context: *allgemein*: general, universal; *Bild*: picture, image; *Bildung*: culture, education; *Dichtung*: poetry, literature; *Erscheinung*: appearance, phenomenon; *Geheimnis*: secret, mystery; *Geist*: spirit, mind; *Glaube*: belief, faith; *Liebe*: love, charity; *Volk*: people, nation; *Wissenschaft*: branch of knowledge, science.

The only other term employed by Fries which has presented difficulties is the word *Ahndung* (an antiquated form of *Ahnung*). There is no exact English equivalent for this word. It is often translated "presentiment" or "presage", but the somewhat ominous tone of these two words, together with their strong reference to the future, make them unsatisfactory. Harvey, in his translation of Otto's *Das Heilige*, renders the words *ahnden* and *Ahndung* in a variety of ways: surmise, divine, inkling. The first two equivalents are misleading because they strongly suggest a speculative and intellectual mode of coming to know; the word "inkling", while capturing part of the meaning of *Ahndung* has a trivial flavour about it which is wholly inappropriate to the German. In the end, I decided to cut the Gordian knot by employing, not a single word, but the phrase "intuitive awareness". It should, however, be emphasised that Fries denies of *Ahndung* that it is an intuition (*Anschauung*). It is, he tells us, a feeling. (Fries employs the term *Anschauung* in the Kantian sense.) *Ahndung* designates a mode of apprehension which is neither the product of intellection or reasoning, nor capable of conceptual analysis.

I have employed Meredith's translation of Kant's *Critique of Judgement* (Oxford 1952) in the short Kant passage cited by Fries in the final chapter on Beauty.

I should like to take this opportunity of expressing my thanks to Mr Roy Woods and Mr Tony Bushell, who both generously placed their time and linguistic expertise at my disposal. Above all, I owe a very special debt of gratitude to my German-speaking wife, Renate. Without her help, given with endless patience and inexhaustible good humour, I should certainly have failed to cope with the tortuosities and obscurities of Fries's often careless and inelegant style.

DAVID WALFORD

Peace I leave with you, my peace I give unto you: not as the world giveth, give I unto you. Let not your heart be troubled, neither let it be afraid.

Verily, verily, I say unto you, Except a corn of wheat fall into the ground and die, it abideth alone: but if it die, it bringeth forth much fruit.

He that loveth his life shall lose it; and he that hateth his life in this world shall keep it unto life eternal.

The vision of these conversations took form in the summer of the year 1811. That vision was inspired by quiet hopes — hopes which were perhaps focused upon a distant future. These conversations are intended as an admonition, for the hopes of the one who speaks were German hopes.

The violent transformation of a swiftly changing epoch anticipated this conversation. Accept in remembrance that which was spoken in hope.

DIALOGUE I

Peace of Soul

Philanthes, an old man, is talking to several young men. . . .

Philanthes: It is not easy to impart a pure doctrine of wisdom which is free from prejudice. Those whose judgement is not already cultivated to a high degree are dominated by an impure mode of thought which always makes it difficult, and frequently impossible, to win them for the opinions of higher practical wisdom, which are, in fact, of such simplicity. And hence it is that he who candidly wishes to learn is, as a result of ignoble presumption, all too easily excited to mocking irony. But this is in no wise appropriate to the clear discourse of reason. The mind which is strong, healthy and pious, despises the titillation of contentiousness and is satisfied only by the unclouded and limpid judgement of reason. I shall, therefore, only offer you what I hold to be true and founded in itself. May it prove its worth by convincing you.

There is something which constitutes a threat to anyone who offers his unprejudiced teaching for consideration: it is the fact that almost everyone of slight education mistakes his prejudices for irrefutable truths. Such a person, though he politely attends to what is said, is only willing to accept what agrees with his prejudices and rejects everything which conflicts with them. I warn you against this danger, noble youths! Nor does this ignoble arrogance arise solely from impure sources. It is, in part, based upon a true idea which is merely misunderstood by the crudeness of the unformed mind. Each person has the same claims to the teachings of practical wisdom and each should acquire them for himself by his own thought. The cruder mind misunderstands this fact: it is no longer able to acknowledge the subordination of the pupil to the teacher, but it esteems itself as highly as its teacher. But I am addressing myself to you on the assumption that your unprejudiced judgement is seeking instruction and knows full well that the truth is only to be found with effort and exertion. My intention is, accordingly, to impart to you what I have heard from those engaged in honest enquiry and which I myself, likewise engaged in honest enquiry, have further developed. What I wish to impart to you is a view of the world which is at once tranquil and serene and self-sufficing, a view of the world which encourages man to energetic action.

Arthur: You are demanding of those who would be your worthy listeners that they should be constantly aware of the fact that what you have to impart to us has been long and carefully weighed and tested by you. Accordingly, should any investigation seem irrelevant, or any doctrine unintelligible, or should the contradictory of a doctrine seem more plausible, we are not, on account of our own opinion, to reject what you offer. We must, rather, challenge you to a clearer statement of your teaching, or calmly explain our own counter-arguments, with a view either to your correcting us or to our finding a better solution. For there still seems to be a great deal which is capable of correction in the practical wisdom of man.

Philanthes: Well spoken! I wanted to make this requirement in advance. With what, however, shall I begin my teaching? He who finds the right entrance to a discourse has gained a great advantage. I suggest that we should, above all, discuss the value and significance of the peace of soul which is the fruit of self-contentment. But I see that my idea does not meet with your approval, Woldemar? What is your objection?

Woldemar: I had other expectations. Our request was that you should instruct us about the higher wisdom of life. From what other idea could such a teaching issue if not from the idea of God and the divine nature of things? Is it not the divine which alone elevates us, and supports and leads us along in all the noble deeds of the spirit? Must we not therefore start from this ultimate source?

Philanthes: You are right! We do want to talk about the divine essence of things. But suppose that the divine of which you speak does elevate and support the whole of our nobler spiritual life. That would, indeed, be not merely the beginning, but the whole content and sum of our teaching. It must be the beginning, the middle and the end of our instruction.

Woldemar: Agreed! But, in that case, the beginning will be the supreme and the purest doctrine of the divinity itself.

Philanthes: It could easily seem so. But you are demanding that we should start with what is the most difficult; but about this we cannot, for the moment, be adequately clear. Let us choose what is easier, so that we may each of us become more familiar with the other's way of thinking, even if this easier starting-point should seem less attractive to you.

Woldemar: I shall happily moderate my desire and follow your lead, whatever you may teach.
Philanthes: What is your opinion of my suggestion, Otto?
Otto: I was wondering why you had given primacy over everything else to peace of soul. I suppose the explanation is this: true contentment is granted to man through self-contentment; its witness is peace of soul, that inner peace of the heart which, independently of man's various opinions about life and regardless of the level of his education, is what every man most immediately seeks and desires. It thus occurs to me that the reason why you wish to speak about peace of soul, above everything else, is probably the fact that, apart from all the conflicting wishes and practical opinions of man, peace of soul is that which each person really seeks and strives to attain, everything else being merely employed as a means to that end.
Philanthes: You have characterised my intention so precisely that I need add nothing to what you have said. On the contrary, I can start straight away by offering Otto's idea to you for closer scrutiny. Let me begin by asking a question. What expression shall we use to sum up, in the most concentrated possible fashion, the full essence of what man desires, wishes, craves? In order to clarify this question, our initial reply to anyone possessed of merely adequate education must be: inner contentment, peace of soul. To take the question of satisfying man's strivings in life: we shall always find that there are conflicting methods of realising a particular objective. But whether that objective has been achieved or not, or whether it remains to a greater or lesser degree unrealised, can only be established from whether or not he has, by means of his choice, arrived at the inner peace of self-contentment. Let us suppose, for example, that someone's desire is directed towards money, or to distinction among his fellow citizens, or to the possession of a woman. By what means will he achieve the object of his will? By acquiring the money, gaining the distinction, winning the woman, or by the opposite? My answer is: Sometimes by the one means, sometimes by the other, for it wholly depends upon whether his desire continues or whether, in the meantime, he changes his mind about the matter. Suppose that someone has made the profit he desired, and that the method and the manner of making the profit is no longer pleasing to him. Of what good is it to him now therefore that he has achieved his objective? His will has not been satisfied. Similarly with someone who has gained the distinction he desired but who does not find the expected satisfaction. Similarly, too, with the person who wins a woman but who fails to form a true friendship with her. On the contrary: where his

desire has changed in good time, he will satisfy his will in precisely *not* gaining what he had previously sought. Or, to take another case, his desire remains unchanged, but he discovers that it is impossible for him to achieve his objective. Will his will be satisfied now, or not? We cannot answer that question definitely, either. For if he becomes aware of the impossibility, and if he is capable of completely banishing his earlier wish from his mind, he will satisfy his will by giving up his desire. What, then, are we to say? When will someone, whom we see striving after the object of some desire, satisfy his will, and when not? You appreciate, I assume, that we may not decide the issue by appealing to the nature of the outcome. It always depends upon how he himself regards this outcome when it is there, depends upon whether he achieves contentment or not, depends upon whether peace of soul is granted to or continues with him, or whether the opposite occurs. If peace of soul remains with him, or if it is granted to him, then he has satisfied his will; in the contrary case, not.

We shall be led to the same conclusion, too, if we enquire, not about external possession, but about the inner value of an action. And we shall be led to that same conclusion irrespectively of whether it is the virtue of a person which strives after that inner value, or whether it is the conscience of the person which speaks thereof. Suppose that someone attaches great value to the education of his mind in some branch of knowledge or art. Will he satisfy his will by acquiring this education, or not? It may happen in one way, or it may happen in another. It is, of course, possible for his expectation to be disappointed, and for him to come to the opinion that he has gained nothing of value in the education he has now acquired. We can, accordingly, once more but answer: if his effort leads to contentment, then he has satisfied his will; otherwise, not. His endeavour can, besides, lead him to contentment in many different ways: in his thinking that he has achieved a noble end, in his giving up an objective he now condemns, even, indeed, in his finding satisfaction in the endeavour itself, even though it does not yield the expected advantage. But it is, above all, in the case where an action is demanded of a person by conscience that, in order to establish whether he has satisfied his will, we shall have to judge by reference to the peace of soul which he has either preserved or come to acquire. For how great is the possibility that a person should be mistaken about that which, in the execution of the action, he regards as leading to the fulfilment of his duty. It does not, therefore, depend upon the outcome. It rather depends upon the contentment which that outcome, no matter what it is, is capable of producing.

All these considerations now lead us to assert that the true objective, which man ought to pursue in life, is the single goal of imperturbable peace of soul. This insight enables us to understand why so many wise men of antiquity regarded inner contentment, intrepidity, unshakeable steadiness, serene peace of spirit, as the supreme good of man, and why they raised it to such heights. Man has achieved everything once he has acquired this unshaken fortitude; it only permits the agitation of desires, affections, and passions, as far as the surface of life, while the innermost core of the heart is preserved in a permanent state of unmoved peace. In like fashion, the storm ploughs up the waves upon the surface of the sea, while the calm deeps of the ocean continue unmoved in a state of serene peace.

But to praise imperturbable peace of soul in this way is of no benefit to us unless someone can tell us how it is to be gained and, once gained, preserved. We have seen that in all human desire peace of soul is the possible outcome sometimes of this result, sometimes of that, here the one, there the opposite. Now, how shall we choose so that in every case it is peace of soul and nothing else which is the secure result. All the questions which relate to how man ought to behave can be reduced to this single question.

Now, one cannot take immediate possession of peace of soul. It is the outcome of what someone is or has. It follows that what we have established so far does not in itself help us a great deal, for the question as to what produces peace of soul probably admits of a vast variety of answers.

Accordingly, let me lead you on to the following consideration. In everything which produces peace of soul and the noble freedom and firmness of spirit which is to be found in such peace, a great deal depends upon the *opinion* which a man has of things, upon his *conviction*.

Did we not earlier see that the way in which a person construed the outcome of his efforts to acquire money, distinction, love, whether with satisfaction or without it, depended wholly upon his opinion of the value of the thing in question. Indeed, we clearly see that it is absolutely impossible for the semi-educated man, at many stages of the development of his view of the world and of life, to achieve peace of soul. And the reason for this impossibility is the opinion he entertains about the value of life. Consider the wild savage who, at the beginning of his development, for the first time notices that, beyond the natural satisfaction of hunger, thirst and sexual desire, there is, in addition, a refining and artificial satisfaction which is capable of intensifying the delight and pleasure to an endlessly diversified degree. Our savage will think that the true purpose of his existence will consist in plunging into the immoderate pursuit of this intensified pleasure, without granting his appetite the peace natural to sense. He gropes around in the darkness of his perverted instincts, destroys himself and never succeeds in finding peace. Similarly, even among educated people, we find many who, led astray by an unhappy education, ruin themselves. Resigned, as it were, to this mistaken life-purpose, they console themselves with the motto: enjoy what you can and suffer what you must. This ruinous path they pursue until, finally, in the chaos of their spiritual faculties, they are no longer able even to utter clear-headedly the motto of their existence. There are others, by contrast, for whom the ideas of a beautiful life have become clear, and who, even if they have fallen into ugly habits, are daily admonished by their better insight and led into a better way of life, until, in their noble effort to achieve a purer beauty in their life, they discover peace.

Otto: I think I detect in what you have said another reason why you mentioned peace of soul at the beginning of our conversation. You wish to impart to us practical wisdom. In other words, you wish to give us insight, you wish to clarify our convictions. It is not the absence of insight which makes what is bad, bad; nor is it the presence of insight in itself which makes what is good, good. In everything which relates to what man wills, it is in connection with peace of soul that insight can help and secure. Insight is capable of affording such peace of soul to each person.

Philanthes: You have given expression to what I was thinking. If we ask about the practical value of our teaching, the practical value of insight, the answer we shall receive will be this: the teaching of wisdom can bestow upon and secure for man a view of life which is at once satisfying and calming, a view of life which guarantees to man an imperturbable peace in the depths of his heart, a peace which is immune to whatever blows of fate may trouble the surface of his life.

Arthur: Certainly, what you have said shows that the preservation of peace of soul is highly dependent upon the fate of human opinions. But when you here praise the teaching of wisdom for purifying opinions and thereby leading to the secure preservation of peace of soul, there is nothing in what you have so far said which could serve as premiss to that claim. On the contrary, we see people in numerous less happy situations actually condemned to uneasiness on account of their opinions. You must, therefore, maintain that the true teaching leads to a view of life which is such that, freeing man's life from all the vicissitudes of external events, it secures man's life for him only in itself. But, of course, this has frequently been disputed by sceptics and such as are ill-disposed towards human reason. Can you, therefore, perhaps now also explain to us how you hope to achieve this objective with certainty?

Philanthes: I shall try. My boast to you is that I have a view of the world to show you which is both joyful and satisfying in itself, and which, were it to achieve nothing else, would secure for each person inner peace, provided merely that he be willing to fix his attention constantly on it.

Each person for the most part forms himself, in accordance with the nature of his insight, into that for which he is taken in the development of his mind and life. The same is true of the means and the end of life.

To begin with a point which is of but subordinate concern to me here: understanding, insight and teaching make the most certain claims on the life of man at the point where, with respect to each person's affairs, the acquisition of skills is required — skills which are the individual's means of establishing himself in society, of occupying and maintaining his place within society.

But, to turn to a point which is of greater and more immediate concern to me here: the same holds true of the purposes of life as well, for it applies to the question as to what purposes are to be designated and how their attainment is to be evaluated. Even in that which least depends upon man's own choice in the play of joy and suffering, of happiness and misery, the supreme judge is opinion and conviction. The joy and happiness of man, and their opposites as well, do not immediately consist in physically stimulated pleasure or suffering. It is rather the imagination which, in memory, in hope, in fear, and in sympathy, is in diverse ways master of man's happiness and misery. Frequently, the conviction of the understanding intervenes and transforms pain and joy, conviction converting the greatest torments into joy, in the enthusiasm of heroic death or martyrdom.

The object of our present enquiry straightway suggests itself in what I have just said: insight and conviction must be capable of becoming the sure masters of man's view of the world and life. But how am I to present this view to you so that you can inspect it clearly and subject it to close scrutiny? Consider, above all, that supreme form of insight, religious conviction. In my opinion, the man who is master of the goal is master of the course which leads to the realisation of that goal. Death is our goal; learn to love it. Love of death in the midst of *joie de vivre* is the doctrine which, immutably guaranteeing peace, must become your guide.

Woldemar: Yes, indeed! I am coming to understand your teaching. Merely focus your attention upon that which is higher, upon the celestial, upon the divine life, and you will find that, in elevating your attention in this way, you have come into the possession of a therapeutic remedy against every pain.

Philanthes: That expresses the matter. The life of man, whether it be of greater duration or less, whether it be richer in drama or in peacefulness — the life of man lies between two limits which are fixed and established, the limits of birth and death. If man, therefore, firmly focuses his eye upon the goal of death, he will have raised his gaze above the whole play of care, joy, suffering, failure and success. Everything ends in death — that is the certain maxim which must fill his heart to its very depths with peace, even when he finds himself in the midst of the most tormenting agitation of life, provided that he can be cheerful in the face of death. The certain guarantee of imperturbable peace is, therefore, being reconciled to death. I am aware that the healthy man dreads death as the termination of the joy he experiences, and that he departs unwillingly from life, for it captivates him and he delights in it. Whether or not it was because my father imparted this view of life to me when I was still young, I do not know, but I have never felt that there was anything harsh about this idea. My constant wish, both in joy and in suffering, is to look death directly in the eye, with tranquillity and desire. It may, perhaps, sometimes have happened that I entertained an eager wish to achieve some object in life — and I have achieved a great many such objects — but I have then always discovered once more, as a result of brief and tranquil reflection in the midst of joyful expectation, the joy with which I straightway wished to follow the ultimate leader. These words of my father have always retained their changeless validity for me: Even if the colours of the rainbow do not adorn the wings of youth, nor smiling joy its countenance, there is nonetheless a solemn beauty which surrounds the form of youth when it reverses the torch of life. We can offer our hand in confidence to our leader. Have no fear of death! Annihilation would not, in itself, be a source of suffering — not that extinction is the fate of the living. Even if terrifying forms should appear to you beyond, the dignity of your own being is more powerful than any misfortune, for even in this life the solemn thought of your own dignity is capable of elevating you above all the vicissitudes of happiness and misery.

When man turns his thoughts to death, all the changing brilliancy of the appearance of things around him — sombre hues as well as bright, joy as well as pain — vanishes from his eyes. But when all sounds have fallen silent, when the whole living world with its play of forms and colours has vanished from beneath our eyes and we find ourselves alone in the dark stillness of death, then do we stand alone, face to face with the Love which rules over all things, then do we feel the embrace of Him who has compassion on all. When death echoes with the message of heavenly expectations, it becomes a purifying and fortifying thought. When you feel the embrace of the Omnipotence which is above you — then do you realise that you are at the heart of eternal goodness.

Someone who, in the moment of overwhelming suffering, looks out upon the magnificent expanses of nature, will once more discover in it the changeless peace he knew before, though he may well be roused to indignation that nature, where everything unfolds oblivious to his fate, utterly fails to notice the immensity within his heart. But, as soon as his calm is restored again, he will be embraced and consoled by the very living splendour which echoes with joy and is radiant with brilliance.

The terrifying and overwhelming power of nature will never be capable of alarming me or causing me to tremble with fear. When I am in peril and there is no possibility of assistance or helpful advice, my anxiety vanishes and the elevating thought of the Almighty seizes hold of me. A friend's jesting rapier or the furtiveness of man can alarm me. To find myself at the mercy of man's incompetent guidance can fill me with apprehension. But when I find myself in the power of nature, with neither advice nor assistance, the fortifying and elevating thought of eternal Destiny presents itself to my soul and my fear vanishes. Never shall I forget the sublime impression made upon me on the evening when I made my first acquaintance with the raging power of the sea. I was sitting in the stern of a little open boat and we were quietly exchanging jests about our unaccustomed pastime. Suddenly the storm fell upon us, ploughing up the floods of the sea and hurling foaming waves against the sheer and rocky cliffs nearby. The imperilled boatmen hauled in the sail. The palid oarsmen exchanged terrified glances with each other and silently struck into the wild flood. On that havenless coast there was no other salvation than that of Fate. A single wave breaking over us from the cliff would have been sufficient to drag us down into the flood. Our little bark pitched to and fro, one moment riding the crest of a wave and the next plummeting the depths of a trough. I turned my gaze upon the roaring tumult and then at the black and threatening heavens above. But of my anxious trembling there was no more trace. I was seized by a sublime thrill at the thought of the holy omnipotence of God. So vivid was that impression that I would today fain issue forth once more to renew my acquaintance with that tumult. And thus am I wont happily to stand, free and proud, confronting the thunder. Thus, in the thick of battle, does the sublime thought steady my nerve and elevate my mind. For, in battle, although it is true that the boldness and composure of the commanders and the valour of the troops secures the army victory, whether or not the individual is to fall a sacrifice to victory, a victim of the enemy sword, or whether, mourning his brother who has given his life upon the field of battle, he is destined to join the celebrations of the victory gained — that is decided by the hand of Destiny alone.

About the time my father taught me these things, when my youthful spirit was moved with greater liveliness by these fresh impressions, I had a dream, which I can still vividly recall. I dreamt that I was lying one lovely summer evening on an elevated spot high above a river, beyond which there was a beautiful panorama of fertile fields and prosperous towns and villages. Beneath me, on the other side of the river, there stood a cottage and before it was a woman with her three children. The boys, in their play, came down to the river, and the smallest of them, at a greater distance from the cottage, fell down the steep bank and was carried away by the river. The two other boys cried out: "We are good swimmers; let us save our brother!" Whereupon they sprang after him into the river, caught up with him and brought him once more to the bank lower down stream. In the meantime, some men had made their appearance at the cottage, had bound up the woman and, having plundered the humble dwelling, had imprisoned her inside. They then fled into the forest. I now turned my gaze to the distance where I saw a violent storm raging over the fields, lightning striking the houses, and the tempest and the hail laying waste the fields. The storm approached nearer and nearer. The boys hastened to their cottage, but as soon as they entered it, it was struck by lightning, and they, along with their mother, perished in the fire. The robbers, however, had made good their escape. Fate's fury filled me with disgust. At this point, the heavens parted above me and I beheld the countenance of the genius who ruled the clouds and hurled the thunderbolts. The face was dreadful in its fury and it filled me with terror. At this point I awoke. But the image was still present to my waking soul, and a sacred thrill possessed me, for the form of this wrathful being was of a divinely sublime beauty. "Destruction is visited upon the earth by the spirit of love, as well," I said to myself. I have never forgotten this image.

This, therefore, is what I above all things expect of our teaching: that, for every situation in life, it provide the man of education, in his innermost heart, with the joyful recollection of death, with its sublime and celestial significance. And I further expect of our teaching that it establish the temper of a God-fearing spirit — a spirit possessed of a bright, religious and unclouded understanding, a spirit capable of steeling all its aspirations and strivings by means of the enthusiasm of this belief.

In this way I hope to be able to offer instruction to your conviction and exhortation to your life.

Otto: I find myself constrained to recall the warning which Arthur gave us. Your words have taken possession of me and they offer promise of sublime consolation in the future. But, if I am to form my future life in accordance with this sublime belief, will not the calm contemplation of the Divine have to be elevated above everything else, so that the only worthwhile form of life will be the lonely life of contemplation, a life remote from action, as practised by many devout persons? But that is not your intention, for our own nation warns us against such an existence, and you, too, value energetic action above everything else in the life of man. For this reason, instruct me further.

Philanthes: In raising that objection, you are like the student of astronomy who, transposed in imagination to a distant star, casts his glance upon the expanses of the heavens and, scarcely any longer able to descry our tiny earth, fears that it will not be large enough to afford him a sleeping-place. But look, you have before you a felicitous image of my meaning. You see the long row of fishing-boats driving downstream and now lining up across the river in order to drop their great net. Now, because the foremost boats are taking up their position below us, do you wish to blame them for driving so far apart from each other and for no longer leaving any room for their fellows, at the same time unnecessarily impeding their own control of the net?

Otto: No. I am fully aware that I only have a clear view of the foremost part of the river, whereas the part beyond I only see in perspective, so that the seemingly narrow band amounts, in all probability, to as much as half its width.

Philanthes: The same is true now. Believe me that the life of man, with all the fullness and beauty of its active motions, has only seemed to you to have retreated into the perspective of the distant background as a result of my discourse, for it led you to the point of view of religious contemplation. What, from one point of view, seems to be but an insignificant and constricted area will, from a closer point of view, appear to you as a rich and vigorously cultivated expanse of meadows.

Otto: Let that suffice for today. We must not detain you any longer now, for the sun has already set behind the mountains.

DIALOGUE II

Beauty of Soul

Philanthes: Now, if I am to lead your thoughts to an acknowledgement of the correctness of what I say, I must first of all refer you back to what was agreed upon as correct in our last conversation. What is important to the individual is peace of soul. The person who has found that has found the satisfaction of his will.

Arthur: Since you are referring to that point, permit me a remark. You maintained that every question relating to what a man ought to do is to be referred back to this striving for peace of soul. But is it not the case that many of the philosophers of antiquity founded their doctrines of quietism and impassivity upon precisely this striving for peace of soul? Will it not, then, be the man devoid of feeling, the man lacking in sympathy, the man without vitality, who will most easily achieve this goal?

Philanthes: You are right. If you can secure for someone a passive state of life-long lack of feeling, then you will have secured peace of soul for that person in the easiest possible way. Such a person has achieved what he wants, though that is not a great deal, for he does not want a great deal. The man of insensibility lives in a state of satisfaction and contentment. In the opinion of the man himself, his affairs are in order. That is not the judgement of an outside observer. The man without feeling is not pleasing to you, even though he is pleasing to himself. Nor is his recipe for achieving peace of soul of any help to you, for you have neither the will nor the capacity to achieve this passive state of insensibility. Accordingly, the man without feeling is displeasing to us; and he is only pleasing to himself on account of error. He could be freed from this error, but then his peace of soul would be at an end. His peace of soul is, therefore, insecure. Indeed, were his error removed, he would perforce look back upon his past life with disgust.

Arthur: I understand you. True peace of soul is to be achieved and secured in life, not through self-contentment based on error, but through enlightened self-contentment. What we, therefore, need is an explanation of how someone can achieve this self-contentment and, having achieved it, preserve it.

Man, as you recently said, is not capable of taking immediate possession of peace of soul. It follows that the man of education must learn to appreciate that it can only result from self-contentment. It further follows that everything depends upon the instruction given for arriving at, and then securing, this self-contentment.

Philanthes: Correct! And I would further maintain that this instruction ought to concern itself with one thing only: the ideals of sublimity and beauty in human life. The reason why I say this is that, for the educated mind, the only thing which has validity in its own right is the intrinsic value of the spiritual life. It is only by reference to the ideals of sublimity and beauty that man can be truly pleasing or displeasing to himself. The only thing which duty commands, the only thing which the purest impulse of our hearts demands, the only thing which every person, in the depths of his being, wills, is the beauty of the life of man — the life of man giving form to itself with the passage of time.

It is this beauty of life alone which witnesses to our heavenly origin, this beauty of life sprung from the idea of the world of life and the idea of spiritual independence. The diamond which, yet uncut, lies hidden in the ground, or which, unrecognised, is trodden in the dust, contains within itself that same inner fire with which, once cut, it gleams in the light. The same is the case with the intrinsic value of the spirit. To be healthy or sick, poor or rich, powerful or weak, educated or ignorant — what are these states but diverse forms in which man is capable of manifesting himself. The intrinsic nature of the spirit is something other, something which is recognised in virtue alone. As the lapidary can only wrest brilliancy from the diamond by means of the diamond, so spirit can only relate to spirit. For the spirit, the value of virtue is to be found exclusively in the life which is spiritual, interior and free. Only in the intelligent spirit, in itself and in relation to itself, does the higher idea of the good, the idea of virtue whose first thought is self-reliance and free independence of the spirit, become clear and meaningful to man, with the I and the You. Thus are honour and justice regarded as the primary requirements of duty: honour, that each man should self-confidently assert his own worth relatively to every other person; justice, that he should respect the worth of the independent spirit in others.

Let me attempt, by comparing two characters, to clarify the first idea which you ought to hold on to firmly in this context.

Some considerable time ago, after peace had been established in our country, I made a journey on business of my father to the capital of a powerful kingdom. Among its morally degenerate people ugly perversions of life jostled each other in filth, cowardice and slavish servility. The extremes of these perversions are no longer known under our superior laws and customs or with our public life. I there made the acquaintance of a rich usurer who had been carefully brought up in the manner of his nation in the house of his wealthy father. He, too, quickly began to practise commerce in the fashion of that nation, where honour was unknown and where the merchant despised no profit for which he could not be condemned by a judge. He thus allowed himself every kind of clandestine fraud which was supposed to be exempt from punishment. His wealth rapidly increased. He succeeded in gaining control of the state purveyancing business. He now defrauded with impunity and on a large scale, and he continued to do so for the rest of his life, cravenly, fraudulently and with brilliant success. While still young he had secured his position. No one could outbid him in the splendour of his mansions, his horses, or, before he married, his courtesans, or, after he married, in the magnificence of his house, or in charitable works. He was a kindly father to his children, and raised them to become men respected in the state.

And now, by way of contrast, let us look at the second character. My father sent me to a small provincial town to visit someone he had known in his youth. I found an aged and ailing man living in a rather poor neighbourhood. He was almost wholly without resources and, indeed, practically without a mattress for the night. I mentioned my father to him, and he replied with seriousness and not without a note of rebuke in his voice: "He was an honour-loving and upright youth." I replied: "And this he remained in manhood, and this he still is today." I hurriedly recounted a great deal to him, but he merely shook his head and gave no further reply. I then talked to him about his present situation. He told me that he had no friends, no valued acquaintance, and that he was one of the unhappiest of men. However, when I responded with marks of compassion he eagerly sprang up, leant with difficulty out of his tiny window and, picturing the charms of his abode, showed me, to the side, between the roofs of his neighbours, a bounded view of the open country, further assuring me that the sun shone into his room in the early morning and in the evening. I now began to think that the old man spent his life in a state of religious ecstasy, inspired by the higher expectations of religion. But when I led the conversation in that direction, he laconically remarked: *"Non liquet.* Of divine matters I know nothing." I felt sorry for the old man, and it seemed to me that it would be so easy to make the last years of his life comfortable. There was nothing to tie him to his place of abode. I wanted to take him to my father, or at least to get my father to help him. But, gently as I introduced the matter, he immediately divined my purpose and indignantly flared up: "You take me for a beggar! But I am still capable of working to support myself, and then I shall be able to die."

From the old man himself there was little to be learned about his earlier life. But from others I discovered that he was the son of wealthy parents, that he had been carefully educated and become a man of wide learning and energetic industry, and that he soon came into the possession of a considerable fortune. He was, however, a man of very great strictness of character; as a result, he was, from early youth onwards, prey to an exaggerated anxiousness in all matters relating to honour and justice. In addition to this, his youthful imagination was dominated by a fanatical ideal of love and friendship. Nowhere did he find anyone of sufficient purity with whom to form a proper attachment. His fortune evaporated under his hands for, when he ought to have made claims on others, his anxiousness always drove him to the fear of doing them an injustice. He was incapable of engaging in any important business, for each undertaking involved circumstances such that he was incapable of reconciling his business activity with his prejudices relating to honour and equity. And so it was that fate soon drove him back into joyless loneliness, and he was even threatened by poverty itself. Not only this but compassion induced him to take under his protection a poor widow and her several children. He married her but was incapable of establishing any ties of warm friendship with her. The children went their different ways, while their mother and step-father grew increasingly needy. Eventually the woman left him and he found himself alone in the world.

His neighbours called him the imprudent old man. Only his landlord, an artisan, judged him differently. When he saw that I was interested in the old man, he said to me: "There was a time when I also called him imprudent. But once, on a journey, I heard your teachers addressing the people on the subject of independence of spirit and telling them that the pure, inner value of man consisted in honour and justice, and I was involuntarily reminded of the old man and I came to respect him for his independence. Since my return home he has lodged in my house. Of presents he will hear nothing at all. However, by fixing the price of what I buy for him at a cheaper rate, and by setting the value of what he earns at a higher rate, I am able to afford him modest assistance."

When I returned home I told my father of my wish that the old man's situation should be improved. But his reply was: "Leave him in peace! You can be assured that this man occupies a higher position in the Kingdom of God than we do with our victories and our laws." — At the time, I did not fully understand my father's meaning, but now I think that he was right.

My question to you is this: Of the two, which would you have preferred to have been?

Arthur: Personally, I should not have wished to have been in the position of either of them. But I think I understand your chief point. What you are saying is this: we must seek the value of a person wholly within that person himself, not in what is determined merely by external circumstances. Could it not, however, be that you have applied your colours too brightly? I respect the old man's unshakeable resolution to adhere to honour and justice; on the other hand, he was not a good husband, nor was he a good father. I despise the usurer for his cowardice, injustice and fraudulence; and yet he was a man of charitable works and he was a good father.

Woldemar: I do not agree, Arthur. For my part, I should have liked to have been the old man. But, venerable Philanthes, explain your meaning more clearly to us yourself.

Philanthes: I should have liked to have been in the position of the usurer, and not in that of the old man. On the other hand, I should have liked to have been the old man himself, and not the usurer. Understand me aright! As Arthur says, we want to judge what the man himself is worth, not what the merely external circumstances either add to or take away from him. The position of the old man, that is to say, his external circumstances, was very disadvantageous, but that was not his fault. The position of the usurer, on the other hand, was very advantageous, but that was not his merit. But I have mentioned no names. We cannot give the innermost ground of a person's character with complete certainty. Let us, accordingly, judge the two men simply as objects of fiction. Arthur reproaches the old man for some of his failings. I cannot agree with him on that point. The failings of the old man were the result of lack of insight and prudence. But these two failings — lack of insight and lack of prudence — were not themselves caused by any defect of will or character. From a religious point of view, a man can be made responsible for his character alone. The failings of the usurer, on the other hand, are defects of character, defects of sentiment. Did not cowardice make him into a man of charitable works? Was it not cowardice and duplicity which made him into a seemingly good husband? Was it not, perhaps, even craven cunning which made him into a good father? No matter, therefore, how commendable the external circumstances of his life may have been, in himself the man was depraved. But no one could seriously wish to be a person who was worthless in himself.

On the other hand, no matter how wretched the external circumstances of the old man may have been, a noble spirit lived within him.

Arthur: Good! Now I understand your meaning! But show us in addition how the inner value of life manifests itself, and, in particular, explain to us how everyone really wills that inner value, as you maintained at the beginning. I have no doubt that you can clarify the matter, but for the moment I do not understand. How can you say that the happy usurer really willed the inner value of the moral life — by which I mean self-contentment and, with it, the satisfaction of his will? To us he is displeasing, but to himself he may have been pleasing. Why do you maintain that he still really willed the moral value of life?

Philanthes: You are pointing, my good Arthur, at the most difficult part of the problem under consideration. And on that matter we shall only come to complete agreement at a later stage. You will admit that if the usurer had achieved self-contentment then that would have been the result of some defect in the formation of his understanding, for in himself the man was worthless. The failings with which we reproach him are not the effect of lack of insight; they are failings of the will. He could, it is true, have achieved peace, but not a truly permanent peace of soul. For if someone had merely succeeded in illuminating the insight of his understanding, he would have recognised the depravity within himself, and his peace would have been at an end.

The human spirit contains within itself the eternal ideas of sublimity and beauty of life. But these ideas can only present themselves to the clear consciousness of the understanding after the spirit has been developed. It is more difficult to show how this work of developing the spirit is to be judged. Let us, therefore, begin by examining the ideas of beauty of life.

In one thing we shall already understand each other better. In whatever direction it may please eternal wisdom to direct our destinies — whether it be in the direction of successful action or whether it be towards the dark, unrecognised and abortive attempt at action — the worth of man lies, not in the outcome of his undertaking, but solely in the deepest power of the spirit itself, the power which leads to our innermost decision. Our question is concerned, not with what happens to man, but with what a man does.

You know that our moral teaching unconditionally praises the moral will and its virtue above all things and equally for each human life. This moral will consist in the energy, vitality and purity of the soul. The health of the soul consists in that vital strength which generates peace, patience, inner valour of spirit and moderation, the antidotes to pusillanimity and loss of self-confidence. It not only draws the life of man along by means of habits acquired from without, but it also lends form to the life of man by means of its own vitality. But then again we say: inner nobility of character is primarily to be found in *purity of soul*, which subordinates the vital strength of the soul to its own conviction of the idea of the good. That vital strength of soul, commendable as it is in itself, can assume a brutalised appearance by surrendering itself to an alien service, or by casting itself away upon base appetites. The sacred seriousness of the moral life is, thus, first of all to be found in the unconditional subjection of the pure energy of the soul to the idea of the good. If we wished to sum up in a single word the type of person who is worthy of unconditional praise, we should say: The man who has *purity of soul*.

If we wish to pass judgement upon or lay down laws for the life of someone else, we shall find that it is impossible to express the law of virtue in strictly regulated prescriptions concerning what ought to be done and what ought to be left undone. Virtue issues commands to the inner life of the character alone, and its essence is freely recognised in a judgement which belongs to feeling. If we wish to pass judgement upon the true worth of someone else's life, we must remember that virtue is not the law. What is important is not the fact that an externally virtuous action has been performed but that virtue has been internally willed and practised. The traditional teaching of Christianity maintains: It is not the law and dead works but the faith in which we live and act which alone makes blessed. Where we pass judgement, not upon ourselves, but upon the lives of others, good works are but the slaughtered body of the mortal angel which you may safely consign to the earth with what pageantry you please. Of us is required the spirit which wishes to be recognised with power and the sense of piety, the spirit which calls its law: purity of soul. The man who, with vital power, achieves such purity, also achieves fullness of life; he will, for the sheer love of such purity, loyally subject himself to all the demands of honour, justice and piety.

> To be but pure in heart!
> To scale the last and steepest slope!
> What wise men thought,
> But wiser yet performed!

And what, now, is the intrinsic nature of purity of heart? It is like the beauty of a garden in bloom! Beside the high-crowned palm — tiny flowers in the grass; beside the mighty trunks of the cedar and the oak — the delicate tendrils of the vine and the liana. Neither reproaches the other. None is valued on account of its usefulness to the others, but each is valued on account of its own intrinsic beauty. So, too, with beauty of soul. Beside the mighty power of heroic greatness — the gentle life of love; beside the quiet sacrifice to understanding and art — the mighty flames of piety and patriotism. No matter how many thousandfold the forms of life, both great and small, purity of soul has no wish either to serve or to control. In the Eden of eternal life, each spiritual blossom unfolds its intrinsic beauty and the sublimity of its growth in purity of heart and in the rays of the higher eternal light.

Otto: You have made clear to me that what is able to please us inwardly in the spirit of man is simply the beauty or sublimity of this spiritual life itself. Our judgement of moral value therefore belongs, so to speak, to a moral taste, to a pure feeling of beauty. What I have reservations about is this: We cannot argue so definitely with each other about matters of taste; in the end we are obliged to accept that each person has his own taste. Now, what is the situation with respect to the strict demands of our duty to adhere to honour and justice?

Philanthes: If you pay proper attention to my teaching, you will find that it is modest and unpretentious. The pure teaching of wisdom will not pander to the pride which deems itself better than others; nor does it aim to settle the dispute between those who are quarrelling about who is better. My teaching is simply addressed to the person who is resolved to be pure of heart and who asks *himself on his own account* what ought to be the object of his striving.

The important point here is this: if the man of good disposition asks what he ought to do, the answer will be clear. If, on the other hand, he asks how the worth of another person is to be judged, let him beware of misunderstanding the answer as a result of vanity or empty curiosity.

Our judgement concerning the moral worth of the life of someone else is, indeed, just such a moral judgement of taste. But do not, for that reason, suppose that the decision is merely made on the basis of vague feelings. Of course, the ordinary, free beauty of nature is left to feelings which are indeterminable. But every beauty which recognises an ideal — and especially the noble beauty which is beauty of soul, the subject of our present conversation — is based upon a fixed law to which it must first pay hommage, if it is to be a fitting object of praise. Merely consider the physical form of man. Must it not conform to a certain symmetry of structure, so that the beauty of its finer formation is only discernible under the law of symmetry? In precisely like manner, the norms of honour and justice are layed down for the ideal of spiritual beauty, norms to which every spiritual faculty, which can be called beautiful, must pay hommage. But the manner of this hommage will manifest itself in the free beauty of life in endlessly diverse forms.

Thus will it manifest itself to you in life. Upon a person's skilfulness or ineptitude you may pass judgement with ease. But concerning who is good or bad you will rarely presume to make a strict decision. For in raising this question the sole object of our enquiry is the innermost spirit. And how difficult it is correctly to take account of the influence of external circumstances in the case of someone else in order to divine the pure interior.

The sort of person whom many people call good is the man who is respectable, reliable, competent, the man who is a good member of society, the man of modesty. But cannot cowardice and lack of character coexist with these qualities? The true worth of a man cannot immediately consist of them. If, on the other hand, someone says: "Let everyone look to himself, as I do! If I meet with an obstacle, I sweep it aside, and what I cannot obtain by violent means I seek to gain by cunning." In such a person, murder and duplicity may conceal great energy of spirit which had simply had no opportunity to develop itself in the brutal circumstances in which it found itself. And then again, to take a contrasting case: gentleness and peacefulness of disposition can easily, though wrongly, be construed as cowardice. Thus, many of us display compliancy and patience in the minor affairs of daily life. It is not that courage is lacking; it is simply that the conflict or the effort is not deemed worthwhile. But when the call of the fatherland rang out, energy of spirit suddenly manifested itself, bold and free, and the good corn was winnowed from the chaff. Now, it is only to a few that the great test comes. And if it does not come, then all we can judge is the skilfulness or the ineptitude of the person concerned; all that we can assess is whether or not the person concerned is able to maintain his position in society. The inner spirit of his behaviour, however, is concealed from us.

Accordingly, energy, vitality and purity of soul is to be found in everyone who wills the good and who is truly worthy. But let us pursue our questioning further: What form will such a life assume? — We can no longer expect a general answer. Our judgement of the life of someone else here parts company from the demands we make upon ourselves. In the latter case, everything depends upon the conviction and prudence of the individual, qualities which are first brought into existence by insight. Our admiration is frequently excited by the devotion and sacrifice to what is taken for duty by those who most lack insight and lead lives of the greatest barbarity — and that quite irrespective of the foolishness of the superstition of many positive religions and the prejudices of perverted morality. Certainly, the beauty and worth of the moral life can unfold with greater purity in the educated spirit.

Accordingly, our further question for each person in himself would be: What ought the person of education and purity of heart to designate as the worthy objective of *his* striving? And once more we must reply: the only thing which counts and the only thing which decides is personal dignity, the pure value of the spiritual life.

Woldemar: What I understand you to be saying is this: the pure beauty of the human spirit consists in the possession of the will to the good. If we were now to ask, "What then is the good?" only the educated understanding could give a correct reply. The decision is no longer a matter of the will but of insight, so that here even the purest and the best in earthly life could err and be mistaken. Furthermore, educated insight will say: The pure appearance of the spiritual life is the good. Many are the demands, indeed, which are made upon our will: we desire pleasure and happiness from sensible delights; we are obliged to concern ourselves in a variety of ways with that which is beneficial and advantageous to us; and, finally, conscience speaks on behalf of the idea of the morally good. Now, you maintain that in all these demands the real object of our will is simply the *pure spiritual life itself* and its temporal development. I am right in supposing, am I not, that this is what you now wish to show us?

Philanthes: What I am maintaining is this: the ideas of the morally good simply tell us about the value of the spiritual life. The one, vitalising thought of virtue is the self-reliance of the spirit and awareness of its intrinsic dignity. But this good, which virtue wills, is the only independent and immediate demand which is made upon the will.

For the purposes of clarification let us follow the distinctions drawn by Woldemar. Man desires pleasure and happiness. But as to who is happy and who unhappy, what the degree to which a person is happy or unhappy — that we do not and, indeed, cannot know. Let us look at life more closely. External circumstances do not, by themselves, decide the issue. The more precisely we make our comparisons, the more elusive happiness becomes, the more we find that every criterion of happiness lacks any fixed meaning. Opinion and dream, delusion and poetry play with the idea of happiness and unhappiness, and deprive every measurement of its yardstick.

If you ask people whom they regard as happy, you will find that some will reply: the rich, the healthy, the powerful, the successful. But what is the meaning of these claims? Laziness, stupidity, ambition and avarice can deprive the man who is so favoured of all his advantages, can condemn him to inward disgust and disquiet. The above claims relate, not to a man in himself, but only to the others who observe him and are able to say to him: you are responsible for your own unhappiness. How often is it not the case that the poor, the ailing and the weak are more cheerful and contented than those who are favoured with riches, health and power.

There are other people who will disagree with this view of the happy man. In their opinion he is the man of spiritual strength, the man who succeeds in healthily developing his spiritual power. Good! But here too you are considering the fate of someone else. Anyone who finds himself restricted in a merely external sense but who can still proudly look into his own heart will find complete compensation in that self-reliance. Anyone who suffers misfortune but who continues proudly convinced of his nobility and the merely circumstantial character of his misfortunes — indeed, anyone who would not change places with anyone else — any such person is happy. The person who is dull and listless in spirit will only rarely and in passing take notice of his own powerlessness.

I have a further question: Who is the happy man — the person who mourns or the one who rejoices? How often does the joyful person lack that awareness which seizes hold of the passing moment. On the other hand, how often does the man who mourns fall in love with his own sadness, making it the high object of his desire and the chief theme of his life. I am at last in a position to tell you the name of the comforter who restores everything to equilibrium. The name of the comforter is "habit". Habit removes the sting from pain and habit takes away the brilliancy of joy. In a thousand diverse ways habit enables us to delight in the unaccustomed and habit gives us the power to bear with ease that which is habitual.

What, then, can we learn from the man who would have us search for happiness in external circumstances? Nothing more than the means to the end, means of which we do not know to what extent they will realise the end. If we are searching for the wisdom which will explain the immediate purpose and value of human life, we shall not need, in the light of what has been said, to ask how happiness is to be pursued. And there is something else: do not our sacred teachings suggest that it is neither pleasure, nor happiness, nor yet advantages, nor any kind of benefit, which the man of education is to call the truly good? Do not our sacred teachings tell us that pleasure and advantage are not what man really desires in the inmost recesses of his nature? Do not our sacred teachings instruct us that it is the intrinsic value of a man's own life which is named in the depths of his heart? And the reason is that what possesses ultimate and true value will not point to something else, as to the master it is obliged to serve. Its validity is independent and free.

Let us begin by considering pleasure and happiness. We see the life of man exposed, through the external workings of nature, to the vicissitudes of changing circumstances which are sometimes favourable and sometimes not. — What else is the succession of pleasure and pain but the feeling of this dependency? What else is happiness than the secure situation of someone with needs who is sure of the means of satisfying them? Pleasure and happiness are nothing but the external circumstances which favour and advance man's strivings. These external circumstances cannot count for anything except in so far as they serve the spiritual life of man. If life itself were a matter of indifference to us, what significance could the means of its sure advancement have for us?

Deeper, therefore, than any wish for pleasure, there is within our spirit the idea of a value, of which life itself is the bearer. This is why we are able to interpret our wish as lying beyond all the vicissitudes of joy and suffering. What limits human life is the fact that it can only be acted out within the boundaries of the external circumstances which either advance or impede it. Pain and enjoyment, pleasure and suffering are but the children of this play of circumstances. The independence of a life freely endowing itself with form and independent of need would be worth more and would occupy a higher position than all the happiness of satisfied needs.

Such a life, independent and free, would know neither pleasure nor pain, and yet it would be more desirable than either.

In order to confirm what I am saying all you have to do is compare the benefit of the simpler morality, adopted by the educated people of our own country, with the distempered and fashionable corruptions of the nations surrounding us.

There is no higher form of sensuous pleasure and passive enjoyment than that involving the sure and efficient satisfaction of natural needs. Every artificial need, of which the end is pleasure alone, is foolishness and the desire for a mere diversity of pleasures, the distempered product of boredom. Man's natural needs — nourishment, habitation and family — are simple indeed. All else is artificial, the need and the desire being equally the product of one's own invention. Where this need is simply invented for the sake of subsequent satisfaction, all effort is a foolish expenditure of energy for the sake of a necessity which one has called into existence oneself and which had far better never been invented in the first place. Such artificial needs can only acquire importance if they confer form upon the spirit and thus serve the intrinsic value of life itself. They thus belong to the healthy life of the development of insight, the spirit and that augmentation of the spirit which is action.

Compare the soundness of our mode of existence which we owe to the magnificence of our public life, with the fashionable foolishness of our corrupt neighbours. Our simple morality despises the effeminacy of their domestic furnishings. Their complex dishes, which are regarded by them as delicacies, are a source of disgust to us. Their motley clothes which are chosen not for their beauty but merely for the sake of a largely tasteless change of form, together with their love of empty show, are objects of contempt to us. Our domestic life, in its healthy simplicity, is not the drudge of empty show but the servant of beauty. And precisely for that reason, the power of beauty is able to manifest itself in our public life, whereas for them that power is something quite alien. Consider the magnitude of our temples, the embellishment of our public places, the dominating and deeply moving power of our simply harmonies, in contrast to the frivolous artificiality of foreign music, which affords nothing but an effeminate and sweet diversion and the like.

Thus, pleasure and enjoyment can only seem valuable on their own account to someone who is less fully educated and too captivated by the charms of sense. By contrast, anyone with a right understanding of himself will have to admit that the ends of his life do not consist in pleasure and happiness. On the contrary, it is the more secret value of life which must itself first impart meaning to pleasure and happiness. How can pleasure and joy be the inner value of human existence when everyone who knows the supreme elevation of feeling or who has experienced pious surrender finds himself raised above all the vicissitudes of happiness and misery. The higher truth of the spirit expresses itself and casts all minor cares aside when the individual discovers his honour in the sacrifice of piety and patriotism.

This, then, is a full statement of the view that the worth of man consists, not in what happens to him, but in what he does. Furthermore, within the field of what he does, true value will be determined, not in the area where his life is subject to some service, but in the area where his life develops with its own peculiar beauty. For it is self-evident that the ultimate purpose of human life is not to be found in benefit and advantage. Implements and tools are only praised if they serve the purpose for which they are made. The same holds of advantage and benefit as well: what is at issue here is not the ultimate purpose but merely the means to its achievement.

What I have said is not difficult to understand. However, there is connected with it a theory of self-interest and egoism, which has found much favour with corrupt nations. In such nations a way of thinking which is not merely crude but also base has become public opinion. There the teachers of wisdom have not merely maintained that people are most easily led by egoism and self-interest; they have gone even further and asserted that egoism and self-interest are the only immediate motives of human action. Now, we are happy to admit that, just as the bull cannot be curbed with the delicate reins of the nobler horse, so too primitive and cunning people must be led otherwise than as men of a nobler turn of thought are led. These same teachers were able to confirm their foolish theory abundantly with examples taken from their own environment. Their error consisted simply in their lack of understanding of how to educate the spirit and, most especially, of how to regulate the life of the individual through the life of the public. It was precisely the assumption of public opinion there, that the only means of achieving anything with people was by crafty cunning, which secured victory for base egoism in the first place.

Otto: Noble Philanthes, a great deal of your present teaching is clear to me. I readily appreciate that the value of things is not to be found directly in their benefit and advantage, for things, of course, are merely means. Furthermore, I recognise how necessary it is to the education of a primitive person that he be dissuaded from egoism and self-interest, that he be shown the disinterested estimation of things, and that this estimation should be made a living ideal for him. I not only understand the assertion being made here, namely, that egoism is not the ultimate purpose in the life of the man of education; I also understand your contention that, for the more correct evaluation of even the most primitive life, egoism cannot be given as the final source of human interests. It would be a very defective judgement which would be satisfied with the information: what I will is simply myself. And the reason why this would be so inadequate is the obvious fact that a further question can always be asked, the question, namely: *What*, then, do I will of myself? And *wherein* am I pleasing to myself?

But although I understand all this in general, I still have one difficulty, and it is the fact that, in the end, it is egoism and interest, after all, which orders all the affairs of men. What other criterion shall I then employ in the ordinary business of life to assess the help, labour and work of others, if I do not employ the criterion of self-interest?

Philanthes: There is much to be said in reply to your words, brave youth. The difficulty which you expressed at the end is a difficulty which you have created for yourself as a result of your concept of human affairs. What you understand by business and intercourse is simply the labour of man and exchange in the market-place. There, each person offers the product of his labour to the other for exchange, demanding for it an adequate recompense. Self-interest must prevail in the market-place, and that is not the consequence of false egoism; it is rather the requirement of justice. There, each contributes to the general work of society, and this intercourse can and ought to continue under the patronage of just reward. In the market-place self-interest *ought* to prevail; such buying and selling is part of the healthy life of the nation. But the market is not, of course, the whole of human life; it belongs to the work which we are obliged to engage in but which itself is only the servant of life. What drives the artisan to strenuous effort and trouble? To whom is the fiercest battle and the bitterest sacrifice willingly dedicated? Examine for yourselves the simpler life of man. Consider the care and the effort of a mother on behalf of her child, or that of a father on behalf of his family. Are they the slaves of egoism? And what of the achievements of the communal spirit, where patriotism and honour inspire to battle, where every heart is filled with enthusiasm for the altars of the nation? None of you will be so obtuse as to want to explain all these things in terms of egoism and self-interest.

Otto: Right! I was simply thinking of ordinary labour, and I forgot the soul of the life of man, which all labour itself serves.

Philanthes: But we can consider your remark from yet another point of view. Self-interest and egoism are the indispensable instrument of all human activity just on account of work, for it is only indirectly that man can achieve his objectives. Each individual must acquire wealth and power if he is to gain and secure a position in society for himself. Here, *his* work is given to him as a task, and his work is distinct from that of the others; for this reason he must be egoistic. But all this selfishness, all this self-interest, ought simply to be the means to the realisation of the higher purposes which are of real importance. To establish what these higher purposes are is worthy of the supreme prize.

If there are some people who find it unworthy that each should care only for himself, but laudable that each should care for all, and if there are some people who wish to erect this into the fundamental principle of the true value of human actions, we can ironically reply to them: What is the advantage you expect to gain? According to the one principle, the concern of each individual for his own good is replaced by the partial concern of all the others on his behalf; according to the other principle — and it is a simpler principle — each individual is concerned with his own good. The result is that, in both cases, there falls to each person just so much concern as amounts to a man's whole concern. The warning against selfishness is not a pure doctrine of wisdom at all; it is merely a sound piece of prudential advice. One is put in mind of Genghis Khan's bundle of arrows: force united is more effective than force divided.

The significance of this is as follows: the person who genuinely knows how to provide for himself with honesty and purity, not in respect of what nature or man owes him, but in respect of what *he ought to do*, pursues the best course. My concern must be what *I* ought to do. But where do I learn what this is? That is the important thing. What we have been saying both for and against self-interest has in no wise revealed the true or the deepest ground of our teaching. This we shall only discover by asking of each person the searching question: What is it which is really capable of rendering him pleasing to himself? And we now reply: Nothing other than the ability to advance his life towards the ideals of spiritual beauty.

Admittedly, if someone simply asks the prudential question as to how people are to be led to specific actions, then the answer will be: if you cannot arouse their enthusiasm for your cause then appeal to their self-interest. But the question which we are here asking of wisdom is: which action is to be promoted as the good action? And here the only admissible answer is: the action which is the product of virtue.

One final question, therefore, remains: What is the product of virtue? To what will the educated insight of virtue point as its purpose and goal? Once more the answer is: self-reliance and independence of spirit. Spiritual life ought to manifest itself in purity, for it bears within itself intrinsic value as beauty of soul. Merely consider all the ideals of morality and see whether they do not harmonise in this one idea.

Truth, beauty and goodness — these are the fundamental forms of the truly praiseworthy life. But the demands of goodness have their own supreme claim, to which all other claims are subordinate. And what is the source of these ideas in us? Simply the task of endowing our spiritual life with beautiful form.

Truth is the law of knowledge. But knowledge is the first foundation of the spiritual life of man. The idea of truth demands that man should acquire inner clarity of thought, that he should win insight for himself. And the idea of truth imparts to this development of insight and to every kind of knowledge an immediate inner value, for it is in this idea that the life of the spirit invests itself with form.

Next to knowledge, character occupies the second place in the life of the spirit, and action occupies the third. But the realm where the character develops in greater independence of action is the realm of the ideas of beauty. Obvious as the power of beauty may be to those in our nation who are educated, it was a long while quite otherwise with other nations. Pure beauty everywhere serves to announce the ideas of the divine life within us. Indeed, it is in pure beauty alone that man grasps the divine. Once again, this truth has become manifest to us more easily because of the magnificence of our public life and the simplicity of our religious teaching. And, provided that the initiation of our youth is free from all false images, it must become ever more and ever more generally manifest.

The purity of our literature in its portrayal of the ominipotence of God and of the deep and pious significance of all natural beauty; the purity of our literature in its simple ideals of the moral power of love and friendship; the simple grandeur of our architecture, the pure form of our sculpture and painting, together with the pure sublimity of our music — all this gives expression in our public life to the essence of enthusiasm and the spirit which leads to devotion, and it does so with far greater vividness and far greater clarity than is the case in the customs of other nations. The barbaric and brazen refractiousness of their temperaments in rejecting the finer development of the feeling of beauty is the worst of the things to support the corrupt morality of our neighbours.

The ideas of truth and beauty thus derive their value from the fact that they are involved in the development of the spiritual life itself. But the most characteristic power of the soul is that of action. The fact that this power of action must be guided by knowledge and by the driving force of character is what first gives to truth and beauty, in subordination to the ideas of action, their true intrinsic worth. Insight and taste, which obey the laws of truth and beauty, are the distinctive and characteristic ornaments of the spiritual life. And yet the claims made by these ideals on the life of people differ a great deal according to the position occupied by each individual in society and the nature of the calling he has taken up. The pure ideals of action, on the other hand, make the same demands on everybody. In honour, justice and piety they validate, in each of their ideals, the single idea of self-reliance and spiritual independence, along with consciousness of the dignity of the human spirit.

To sacrifice nothing of the subtlest feeling of honour, to deprive no one of any part of their rights, to acknowledge, in pious submission, the higher meaning of the life of man — these demands, with their sacred necessity, spring solely from the inner nobility of the spirit and are, indeed, wholly identical with the consciousness of that nobility.

And all the other ornaments of the moral life — honesty of character, all the purity which is the product of moderation, innocence and prowess in life — we praise them because they serve the independence of the spirit. The ideals of love and friendship, ranging from the gentlest touch of sympathy, through family love and the closest bonds of friendship, to the holy fire of public spirit — we praise them because in them the dignity of the spirit is acknowledged in the life of others, and because recognition is given to the power of the spirit in human life.

Accordingly, it is the idea of the dignity of the spirit, the idea of self-reliance, which is *the idea* from which all the ideals of the moral life take their rise. And how is it with this idea? How does it apply to the life of man? We shall now be agreed on the truth of what I have been maintaining. The requirements of virtue are given to us with the idea of our intrinsic spiritual dignity, and they are given to us in such a way that every educated person must say: no matter how often barbarity, deformity or weakness may vitiate my pure will, I nonetheless wish and will, in the depths of my heart, one thing alone — that my life should correspond to these moral ideals, that I should raise myself, in accordance with those ideals, to nobility and beauty of soul.

The idea of the sublime demands justice of honour, and piety stands before your soul, sternly issuing its command. But this command is not something alien to which you are forced to submit by someone else. It is the purest idea of your own spirit. Its holy necessity simply tells you the name of your own truest will. Learn but to understand yourself and you will find that what is here required of you is nothing other than your own will, the dignity and power of your own being.

Arthur: The beautiful truth of your teaching is very clear and very easy to grasp. If a man considers the matter properly, he must find that happiness and prowess are never what he truly wills in the depths of his heart. They are both of them merely means to purposes beyond themselves, are both of them merely servants of the will. And if we then ask: where does the ruling power of the purpose which is valid in itself, where does the ruling power of the true and most inward will, manifest itself? — then there is but one answer: it manifests itself in the inner power of the spirit and in the beautiful development of that power.

DIALOGUE III

Moral Development of the Spirit

Woldemar: Noble and venerable Philanthes, we followed your teaching yesterday with particular enjoyment. The doctrine of moral self-understanding, in which all the demands of morality issue from the single fundamental idea of self-consciousness of spiritual dignity, is both simple and clear. Indeed, I find this doctrine so straightforward in its truth that I only have one more question left: How could such a simple doctrine remain for so long unrecognised? And how, once it had been recognised, could it be subject to such frequent misinterpretation?

Arthur: I wanted to make the same point. But there is another question which I should like to raise: How is it that such different and such conflicting views of life have arisen from such simple and fundamental ideas?

Philanthes: There are many superstitions, many prejudices, many factors in the involved affairs of man which obscure our view of that single, central, fundamental idea, which dominates everything.

If I am to give you a general view of the whole matter here, we must, as I recently said to Arthur, consider the gradual development of the spirit. We must, therefore, speak of man's great task, must speak of man's obligation increasingly to develop the power of the spirit, progressively to develop the spirit, through his own life and by means of his own inner power. It is only in relation to this great communal work of mankind that our teaching can acquire its full significance. I have shown you that, for the cultivated person, the only thing which is desirable is to make the dignity of the spirit the fundamental law of his social life. It follows from this that, for the evaluation of the life of someone else, it is solely vital energy and purity of soul which can render such a life worthy of praise. However, it is the conviction of the individual which first determines what the pure will of that person performs in life with vital energy. But this individual conviction can only advance towards perfection little by little as a result of gradual progress.

What a great achievement was the gradual maturation of the human spirit, what a great achievement the taming, in diverse ways, of the wildness of the sensual appetites and their conversion into something subtler, what a great achievement the slow acquisition of the habits of order, skill and industry, and, when all that had been achieved, how impressive the battle which was then fought against error, against subtle prejudices and subtle superstition. So great was this achievement that the majority of those who enthusiastically recognised its magnitude preferred to attribute it to immediate divine assistance rather than to credit man with this achievement in the supreme task given by God to man. But you will readily appreciate that had this achievement been the immediate work of God it would not have prospered so feebly or so imperfectly. Man himself must bear the responsibility here. Of all the things which man is capable of knowing, that which constitutes the especial dignity of his being is his capacity to shape the beauty of his own life.

How great must the past civilising wisdom of our forbears have been to have enabled us to rise from the first curbing of animal lust, the first foundation of order, the first introduction of cleanliness and modesty, to the present level at which the meanest member of our society today stands as a result of science, commerce, habit, custom and law, and, above all things, as a result of language, the mediatrix of all man's spiritual life.

To begin with, what was important was the curbing of the wildness of the physical appetites and the restraining of wild sense so that the sensual nature of man accorded with justice, modesty and cleanliness. After that it was necessary to establish fixed rules of custom to regulate the manner of life, and to control morality, commerce and law. Finally, it was important to maintain the vitality of the spirit responsible for change and progress. Consider the life of primitive peoples, the life of the more civilised peoples of Asia, and our own life under European culture. Among primitive peoples you will find that what dominates their whole spirit is the wildness of their sensual desires. In Asia, however, among the descendants of our most ancient teachers, you will find the power of blind habits devoid of all spirit of its own. With us, by contrast, the restless spirit of progress is everywhere still alive. Now, where this restless spirit prevails, error also makes its appearance, and the battle of the spirit with such error is the most difficult thing of all. Education is corrupted by false ideas. Feeling will probably soon show itself superior to any initial lack of constraint, but then we shall be in danger of seeing the emergence of lassitude and prostration, and the disappearance of our health of soul. In the past, this has often been the cause of the vanishing of a nation's culture and the death of its vital spirit, or, at least, it has been the cause of the triumph of a timid and action-shy outlook on life, in which the spirit grows confused and loses its earlier light.

In this general situation, where insight must gradually be re-created and error checked, there is such a diversity of needs crowding each other that, in the absence of a certain higher level of self-understanding, a great deal of confusion will inevitably continue to prevail. The understanding is still unable to distinguish moral and religious ideas, and it confuses images of the latter with the thing itself, so that, as a consequence, it imposes many foolish limitations on man's way of life. In addition, the rules regulating the satisfaction of needs, such as the attainment of pleasure and comfort, will be confused both with the demands of spiritual progress towards insight and taste and with the prescriptions of morality.

There are, to be specific, four relations which I must explain to you more clearly: the relation, namely, between religious and moral ideas; the relation between prudence and wisdom; next, the relation between duty and beauty of soul; and, finally, the relation between the individual and the public life. We must take account of them all if we are to avoid misunderstanding in our moral evaluations.

The most important of these relations — and the one which has been most instrumental in causing confusion in the history of man — is the relation between religious and moral ideas. I should like to draw your attention to the matter by means of a single example: religious consciousness of our own guilt. I am addressing you young men whose intelligence is sound, whose attitude to life is one of cheerful courage and whose hearts are full of confidence. It will be no difficult matter for you, therefore, to understand and approve the teachings of bravery, courage and confidence. You will, however, recall that, in all the religions belonging to the Asiatic tradition, consciousness of one's own guilt is the fundamental idea for the interpretation of life. From that one idea derive both rules for living and attitudes to life, and with them enthusiasm for self-reliance can easily come into conflict.

It is true that this consciousness of guilt and our own moral weakness is to be found in the heart of every man whose religious feeling is at all developed. It is this idea of guilt which gives to man's devotion that spirit of humility which accompanies him in his worship of God, and in his cleansing and purification through prayer.

This idea of guilt gives to all man's enthusiasm for self-reliance that spirit of sacrifice, without which nothing great is achieved in the life of man.

All that is noble on earth vanishes away. Only in death is man deemed to be happy. Consider the noblest figures of history. Timoleon had to bear the melancholy pain of fratricide within his heart. With greater cheerfulness, Epaminondas died victorious for his country. In poetry, Achilles and Siegfried both chose the brief, bold, heroic life with an early death.

This consciousness of guilt inevitably shapes our religious view of life. The clear and cultivated spirit, of course, recognises that confidence in the higher divine origin of man is not thereby destroyed, though the ideas of someone less educated are bound easily to fall into confusion here. This humility has been converted into a false and seductive idea, which has misled people of less education into attitudes ranging from pusillanimity to self-contempt, and into behaviour ranging from the life of remorse to repulsive indulgence in penetential practices. This misguided religious teaching has generated the prejudice that man is weak, fundamentally corrupt and wretched. It is this misguided idea which, issuing from India, has so frequently been instrumental in corrupting man's whole moral outlook. Instead of courageously pursuing the works of honour, justice, love and friendship, instead of patiently practising the endurance of misfortune and striving after all that is true, good and beautiful, those who have been corrupted by such misguided religious teachings have lost themselves in the ceremonial service of fantastic purificatory and expiatory practices. They have mistaken the true spirit of the moral life and come to equate it with the mere expectation of God's miraculous assistance, the renunciation of action, contempt for all self-reliance and a naive, indeed, a craven quietism of spirit. Once the mistake had been made it was, of course, difficult to give a proper hearing to teaching which was sound and pure.

Otto: I think that we shall now all understand you in this present matter. Man ought to seek his inner moral dignity in the capacity to restrain, with healthy self-confidence and clear sober-mindedness, his sensual desires and his emotional ebullience, and in his pure and honest espousal, in the cheerful enjoyment of action, of honour, justice, friendship and every beauty of spirit. We are put in mind of the warnings against the affected piety which good naturedly wallows in meek or mawkish sentimentality, in the process forgetting or even coming to despise action. The result is that this good-naturedness easily serves as a shield for superstition, which is constantly renewing the attempt to replace moral ideas by purificatory practices. Let us hope that we are saved from such error.

Philanthes: That is right. Be loyal to this venturesome and enterprising attitude to life, and beware of all empty dallying with religious feeling.

The second relation which we wanted to examine was that between wisdom and prudence.

The eye of wisdom is constantly focused on one thing alone: the ultimate purpose of inner beauty and sublimity of soul. But life requires a great deal to realise this purpose. It is to prudence that we must turn for advice in these matters. If wisdom is able to separate all the subordinate strivings after pleasure, happiness and the progress of the spirit, from the higher laws of morality, which pays exclusive hommage to the pure idea of spiritual dignity — it will, nonetheless, be the case that a complete rule of life relating to moral ideas will depend, for the sake of prudence, on the making of many provisions in life. Here, too, prudence and wisdom must be of equal importance. It will be important to distinguish the precept of the one from the law of the other, though it will not be so easy strictly to separate these different demands.

As an example of how wisdom is in need of the advice of prudence, consider our strict, indeed, severe, laws relating to chastity. To them, and to the noble spirit of our public life, we owe the purity and earnestness of family-loyalty in our nation. What extensive and artificial auxilary considerations of prudence were necessary for the ordering and justification of these laws! Now, do we wish to claim for this aspect of our morality and law that it is universally binding on all human beings? I think not. It is merely a positive law, which prudence recommended for the health of the soul. We are happy to admit that, in this matter, wisdom leaves a choice to the nations as to which of the many forms of morality and usage they should adopt. We merely sought to make the choice in the way which was most advantageous to the beauty and soundness of our lives. The barbaric lives of savages, which know almost no shame and no restraint to sensual desire, are more natural than our morality and law. Among our neighbours the police have a more indulgent outlook and their major cities are dirtier than is the case in our own country. We shall have to regard these defects as having almost the status of needs with these more barbaric and more corrupt peoples. We, on the other hand, know that the inner contradiction in such moralities has a deleterious effect on family life, for it indirectly fosters the spirit of falsity and deception. We also know how this, in its turn, so aggravatingly leads to the corruption of the rulers, and engenders villainy, brutality and venality in government officials. For this reason, we have thrown aside all profligacy of this kind as something hateful. We have, on the contrary, by limiting the barbaric love of magnificence and by means of the communal spirit, made it easier for each individual to establish a family.

What I have just said shows how the work of wisdom, and even that of duty, can only thrive with the help of prudence. As a result, you will have a clearer idea of this relation which, it seems to me, impedes the moral progress of man's convictions. But there is another point I should like to make as well. Even among the pure requirements of wisdom we find important differences. The most important is that between what duty commands and beauty of soul commends.

Wisdom, with strict necessity, commands us, in honour and justice, to respect the dignity of the spirit. But there is much, which is not identifiable with honour or justice themselves, which is commended on their account alone. As a result, the demands of duty part company from the requirements of spiritual beauty. Anyone lacking an exact knowledge of this distinction will easily fall into confusion in his moral judgements.

In order to clarify this distinction between duty and the spiritually beautiful or noble, which is distinct from duty, consider a famous example taken from the last war waged by our neighbours. The enemy attacked one of their cities. Some soldiers plundered the house of one of the citizens, and ill-treated both him and his family; they then drank his cellar dry and fell into a drunken sleep. Too late to be of assistance, the bridegroom of the daughter arrived on the scene. The young man embraced his bride with eagerness, though she was scarcely any longer mistress of her senses, and cried out: "Our vengeance will be easy!" — "Not so hasty, my friend," replied the young girl's father, "leave the matter to me." He carefully picked his way among the sleeping soldiers and removed their weapons. He then took two rifles, gave one to the young man and said: "Friend, our revenge is now certain! There can be no question here of injustice; the corpses can quickly be concealed and no one will look for them here. But first listen to me, and then make your choice. Slaying them will not expiate their wicked deed. Of the thousands we have only met a few. How would it help? Do not stain your pure hand with this ugly murder of revenge. When the time is ripe — then we can speak and act." The young man mastered his fury, and silently left to bring both mother and daughter to safety. But as soon as the opportunity offered itself, they presented themselves before the townsmen of their city and the citizens of their country: "Dishonoured people!" they cried. "You have been robbed of your possessions; your women and children have been dishonoured and slain. Such is the fate of the man who knows no honour and awaits his enemy unarmed! Let us now bestir ourselves, let us arm ourselves, let us wipe out our old shame and save ourselves from new dishonour!" Their appeal spread through the whole country and a fierce struggle began. Thousands fell, cities and villages went up in flames, but courage and honour lived in the hearts of the survivors. After a few years it was no longer possible for enemy troops to set foot on the sacred ground of the fatherland without leaving its fields covered with their corpses. If we consider the self-mastery of the young man, we shall not say that it was strictly speaking demanded by duty. And yet we shall, on account of spiritual beauty, call it noble.

The law regulating our family life is not prescribed by the strict command of duty. The self-mastery of the young man was not obligatory, though it was noble. Similarly, you will have to distinguish many degrees of praise in the value of human actions. But these gradations cannot be clear to the human spirit from the very beginning, and the seemingly contradictory demands which they make must often lead to confusion.

Our teaching, with its distinction between these various demands, must be formulated and developed with special art, if it is to be made convincing. Consider for a moment the education of children. The teacher must command them, sometimes in respect of what duty requires in the matter of honour, loyalty, truthfulness, sometimes in respect of what is required by mere orderliness, physical cleanliness, or even the prejudices of society. How shall the teacher explain to small children the exact nuance of each demand? Instead of attempting to do so, he will often simply rely on the child's love and respect, demanding obedience for its own sake. So too in the tricky matter of instructing the common people. The teacher does not venture to appeal to the insight of the less well educated. He rather appeals to the commands of God and the obedience due to them, relying on the motives of the love or fear of God. This leads to the teaching of wisdom being presented in a way which all too easily misleads the teacher himself into being insufficiently precise about his own insight. In educating children and instructing the common people about wisdom, appeal ought to be made to the insight of those receiving the instruction. But you will readily appreciate that this presupposes on the part of the teacher a spirit which has been subtly prepared, and seriousness in the instruction itself as well. The first of these two factors, the development of one's own spirit, is not something which can be achieved under all circumstances: for mankind can only make this spiritual progress gradually and by means of its own energy of spirit.

In moral instruction it is extremely important to learn to avoid the error of many teachers who employ the single form of strict command to express all that is expedient, beautiful and noble. But the situation is more complicated than this. Our morality and custom, our order and art is valid *for us*, but not necessarily for others. If, therefore, I am going to convince the pupil who is young in spirit, I must show him the situation as it really is. I must explain to him how he feels a strict obligation, admitting of no exceptions, to observe the demands of honour, justice and piety. And I must explain to him how other obligations — of spiritual excellence and purity, love and friendship — vary in their validity according to the individual and according to a thousand distinctions of degree. I must show that such obligations do not issue their prescriptions with the strictness of the commands of duty: they allow the individual a choice. And then I shall also show that, although these obligations are not duties, they do designate that which is alone truly praiseworthy. I shall explain to my pupils how these obligations, which do not amount to duties, invite him to choose the spiritually beautiful and noble, and to reject the vulgar, the ugly and the base. I shall in other words show how each person, provided only that he correctly understand the innermost wish of his own heart, will keep the inner eye of his spirit fixed in love upon these ideals of excellence, purity and friendship.

The failure to observe this subtle distinction may well lead to a situation in which full obedience is no longer rendered to any commands at all. In so far as the growing youth comes to suspect the binding force of some of these prescriptions, he will easily come to suspect them all, and no longer wish to obey any of them.

By contrast, if someone is shown the difference between the pure ideals of duty and those of spiritual beauty, he will recognise that what is here being expressed is not the compulsive force of an alien ruler but simply the clarification of his own will, the innermost drive of his own heart.

The confusion of duty with the requirements of beauty of soul will, on the other hand, easily produce resistance to the ideals of morality themselves. Such a confusion also serves to flatter an effeminate and affectedly superior moral view of life, which is unacquainted with the true moral force of the spirit.

Honour and justice are the fixed demands of duty, and not one iota of these requirements may be sacrificed in the vigorous and morally healthy life. Not all the fullness of benevolence and love can compensate for your furthering your interests in life by means of fraudulence, subservience, or any other crime against these sacred ideals. Benevolence and love are the splendid ornaments of the moral life: they will joyfully flourish like the foliage and the blossom on a healthy plant. But honour and justice are the work of duty, incomparable and incapable of being outweighed or replaced by anything else. Here, strict obedience is what is required. All else will follow! And he who withdraws the least part of his obedience will seek in vain to excuse himself and extenuate his shame.

Woldemar: Certainly, the subtle observation of this distinction must have the most important effect on the spirit of moral instruction. Such superior instruction will above all impart to the pupil the more lively feeling that moral ideas are never a dead instrument of skill or slavish obedience, but rather involve free respect for the pure force of the spirit alone.

Arthur: You have now made it perfectly clear to me how so many different opinions, all of them deriving from one pure, fundamental moral idea, were bound to arise. I now understand that these different views reflected different levels of spiritual development: at one level of development, religious feelings and their symbols were confused with the demands of morality themselves; at another level of development, consciousness of the demands of morality itself led to a diversity of opinions corresponding to the way in which prudence advises, and wisdom sometimes merely commends and sometimes positively commands. You then went on to mention what recently made such a lively impression on us in your speech to the people: the influence of the communal spirit in the nation, an influence which also extends to the individual as well. Give us a fuller account of this latter point.

Philanthes: It was this point upon which I wished finally to touch. Just consider what happens when you want to give greater precision to the teachings of duty and honour, in relation to the life of the individual. At every point you will be referred to the ideals of public life. And these ideals are ideals which the individual will not even be able to follow, unless he is favoured by the beautiful form of the communal spirit. We are here making claims upon the public life of nations, and we are doing so in the name of moral ideas. A nation ought to display character internally within itself and in its own inner justice. But it ought also to display character outwardly, partly, in the love of honour – by means of which it asserts its own independence – partly, in the love of its native country – by means of which it fights to the bitter end rather than allow itself to be enslaved – and partly, in the love of justice – by means of which the people acknowledge the rights of others, an acknowledgement which is free from any wish to dominate others and which is ready to accept others as equals.

These demands made by the ideals of public life will confuse and mislead the man who understands himself insufficiently clearly when he makes moral judgements about what is and what is not allowed. The purest claim that I can make upon the moral life of the individual is that of the sense of honour, which insists on resistance and tolerates nothing unworthy. The demands of justice are no longer directed purely to the individual. All that I can ask of the individual is a peaceful disposition. By this I do not mean that effeminate disposition which takes no notice of insult but readily ignores it. What I do mean is the disposition which is opposed to presumptuousness, and is careful not to encroach upon the honour or trespass on the rights of someone else.

How else, therefore, can you inspire your life with the idea of law and justice than by the legislative spirit of the whole nation? And all the friendly and joyful blossoms of beauty in life – love, friendship and family life, indeed, the lovely form of serene sublimity in devotion – how else will you achieve all these things than by means of a morality which has been sanctified in the public life of the nation by means of that vigorous communal spirit which lives in patriotic honour and religion?

The final part of my teaching thus leads me to the theme of my recent speech to the people: justice, energy, and health of soul can only be won for our nation – can only be won for *any* nation – by means of the force of the communal spirit and the noble form of its public life. The inner being of the development of spiritual sublimity and beauty evidently presupposes the vigorous and healthy development of the state.

Even when the moral teaching of a nation has been developed in the most subtle fashion, it will be incapable of anything more than a merely imperfect manifestation of spiritual beauty, unless the sublime enthusiasm of patriotic love and national honour inspires it and soberly regulates its affairs.

Otto: If we interpret what you have just said from a different point of view, it brings us very close to our main question. You have drawn our attention to the fact that the moral development of man depends to a large degree upon the level of the development of the state and the public life inspiring it. However, since the moral development of the spirit is what is supremely important in human life, this very same observation also tells me what we have to refer to if we are to assess the purpose of the union of the people in the state. Is it not true that beauty of soul is the one clear ideal of the moral life? The state ought to serve beauty of soul, and in it alone find its purpose. But the spirit lives solely in the individual. Accordingly, a state is only happily and well ordered if all the elements of its life conspire together to realise the following situation: each person in the state should be filled with inspiration, to the proper degree and in freedom, for this moral life and its beauty, and all the circumstances of public life should do as much as possible to protect and nurture this beauty of soul in each individual.

Should the question therefore arise as to what the purpose of the state is, then our answer will be that the most important thing is not wealth or flourishing trade, nor the long continuance of peace, still less victory and conquest, nor a continuing and unchanging constitution, nor anything similar — but the ideas of beauty of soul alone. Nothing else possesses any value except in so far as it serves to develop beauty of soul.

Accordingly, the most important thing in the history of mankind as a whole is the moral development of a whole nation in its public life, a certain uniformity in the formation of the spirit in all its classes in respect of all purely human interests. I fully realise that what is meant by this is something more and something more vigorous than merely the development and dissemination of a correct system of morality among the whole people. What is intended in particular, namely, is enthusiasm for moral ideas — an enthusiasm which, it seems to me, is a gracious gift of fate to individual nations.

Philanthes: Surely you do not wish to attribute progress so completely to chance! After all, a sound spiritual inheritance is certainly a great advantage.

The highest possible achievement in human history is teaching nations moral truth. But, of course, teaching is not enough on its own. In public life we also need the vigour of a forward-striving spirit, with its moral strength of will and its subtle feeling for honour and justice. But neither school nor the education of the youth will, by themselves, grant us these things. And yet we shall not have to depend exclusively on the happy gift of a special popular enthusiasm

— an enthusiasm which, it must be admitted, only a gracious Fate can grant us. On the contrary, there is a great deal in the habits of life, in customs and laws, and in the rites of positive religions, which must be employed to realise the supreme purpose, the education of nations. Is it not true that the first and easiest requirement which can be made of the moral life of the individual who wishes to rise above the savage is that he should be able to moderate his sensual appetites and the violence of his emotions. But how far has the majority of so-called civilised peoples advanced in this matter? Is it not true that a firmly founded habit, a truly tried custom, would be capable of effecting a great deal here? But how much is there still to condemn here in the morality of the rich? How little has gluttony, lust, stupid pride and the barbaric desire to dominate been restrained. All these social forms of life still very much belong to the childhood of man's moral life. Is not war itself, for example, with all its horrors and cruelties, not itself a consequence of our sensual barbarity?

My view is that, where this moderation blossoms into a peaceful and firm force in public life, the nobler blooms of the moral life will easily unfold in their beauty. It was for this reason that the Greeks rightly called such moderation the health of the soul. . . .

All moral education is based upon moderating the sensual desires and restraining the emotions. You no doubt know that, in addition to such moderation and restraint, we also need the nobler gifts of honesty and purity of heart. If, however, public life were to achieve such moderation and restraint, the major seductive impulses would disappear for the individual, and education alone could then effect a great deal to advance honesty and purity of heart.

You will be familiar with the fact that Aristotle concludes his system of morality with the observation that the most important of all the state's concerns was to provide for education, and that the only state in which the legislator had made such provision was that of the Lacedaemonians, whereas in the majority of other states each person conducted his own life according to his own lights, ruling over wife and child in cyclopic fashion as he saw fit.

If we compare modern civilised states with the above situation, we shall probably find that public provision has been secured in particular for general religious instruction, and that an effort is constantly being made to improve these institutions. But I see no public provision made for moral education alongside such religious instruction. Indeed, most people will probably regard it as impossible, for one half of man, namely, his body, has been completely forgotten in public educational institutions. But, in this respect, I cannot commend our new practices sufficiently highly. Spirit and body are so closely connected that the neglect of the one leads to the damage of both. Merely consider how much our nation has benefited by expending so much more effort and time on the training of the body than other nations do. In your youthful life together, you highly esteem the appearance of physical strength, stamina and skill. Is it only your body which benefits as a result? Certainly, you know better than I do what a great protection such training provides against wantonness and effeminacy. It is precisely this public provision for physical training which is the chief institution of the state for moral education, for it gradually accustoms everybody to that moderation which is the first requirement of morality. And in all the exercises of such physical training the participant must be honest, for here cunning is of no help to idleness, nor is fashion either — traditionally both of them, cunning and fashion, so easily putting an exaggerated premium on low trickery.

Otto: Certainly! The provisions made by the state must be capable of securely advancing the vigorous moral development of the nation. And provided that we keep our eye focused on the ideals of beauty of soul in our laws, customs, and, especially, in the arrangements made for public education, that advance will be made.

DIALOGUE IV

Julius and Evagoras

The old man had discussed various matters with the young men in this way. Then when they were gathered together again one evening, he came to them with some volumes he had written himself. "You know my opinion;" he said to them, "before I say any more, read these volumes among yourselves. You know the work and deeds of our liberators but there is much in the lives of the princely brothers Eugene and Julius and my father Evagoras that will make matters clearer and more vivid. From my own early memories, I have re-worked and completed what my father put together from Cecilia's papers." The young men took it in turns to read the volumes out loud, as follows.

It was our great Julius's favourite ambition as a child to travel through the Swiss mountains on his own. As a young man he put the idea into practice and on the journey he met Evagoras. Julius gave his brother the following account of their discussions. . . .

Evagoras: Look around you at the full and joyful life of nature. Does there not echo from every crag, from every mountain meadow and every Alpine peak, and does not every shimmering wave of the lake declare: "Language is but sound and smoke, cloaking the heavenly fire with cloud." Why should we wish to inherit, or borrow or prune, or affect faith and feeling? Faith, after all, is the Son of God, innate in every human breast. Faith is the first possession of every human being, the spirit's only guide. Such is the life of the straightforward and simple development of the spirit. It is only clumsy and measured speech, intended to give scholastic aid to faith, which first produces doubt and fear of corruption.
Julius: Do you wish to disallow, as I am told some people do disallow, all validity to scientifically measured language about faith, insisting that we trust to feeling alone? But where does the certainty of feeling reside? In the realm of feeling, is it not open to anybody to

say whatever he wants? In this sphere, is it not open to anybody, either in tears or with laughter, to censure or mock you and your claims?

Evagoras: I doubt whether I can give you an adequate answer straight-away. But we have plenty of time, so let us continue our conversation.

We proceeded on our journey, keeping close to the shore, from Stanzstade, round the Rossberg, to Fahr. From there we walked through flowery meadows to Sarnen. On the way, we continued with our conversation.

Evagoras: Just consider for a moment the following point. What do we really hope to achieve with our questions about God and eternal life? Are they merely the product of curiosity? If they are not, what is their motivation? The way in which a person expresses his faith is normally regarded as an important matter. To be irreligious, or an heretic, or an unbeliever, or, as others put it, to deny God's existence, to express contempt for God, or to blaspheme Him — all these things are supposed to be the most dreadful of crimes. But, on the face of it, I can see nothing there except the poverty of human knowledge, which is so unstable in its judgement of the most important things. What difference would it make to the world if the whole human race had cried out for thousands of years: There is no God and no eternal life. Would it make the slightest difference to whether there was a God or eternal life? In my opinion, it is enough that there is a God and eternal life. Let people say what they please. What is there, in such matters, that a man can do, either for or against? Everything remains the same, just as it was without his interference. Everybody will die soon enough, and then each person will, presumably, find out for himself whether he was right or wrong. Take someone who has firmly convinced himself by demonstration that there is nothing apart from the life which is bounded by birth and death, and who now finds himself ushered suddenly into the glory of a higher exis-tence. What more would his feelings be than the surprise of a child at a festivity? Surely, we are not going to be afraid that God will be angry with his erring, scoffing, blaspheming children? Even in the case of a good ruler on earth, we expect that, if he have a clear conscience, he will let his subjects speak, provided only that they are obedient to him.

Julius: What you say seems very one-sided to me. Our concern is not merely with the truths themselves. Opinion on these matters of belief has, after all, the greatest influence on human life itself. If man believed that there was eternal punishment to fear and everlasting reward for which to hope, would not this give him an outlook on life which was entirely different from that which the opposite belief would engender in him?

Evagoras: There are two things I wish to say in reply to your question. The first thing is this: you have arrived at the point to which I wished to lead you. You admit that the great value attributed to religious belief in positive religions is to be sought, not directly in man's conviction of their truth, but in the influence which this conviction has on his view of life and way of living. Is this not true?

Julius: I agree.

Evagoras: We must therefore see what the influence of religious conviction on man's view of life is really supposed to be. Now, you yourself maintain — and this is the second point which I wish to make — that this influence consists in the fact that man's outlook on life will be radically affected by whether or not he believes in eternal reward and punishment. But, whether the story of a retributive God and eternal life be true or false, the situation is, in fact, simply this: in this life, the rod is not prepared for the vicious, nor do they receive their stripes, and the virtuous day-labourer often fails to get his reward. We must, accordingly, try to make people believe that this injustice will eventually be rectified in the world to come: punishment will be meeted out to the one and reward will be given to the other. This whole doctrine is infected with a serious misunderstanding, which could only deceive someone of mediocre education. Without parrotting phrases you have learnt, what would your own opinion really be? Supposing that you were firmly convinced that the eternal torments of hell were being prepared for you because you were leading a life of love and friendship, and pursuing honour and justice, and that the delights of heaven were to be won by pursuing a life of hatred, contention, deception and duplicity. Would it then be right and good to act so as to avoid the torments of hell, or not? Must we not say of someone who lived in this belief that, while he would, of course, be very much excused if he adopted a dishonourable and base life, he ought really to act in the opposite fashion?

Julius: You are taking the torments of hell and the delights of heaven much too literally. How is it possible to make the distinction you have made? The belief in heaven and hell simply *is* the belief that goodness will be rewarded and evil punished.

Evagoras: As far as taking it literally is concerned, my view is this: anyone rightly understanding these things would speak in such a manner that what he said could be taken literally, image for image, and thing for thing. He would not talk in such a way that image and thing ran into each other, for then nothing would have any specific meaning. But let us leave this point. The second point you make concedes everything I need. Goodness, you say, is rewarded and evil is punished. So you already know what goodness and evil are, quite independently of reward and punishment. Love and friendship, honour and justice can only lead to heaven, not to hell. You have no wish to hear the opposite view at all.

Julius: Such, indeed, is the case.

Evagoras: If such is the case then it follows that an upright, trustworthy and pious life has its own commendation in itself, possesses its own value in itself and has no need to borrow it from rewards. The ideals of honour and justice, the ideal of beauty of life, are valid for the spiritual life of man even apart from any heavenly recompense. It is in these ideals that the beginning of human wisdom is to be found. If someone thought that God did not exist and that there was no eternal life, life would, indeed, apart from these moral ideals, have nothing to offer him in which he could truly delight. The energetic, pure and sincere espousal of honour, justice, and every ornament of beauty in the spiritual life would be for him, as it is for us, the only thing worthy of praise.

Julius: My feeling is that you are right, and that believing or not believing in eternal retribution ought not to affect a man's innermost view of life or its precepts. However, will not someone who lives in the happy expectation of eternal reward not fulfil his duty with greater confidence and more cheerfulness? Does not man need to be encouraged to goodness by the hope of reward and dissuaded from evil by the fear of punishment?

Evagoras: You are once more saying things which you have in all likelihood heard from other people and which you do not really believe yourself. Of course, someone who is still so crude as to be incapable of distinguishing virtue and beauty of life from casual labour undertaken for daily wages, must represent the matter much as you have done. And again, the majority of our nation is too lazy to give any thought to such things, and thus adheres to the old and mistaken way of talking about them. But you will have the courage and energy to realise that virtue can only display its power in life by being mistress of the crude appetites for the sake of duty and the beauty of the spiritual life. But how will the power of virtue prove itself in an action performed for the sake of reward? Such an action is valuable, not, indeed, for its own sake, but because of its reward. It is, indeed, the mere slave of an alien command. You will, perhaps, thus appreciate that enthusiasm for the ideals of the sublime and beautiful spiritual life — an enthusiasm in which these ideals are acknowledged purely for their own sake — is alone capable of securing and increasing the power of virtue.

Julius: You are right.

What, then, is your opinion? Is it a matter of indifference to a man's view of life how his religious convictions, how his belief in God and eternal life, are developed?

Evagoras: Have I then denied that the healthy development of the religious conviction has an advantageous influence on man's view of life? Was I not rather merely denying that the ideas of eternal retribution were capable of modifying the educated man's view of life? I am simply opposed to the idea of the divinity being worshipped under the image of the world's chief criminal judge.

But, apart from this, you have a choice. Which view of the world would be the more beautiful, the more harmonious in itself? The view which is embodied in belief in God and eternal life, and which connects our views about the value of human life with our idea of the origin of all things, according to which all life flows from one sacred source of all existence, and which senses that the dominion of the world is eternal goodness? Or some other view of the world which — with no belief in God or an eternal life — establishes no connection between man's own conviction about what is capable of giving value to his life and his knowledge of the world, or which even makes them actually incompatible, and which is constrained to regard the dominion of the world as surrendered up to the dead Fate of necessary natural laws. Who, if it were merely a matter of choice, would not give preference to the former alternative? In it alone is inner beauty and sublimity to be found. Furthermore, it is this view alone which gives completion to the moral ideals of life. Piety which, in enthusiasm and devotion, endows life with a quite peculiar beauty, is animated solely by this belief in God and eternal life. Certainly, then, the right and true development of religious conviction is of great importance to man, for without it we cannot perfect the ideals of the moral life, nor can we reach that higher understanding of the self which guarantees assured peace of soul.

And, in this connection, take careful note of these two points: whoever wishes to make religious convictions about God and eternity the ultimate foundations of his whole view of life will never attain to full understanding. In life, faith is one with the moral ideals of the good and just; it is given with them. But once someone falls into perplexity, and starts to ponder and doubt, and seeks the grounds of sacred truths, he must first of all come to some decision about the inner moral value of life, must acknowledge the ideals of sublimity and beauty of soul, and only in the second place consider belief in God and immortality.

The second point to notice is this: whoever seeks the higher understanding of the self in order to arrive at peace of soul should avoid snatching after promises as to how happiness can one day be securely attained. The true spirit of this understanding of the self is submission. Man should learn to feel himself equal to coping with every shift of happiness and unhappiness, should learn, indeed, to rise superior to it. Man should learn to appreciate that all the vicissitudes of joy and affliction merely belong to the trifles of our finite existence, whereas eternal significance belongs to the pure spiritual power of virtue alone.

With these conversations we arrived at Sarnen towards midday, and in the afternoon Evagoras took me up the valley. I commend to you the upper lake, in particular, and the position on it of the village of Lungern, with its waterfall. The last rays of the setting sun were playing over the region with the most wonderful magic when we once more reached the foot of the Kaiserstuhl mountain, where one has a view across the valley of Gyswyl and the Lake of Sarnen. In a short while darkness fell; the stars began to shine brightly and the moon rose. The region, with its dark masses of high mountains, displayed an entirely new beauty. Once more, we took our places opposite each other in a boat, and allowed ourselves to be carried slowly through the gentle night across the surface of the lake. The boatman innocently entertained us by telling us about his faith in Friar Claus, whose bench still performs miracles, for splinters from it heal the sick. I asked my friend: "Why is it that stories such as this, which are innocently acknowledged everywhere, always take the same form?"

Evagoras: It seems to me that perhaps all our boatman's stories are superstitious dreams, like the forty-year fast of his saint. On the other hand, perhaps all his stories, with the exception of the long fast, really did happen as he describes.
Julius: You mean as a result of a coincidence?
Evagoras: Oh, by no means! Healing the sick is, without doubt, the least and the easiest of the feats of the prophets. I had better explain my self at some length. Consider, for a moment, the power which our minds have over our bodies, in quite familiar and everyday

things. Consider the way in which someone who is taken by surprise or seized with terror displays quite unbelievable physical strength. Consider how often that happens in the case of fire or war. You are, doubtless, familiar with the way in which people, such as generals or absolute rulers, who are engaged in incessant and intense mental activity, can survive on very little sleep — so little that it would be quite impossible for us, in everyday life, to emulate them. And yet it does not exhaust them; it actually preserves their health. Consider, again, how often it happens that, when the wounded, both victorious and vanquished, are born from battle and carried to hospital, and there given entirely equal treatment, the victors quickly recover, while the vanquished irresistibly hasten to their death. Courage and hope animate the one, and despondency destroys the other. Consider, yet again, how often it happens that someone predicts his own death and dies as a result, while others, in exactly the same fashion, recover as a result of prophecy. Phenomena such as this eventually generate that extreme volence of emotion which we call fanaticism and which, so to speak, makes the impossible possible. The fury of the flagellants at the graves of the saints raises the intensest pain to that level of happiness which is deemed holy. The same thing is true of all enraptured bliss, and of the most bizarre and often sudden healings of illnesses.

Julius: Do you take all that completely seriously?

Evagoras: Many such stories are fabrications, many are dreams, but doubtless, too, many are, in all seriousness, facts. We can now test these things on a small scale by, so to speak, experimenting on people with very weak nerves.

Julius: Nature moves in a mysterious way. Your claim that there is no higher mystery in these things seems to be making me confused about what I have been taught.

Evagoras: I have no wish to confuse you. There is probably no real mystery here at all. For us the mysteries lie elsewhere in a higher realm. What is certain is that all these things occur as much in accordance with the laws of nature as do those things which we understand. Our comprehension of the structure of our own bodies and the cycles of their motions is as yet imperfect. The science of the future will make discoveries which have hitherto proved beyond our power. I am confident that then everything will be found to be capable of explanation.

Julius: Well, in that way superstition could be defended on the grounds of its utility.

Evagoras: Certainly! Here I am looking at the bright stars and the extensive landscape, with the moonlight around me. Why should I not be ready to speak in defence of superstition on this lovely superstitious evening? But I began differently. If we did wish to praise superstition for its usefulness, all the deaths caused by the wars of religion and all the flames of the stakes prepared for unbelievers would be testimony too horrible against us. There is no point in once more describing the dreadful consequences of error in the history of mankind. You are already sufficiently familiar with them. As I said, I am more inclined to praise superstition than to inveigh against it. For, among our peoples, faith wanders, naked and bare; it is forced to flee to superstition for protection. And who can blame it, if it petitions superstition for rags to cover its own nakedness, or even to adorn itself?

Raise your eyes to the peaceful light of the stars, regard the bright disc of the moon, look around you at the dark walls of the mountains, consider the waves of the lake. What is it that presents itself to our eyes? Inert masses formed into conglomerates by gravitational attraction? Or divine ideas, the higher spiritual archetypes in the eternal essence of things? Certainly, they are masses formed into conglomerates by gravitational attraction. But what about the other question? Do not the higher ideas of the spiritual life manifest themselves to us in all the sublimity and magnificence of nature around us? To me, this question is both truth and foolishness. Anyone who seeks to convince others that this way of talking is high wisdom is a fool. On the other hand, anyone who refuses to acknowledge the symbolic truth and significance of such language, on the grounds that it cannot be given a purely factual analysis, is a one-sided scientific pedant. We thus stand between the two positions, allowing to feeling its due. Holy intuitive awareness raises us above all scientific language. And we, recognising the rights of that intuitive awareness, will never seek to make it scientific.

And this is what will inevitably happen in life. A healthy love of truth makes one irresistibly averse to superstition, while a healthy love of beauty, standing next to and loudly contradicting the love of truth, lovingly protects superstition. And so superstition pleases us wherever it innocently presents itself to us in peaceful unpretentiousness. We are happy to leave the common man in undisturbed possession of superstition, for from him we expect no scientific education. Likewise, it delights us in a friendly and gentle girl, and in a woman of similar nature. But, in the case of a man who speaks with a pretence to scientific education, the grimace of superstition incites us to ridicule and contempt. Did we not this very morning benevolently watch a young girl as she decorated an image of the Blessed Virgin with fresh flowers? Will you not silently allow each dreamer, like our boatman here, his own opinion? For how will you induce those, who have no part in our learning, to distinguish things from their symbols? Take care that, in the effort to eradicate all error from their understanding, you do not also rob them of their picturesque dreams. With a harsh hand, you would be simply stripping the flowers from their lives, leaving nothing behind but the bare stalk of understanding. It is in this respect that the life of our peoples is deficient. It displays rigid forms in the service of truth, whereas the life of our peoples lacks the sacred power of beauty. For this reason, be indulgent when you see these altars being set up, no matter how small or poor they may be....

Julius: Certainly, you enlightened me a great deal about the true value of religious conviction. But what is religious truth? How is it to be — how can it be — secured? You say that faith is the divine element in human conviction, and you condemn the usual measured way of talking about it. But how is it to be changed? And how will you protect faith?

Evagoras: There is still a great deal to be said in this connection, but for the moment we shall only be able to touch on a few points. Let us ignore the issue of the correct expression of faith, whether it be the way it is formulated in this locality of that, and attend, first of all, to the following questions. What is faith in general? And how do we come into possession of it?

Evagoras here now began to make some seemingly dry distinctions. But they afforded me capital entertainment in the fresh morning air. I understood them straightaway, and I also found them very illuminating and important as well. So, permit me to tell you about them....

Evagoras: Let us, for a moment, examine what the situation is in general with respect to the certainty of man's assertions. Suppose that you say something and someone asks you: How do you know? You will answer in one of the following four ways, depending on the nature of the circumstances. In many cases you will reply: Someone told me. In other cases you will answer: I perceived it myself; I saw it with my own eyes. Then again, thirdly, in other cases, you will respond: Listen, I shall prove it to you. Finally, and fourthly, your answer will be: It is self-evident. Now, if we ask in general about the source of the certainty of man's assertions, we must exclude the first answer. For if I appeal to what someone else has said, and that person does not in his turn appeal to a third person, then he must either rely on his own experience, or he must know a proof, or the matter is self-evident. In the last analysis, therefore, we always arrive at one of these three last cases.

Let us begin by considering for a moment the meaning of the phrase: I wish to prove it to you. Obviously, I look for premises, about which there is agreement on both sides, and from which I draw conclusions which must eventually lead me to the assertion I wish to justify. In the absence of premises which are agreed upon, I cannot draw any conclusions, nor can I produce a proof. Would you not agree?

Julius: That is obviously so.

Evagoras: We are thus freed of one of our four cases, the one which is of no possible immediate use to us. Depending on the nature of the conclusions, each proof simply asserts that this or that assertion is to be regarded as certain because something else, which is presupposed, is itself already known for certain. Each proof, therefore, merely repeats the truth of its premises. So you see that, with respect to the certainty of our convictions, everything depends on immediate premises, which do not in their turn appeal to any proof. Accordingly, proofs, while they may be of the greatest importance for the order of our thoughts, cannot be called the first, pure, source of certainty at all.

Simple as this correct observation was, it nonetheless struck me forcibly. I considered how much effort had been expended, especially in divinity, on proofs of the existence of God and the immortality of the soul. I saw in advance that this observation would be bound to have very important consequences. But I should like to let my friend speak further.

Evagoras: I have mentioned four sources of certainty in our convictions: what others tell us, proof, perception and self-evidence. Of these four sources, we are now left, therefore, with only the last two as the pure sources of our convictions: our own perception and self-evidence. Now, let us start by considering your own perceptions. To what are you really appealing, when you assert something on the basis of your perceptions? We call this mode of knowledge sensible intuition, taking as our model the clearest type of perception, that afforded by the eye. These intuitions are cognitions of individual objects which are present to us. It is in this way that the eye and the ear and the other outer senses provide us with immediate information. It is in this way, too, that inner sense informs us; it enables us to perceive which thoughts, ideas, desires, emotions, are within us at the time. In the case of perceptions, we, therefore, assert something simply because we have come to know it in sensible intuition. Now, to what are we really appealing here? You will not be able to express the matter better than this: it is self-evident to the human mind that the coloured objects outside me, which a healthy eye sees, exist, that the sounds which a healthy ear hears, exist; and so on with the objects of the other outer senses. Likewise, finally, the states and mental activities, which I apprehend with the inner sense, are within me. — Many philosophers, it is true, misled by an erroneous view of the nature of proofs, refused to accept the immediate certainty of sensible intuitions. Instead, they maintained that the ground of the validity of knowledge was the effect of the object upon our organs of sense, and, through the mediation of that operation upon our sensibility, its effect upon the mind itself. But you can easily see that that is not the case. I see colours, and, in virtue of that, I immediately know what coloured objects surround me; I hear, and, in virtue of that, I immediately know what sounds there are around me. These, and similar assertions, made by everybody endowed with sight and hearing, are not to be derived from the assumption that objects are the causes of the impressions made upon my senses. This view has no meaning, if only because that which is immediately perceived is wholly absent from it. How do I know that an impression is being made upon my sensibility? If we adopt the above explanation, I must say: because it was the cause of another impression on my inner sense. And what is the source of my knowledge of this impression on my inner sense? Once more, because it is the cause of a third impression, and so on *ad infinitum*. This explanation thus affords no information about the perception which really occurs. Furthermore, if we examine the circumstances of the individual outer senses more closely, we shall find that the usual philosophical view makes the mistake of attributing to every child, every savage and every common man, certain purely scientific insights, of which they know little or nothing, and by means of which it is not possible to achieve one's objective anyway. What do children or ordinary people know of the physical oscillations by means of which sound is transmitted? Or what do they know of the reflections of rays of light by means of which light plays between the coloured surfaces of objects and the eye? And yet, these oscillations and rays of light are the only means by which things heard or seen operate upon the ear or eye. It would follow that someone who did not possess this scientific knowledge would not be able to see or hear anything. But even with such knowledge, nothing substantial would be gained for our case: since neither eye nor ear is the sense of our mind itself, but only its physical organ, no real explanation has been given of why we hear sounds rather than oscillations, or why we see colours rather than rays of light. You will therefore, presumably, agree with me that our conviction of the certainty of our perceptions consists in the fact that it is self-evident to the human mind that what presents itself to sensible intuition as present, is present.

You thus see that, with all our questions about the sources of certainty in our convictions, we have really arrived at the last of the above-mentioned four cases. We have, namely, arrived at the question: What is the meaning of the claim that something is self-evident?

Julius: Good! I appreciate that, if we rely on tradition or on what someone else says, or if we assert something on the basis of proof, this simply amounts to an indirect securing of our convictions: we are referred back either to perceptions or to something which is supposed to be self-evident. Furthermore, these perceptions themselves are simply a special case of that by reference to which something is self-evident to us. Thus, the riddle of certainty and truth for the human mind consists in the fact that certain assertions are self-evident to it. But this, it seems to me, merely introduces the most awkward question of all: What is self-evident? Indeed, what can be self-evident? Whatever I assert, I assert with my understanding, which thinks and expresses thoughts. It is precisely the assertions of the understanding which are exposed to error. We can err. Must I not, then, always raise the further question: What justifies me in asserting this or that? How can I say that something is self-evident here? Must I not always first be in a position to defend my assertion against error? If someone asserts something, then it is never self-evident that he is right. His judgement can always be mistaken. He must embark upon the defence of his assertion. Now, this seems strange to me. First of all we say: everything which is really certain in our convictions is self-evident; — but then, on the other hand, I must also say: no assertion of our understanding is self-evidently true. Am I mistaken, or is there a contradiction here?

Evagoras: You are absolutely right. But your two views do not contradict each other, provided that you make a proper distinction between what belongs to the immediate knowledge of reason, and what merely belongs to the repetitive understanding.

The assertions of our understanding, the propositions, the judgements in which we really become conscious of the completer kind of knowledge, can never, as you say, be strictly speaking immediately self-evident, for it is precisely these judgements which are exposed to error. Our understanding is frequently mistaken, in that it asserts propositions which are false. We must distinguish true propositions from false. We must, accordingly, in the case of every proposition, be capable of offering a justification of its truth, if it is to have any validity. What, then, is the meaning of the claim that an assertion of the understanding is self-evident? In this connection, pay special attention to the following point: All the assertions of our understanding are judgements which are expressed. How things are is not expressed in them *immediately* (for otherwise we could not admit that error could creep in). The situation is rather this: the understanding does nothing more than immediately *repeat* the knowledge and the convictions, which already exist in our mind independently of their expressions.

By this means we now see the meaning of the phrase: an assertion of the understanding is self-evident. When, namely, I prove something, my understanding derives one assertion from another. It asserts what is proved simply because it is entitled to assert that from which it is proved. Here, the truth which is proved does not need to be self-evident to the understanding; it is rather indirectly self-evident, for it is derived from other assertions which it has already made earlier. If, on the other hand, the understanding does not appeal to earlier judgements to justify its assertions but rather to knowledge and convictions which are immediate and independent of itself, then we say that the propositions are self-evident, for they cannot be derived from other propositions, but only from the immediate convictions of the mind.

We thus say: a truth is self-evident if the understanding is not able to inform itself on its own about that truth by merely appealing to other truths which are already known to it, but rather derives it from the immediate convictions of our mind alone.

Julius: In this teaching everything seems to depend on your distinction between the understanding, which thinks and judges and which is merely repetitive, and reason, which really has the first word, which is simply repeated, and which is, so to speak, the original which is copied by the understanding. Now, the first copies, which the understanding has itself copied from the original and which are not merely copies of copies, are the assertions which are self-evident.

Evagoras: Perfectly correct!

Julius: Now, what then are these originals of reason itself? What are the first copies of the understanding?

Evagoras: These immediate convictions of our mind manifest themselves in different ways. To start with, sensible intuitions are instances of such immediate convictions. I see and hear and, as a result, I am immediately convinced that the objects, seen and heard, are present around me. Now, if the understanding in its judgements merely repeats what I have seen or heard or, in some like fashion, perceived, then it is self-evident that its assertion is true, for the assertion is not to be proved from other judgements; it is simply the expression of a conviction which is immediately certain for my mind.

But we also have many convictions of things which cannot be intuited at all, and of which we can only become conscious as a result of reflection and the insight of our understanding. Once more, proofs are incapable of validating this type of assertion, for they, of course, depend on assumptions which come from elsewhere; and here, too, all the proofs must be based upon assertions which are self-evident. There must, therefore, be immediate convictions in our mind, which we can find in ourselves simply by reflection and the insight of our understanding; and these convictions have as much immediate validity for the human kind as the intuitions of sensibility themselves. Indeed, if you pay close attention to the matter, you will notice that our understanding is incapable of asserting a single proposition, without adding something to it; and this addition is not something which can be immediately intuited; we rather become conscious of it as a result of reflection alone. What we immediately intuit, for example, we know simply as the changing properties and effects of things. But that these same things have a permanent being, to which properties belong, and that they are the causes of those effects — that is something which we add to them in thought. Just consider your flute, for one moment. You see its colour, you hear its tones, you feel that it is sometimes warm and sometimes cold; but the unity in the being of the thing, to which all these properties belong, and in relation to which you say that it is made of wood and ivory — this is something which you cannot intuit; you can only add it in thought. This is even clearer in the case of causes and effects. Over yonder you see the shadow of a cloud flying across the mountains. But what do you really see? You see alternating patches of darker and lighter colour on different parts of the mountain, and up there in the sky you see the clouds and the sun. Now, if you say that that shadow comes into existence as a result of the interposition of a cloud between the sun and the mountains, you are adding in thought this *as a result*, this producing of an effect, for, in fact, you are merely aware of several states of things *next to* and *after* each other. Now, how do we come to talk of the being of things, of causes and effects? Obviously because it is self-evident to the human mind that there is a permanent being underlying all the changing properties of things, that there are causes underlying all the changes of these properties. There must be such an immediate conviction in the human mind, though it can only become apparent to the human understanding as a result of thought. In necessary and universal assertions, where I speak of all the members of a class, I assert something which no one can explain by means of sight or intuition. For who has made the intuitive acquaintance of *all* human beings, of *all* animals? This therefore shows how our ideas of God and the immortal soul refer to such self-evident and immediate convictions which are not to be found in perceptions. Such convictions must be found in our mind. Do you agree?

Julius: Certainly. But explain the matter in more detail.

Evagoras: From what I have just said, I can start by explaining what faith, as opposed to knowledge, means in divinity. Faith, like related words in other languages, really signifies trust. Faith in a truth is, of course, initially said when I accept a conviction because someone, whom I trust, has assured me of it. But, as we are now mentioning faith and knowledge in the context of religion, we must relate the difference between them to what I am here saying. I have knowledge of a thing if my knowledge of it has been gained somehow through intuition. I believe something if I have not myself seen it, though it is still my conviction. I believe something if I have a conviction in relation to it, which I only find within my self by thought. Among my cognitions, knowledge goes a long way, for, even if I am only able to think certain relations, such as those of cause and effect, and am not able to intuit them, I can still frequently point out the thus related objects in intuition, and in such a way that the above relation becomes intuitive and clear by example, as was the case with the cloud and its shadow. I do not know intuitively that a thing is a cause or an effect, but I do intuit the thing which is the cause or the effect. On the other hand, the immortal soul, God, the eternal being of things, the totality of the world — these are objects which are wholly foreign to intuition, and for which no intuitive evidence, through examples, can be given. Now, these objects belong to precisely those convictions which we entertain in religious ideas. They thus belong to the belief of which we can only become aware by means of reflection and through our own insight.

You will thus recognise that religious belief is the conviction in man which dwells within him independently of all intuition. It is the first possession of human knowledge. It belongs to the convictions which are self-evident for man, and it must dwell in human reason in a uniform fashion.

In order to clarify this last contention, consider the following point. Let me show you, namely, another condition, in the absence of which no error, no groundless fantasy, no deception, would be possible for man. Do you suppose that a blind man could create for himself a world of colour, or a deaf man a world of music?

Julius: No, that seems impossible to me.

Evagoras: And why?

Julius: I suppose because, when we create something we can only use such objects as are already known to us. New and strange as the paintings of imagination may be, they are nonetheless merely compositions made up of parts which are already known to us and which are simply arranged in a different way. Imagination will not invent anything which is wholly new. It may make a drawing of the chimaera for itself, an animal which nowhere exists. But a chimaera is an animal which is formed from the juxtaposition of parts with which we are already familiar in other animals.

Evagoras: Good! Is it not exactly the same with deception and error? The blind man cannot be deceived or fall into error concerning colours, and the deaf man cannot be deceived or led astray in what relates to sounds, for they are completely ignorant of such things. I can form a false opinion of a thing, provided that I already in a way know the thing. But in relation to what is absolutely unknown to me, deception and error do not occur. Deception and error are not primary in my ideas; they are always merely derivative in character. About something of which I know nothing at all, I cannot succeed in asserting anything. Only that which is known to me, albeit imperfectly known, can lead me astray into deceptions and errors.

Julius: That is incontrovertibly true.

Evagoras: We shall thus be able to decide in the case of any question whether it can be wholly based on error and deception, or whether it has not rather arisen from a sure and immediate conviction within us. For it is only that which is composed indirectly of other modes of representation which can have originated from error. On the other hand, the first content of an idea necessarily refers back to an immediate conviction in our mind. Take, to begin with, and by way of example, the question: could accounts of griffins and unicorns be nothing but fables?

Julius: Certainly! Experience has given me images of the lion and the eagle, and the image of the griffin can be formed from these images. The form of the unicorn deviates even less from the familiar forms of animals. These forms can, therefore, be the products of imagination, and it is observation which first decides whether they are real or not.

Evagoras: Here is a second question for you: could the accounts of ghosts be mere fables?

Julius: I certainly think that they are fables.

Evagoras: This is the same problem as before. A ghost is supposed to be the spirit of someone who has died and who then reappears in physical form, though not according to the ordinary appearance of human life with rebirth, growth and death, but merely in occasional fleeting appearances, sometimes merely in sounds, sometimes in a blow, sometimes in a misty form, or, perhaps, even in a real human being, who then rapidly and suddenly crumbles away or disappears. In all this you merely see representations borrowed from the ordinary experiences of human life; from them the creative imagination was able to compound its images. But here we can go even further. Indeed, we can even prove that stories of ghosts are certainly nothing but inventions, and that they have nothing to do with experience or truth. Cast your eye back. Only observation can establish whether or not there are unicorns. Natural history, presumably, can prove that there cannot be any griffins, for the biological process which is able to produce and preserve a lion will not be able to form the feathered wings and skeleton of a bird, as well. Finally, in the third case, relating to ghosts, the matter stands differently again. Every sensible perception gives us a single image; this image can be exactly observed and retained, and judged in strict accordance with the laws of nature. On the other hand, the images of the imagination are frequently of such an unstable and indeterminate character that they dissolve as soon as one tries to fix them exactly with one's eye. This is the case with the phenomenon of ghosts. A ghost is supposed to be a rational spirit which appears in a changeable and nebulous body. This is really a theme for natural history. Is there such a type of animal in the world, or not? But someone who tells such stories of ghosts does not wish to be construed in this way. The image is not to be subjected to such close scrutiny. How the matter stands emerges most clearly when we ask what makes something terrifying and what arouses our interest in such ghost stories. The real motive for these fantasisings is to manifest the spiritual, independently of all corporeal mediation.

Human knowledge, however, affords no example of such a phenomenon. The imagination, accordingly, helps itself by means of the seeming diminution of corporeality, for it construes the body of these spirits as vanishing, or as invisible, or as lacking in solidity, and so on. The whole thing is a fantastic invention, where the attempt is made to give an intuitive character to the idea of an incorporeal spirit. This idea itself, however, has arisen from our religious conviction. In virtue of its religious origin, it is the indirect cause of the interest taken by most people in such stories. An example of what I am saying is the dream: it takes its immediate origin at some point from our fixed and underlying convictions.

All ghost stories are the work of the human imagination. But the immediate basis of such stories is to be found in the convictions, by means of which our imagination is stimulated, that is to say, in the belief in the incorporeal and independent existence of the spirit and that which has life. The dreams just mentioned attempt, in their clumsy fashion, to give sensible form to this belief.

This should enable you to understand the truth and meaning of my claim that everything which is invented or erroneous in human thought is mediate in character.

Julius: Your explanation has made clear to me that poetic invention, deception and error can only occur in the mind mediately and derivatively, and that they always presuppose the presence of an immediate and sure conviction in the mind — always presuppose that truth exists within us prior to error. But if I now consider the matter from a different point of view, this immediate conviction can itself be subjected to examination and the question raised as to whether it is not, perhaps, vain delusion and foolishness?

Evagoras: What I wanted to make clear will soon be plain. What I am saying is this: all human conviction is founded upon man's first and immediate belief in himself, upon the belief that his reason is of value, that truth lives in reason. This belief is the innermost possession of every human spirit in its immediate conviction, a possession which can never be lost. Its truth, we have already said, is self-evident. No man can diminish or increase this truth. But the other truth, the truth which combats error, the truth which may sometimes prosper in the human spirit and sometimes fail to prosper, is simply the truth which is not self-evident, the truth which is first acquired as a result of the proofs of the understanding, and which, for that very reason, is always indirect and, in the last analysis, always rests upon an immediate and unassailable foundation.

If someone says to you that the whole of human knowledge could easily be a dream or even madness, and if you carefully consider the matter, you will not allow yourself to be inveigled into such a dispute, for, supposing that you and your entire life were merely a dream and madness, then it would follow that there was nothing in you which was receptive to the truth, nothing in you which could settle the dispute. The whole dispute is empty, for who would wish to convince a real madman that he was mad? Each person lives in the conviction of his own truthfulness, and he does so irrespective of what the understanding may say. In the philosophical schools there may well be many people who, as a result of misunderstanding, call themselves sceptics. In life, however, everybody knows what to expect from his neighbour and the morrow.

All the misguided talk of scepticism in philosophy is the exclusive product of confusing these two views of truth. In man the understanding errs, but it is also capable of being instructed. But for reason, which instricts the understanding, there is no conflict between truth and error at all. In reason, there is, in virtue of the belief in self-reliance, nothing but immediate, self-evident certainty. Beyond this human language cannot proceed. You must admit this.

Julius: Yes, I must certainly accept what you say. The understanding of man can only repeat, can only copy the original in reason, an original which is inviolable for it. Its scepticism and negation, if it concerns the first convictions themselves, is always merely a false copying, for these first convictions are present in our mind quite independently of the understanding. This is already manifest in scepticism, dreams and error themselves, for they only arise indirectly, and thus only as a result of something else — the prior first truth.

Evagoras: This conclusion, that all falsity, error and dream in human opinions is merely something indirect, which derives, in the last analysis, from inviolable truth, is a conclusion of the utmost importance.

If you examine the history of man's opinions, and if you take note of all the barbaric madness of religious superstition and all the contradictory opinions about goodness and beauty, you could easily begin to wonder whether any of these opinions had any firm foundation of truth — whether they were not simply dreams. It is difficult to determine to what extent the operation of the dreaming imagination enters into our religious convictions and our ideas of goodness and beauty. In all this, it will be difficult to determine the genuine foundation of necessary truth. But you will agree that we have gained this much: we are certain that, with the immediate convictions of the mind, we possess *some* such necessary foundation of truth, whatever it may be, because the merely mediated opinions, whether they be false or dreamt, must be based upon *something* which is immediate; and that can only be inviolable truth.

You will thus concede that all our assertions are based upon assertions which are self-evident, and that the immediate convictions of the human mind are expressed in these self-evident assertions. About them there cannot really be any dispute, for they are valid for every human being *qua* human being, and that validity is uniform in character and independent of the individual will.

With this I was in agreement. We now proceeded to discuss religious conviction in greater detail. On the basis of what had been said so far, Evagoras now showed that our religious opinions must be founded on a conviction which was immediate and certain for every human being, religious beliefs admitting neither of validation by mere proofs, nor yet of rejection as delusion and error.

Evagoras: You will concede that, in order to show that the religious opinions of man cannot be simply dream, deception and error, all I have to establish is that they contain immediate and distinctive ideas of their own, which are not merely compounded from other ideas. But this is easily established. At the centre of our religious opinions are to be found the ideas of God and eternal life. Whatever images may be used in talking about the divine, the transcendent and the heavenly, as opposed to the temporal, you will find in the fundamental idea of God and eternal life something distinctive, which is not derived from natural cognitions, and which cannot, therefore, be the mere product of the imagination. The idea of God designates for us the one, holy, first cause of all things. The idea of eternal life designates for us the being of things, which is distinct from all the finite existence of the empirical world. Now, even if I say nothing about the existence of God or the immortality of the soul, our concepts of both contain the idea of the unity of all things, and the idea of an absolutely perfect, infinite and unconditioned being of things. Moreover, if we wish to develop these ideas of God and eternal life, the mode of thought which we employ is that of progression, which involves advancing to what is supreme — the ideas of omnipotence, omnipresence, blessedness, and the like. It is true that the imagination can employ these ideas in many ways to develop other notions, but, according to what has been established so far, there must necessarily be a place in our immediate convictions where these ideas of perfected unity and of what is supreme take their rise in our representations, and from whence they can then be first given an indirect employment in poetic creation. Now, since none of these ideas contains anything intuitive at all, it follows that the place we are seeking in our mind must be that of faith, the first home of religious convictions. This same conclusion also emerges if you consider our idea of the eternal goodness which has created the world, or our idea of the beauty of nature.

This is also the real reason why our religious convictions cannot and may not be defended by means of proofs. But this last point will become clearer when we discuss it in greater detail. This morning you had no difficulty in understanding me when I said that every proof presupposed something which was distinct from what had to be proved, something which had to be determined in advance as certain and from which the proof merely derived the new truth. If, therefore, in matters of religion we are, as has just happened, referred back to an immediate ground in our convictions which is itself religious in character, then it follows that the first and true life of religious conviction for man can only be found in this immediate ground. But if you are to understand me aright in this matter, we must pay yet closer attention to the many types of proof which occur in thought, and to the type which is alone involved here. I can, perhaps, begin by saying — and I hope you will agree — that if there is talk about eternal life and God in your convictions, then these ideas must, of course, necessarily be the ideas of the beginning and the origin of things. To regard the existence of God as something derivative would, indeed, be meaningless. If my idea of God is to have any meaning at all, then it must designate that which is first, that which is supreme, that which is the origin, that which cannot, in its turn, be derived from anything else. The situation is similar with regard to all the other religious ideas, the ideas of immortality, freedom, and others too. It is possible that there is a great deal which can be proved from immortality and freedom as from the existence of God. But these ideas cannot themselves be proved from anything beyond themselves.

Julius: Yes, that seems very convincing.

Evagoras: But take care. We can also conduct proofs by inferring the ground from its consequences, by inferring from that which is dependent that upon which it is dependent. Here, we must be completely clear as to why this type of proof is of no help to us in this present case. If someone were to say to you, for example: "Look, here is God's work! Look, this miracle, this beauty, this purposefulness in nature is the work of God! — Must there not, therefore, be a God who uttered this word, who executed this work?" — the person in our example has succinctly proved the existence of God from his premiss. We could, however, subject the premiss itself to attack by showing that no one could certainly prove of anything that it was the word or the work of God. But this would get us involved in the unresolved dispute with superstition in positive religions, where it is so difficult to see clearly because image and thing are constantly being confused. But none of this is necessary for us. Let us merely examine more closely the type of proof which seeks to derive the ground from the consequences. We shall reach the conclusion we need straightaway.

Here is a simple example: you hear my voice without actually seeing me, and from that you infer my presence. Someone else, who is not acquainted with me, will only draw the imprecise conclusion that someone or other is present. Finally, a third person, with even less knowledge, will merely infer the presence of some object or other which is making a noise. It is clear from this series of gradations that we are capable of coming to know the ground from its consequences only to the extent that its nature is already known to us beforehand. Someone who is to recognise me from my voice must already be acquainted with me and my voice. And the same thing holds in all similar circumstances. If I am able to infer the ground from the consequences, then there must already have been talk of this ground at an earlier stage in my knowledge. So too, therefore, if the inference from the works of God to the existence of God is to be intelligible to us, the idea of the divinity must already have been mentioned to us on an earlier occasion, at a higher place in our mind. Belief in the existence of God must have been inscribed immediately into the heart of man. This belief must have a life in man's thoughts which is both prior to and deeper than any indirect attempt to prove God's existence.

If, therefore, you consider error, dream and delusion about religious objects, it will emerge that there lies hidden deep within us a source of religious truth which the energetic enquirer must be able to find within himself, provided only that he hold fast to the question: where within me is the conviction which is immediate and from which the understanding borrows its words and the imagination its colours?

At the beginning I said to you that believing something really means regarding something as true in virtue of one's trust in the person from whom it is derived. Later, looking at another aspect of religious belief, I contrasted conviction without intuition with knowledge with intuition. If you compare the two more closely you will find that this religious belief also lives in *trust*, in the higher trust, namely, of spiritual self-understanding. This self-understanding is twofold: firstly, moral self-reliance which is based on the dignity of my own spirit, and, secondly, religious trust in the universal rule of eternal goodness.

Let us now draw two conclusions from these reflections.

The first conclusion is this: faith lives in the innermost part of the human spirit, a firm conviction existing in every person in the same way. The whole play of religious opinions in history can only have arisen from the more or less imperfect attempts to express this one faith. Our second conclusion is this: if we now ask how this one faith is to be truly expressed, our reply will be: this truth can only be acquired for the understanding by the gradual development of one's own insight. Outside instruction is of no use to it. For the human spirit, the truths of religion do not depend on history, or narratives, or tradition. They are innate in the innermost being of our spirit. Man can only find them within himself by means of clear self-consciousness and confidence in his own powers of reflection. You will have no difficulty in conceding these two points. For that which, in the destinies of temporal human existence, is announced in immediate knowledge to one person in one way and to another in another, is nothing but the intuition produced by sensible stimuli, intuition by means of which we become aware of the particulars which are present both within and around us. But in everything which does not spring from intuition, no such accidental Fate rules over the human spirit. The changeless heart of man gives the verdict of conviction. That heart is the same in every human being: from it nothing can be subtracted and to it nothing can be added, without changing the human spirit itself. Now, religious belief is that conviction of our spirit which is furthest removed from sensible intuition. Whatever form it may take, it lives, the same higher possession for everybody, in the invulnerable heart of our spirit. Faith is, so to speak, the deepest region of the spirit, peaceful and unmoved. The waves of life, which are stirred into agitation by sensibility and understanding, only play upon the surface of the spirit. Or, to express the same thing in different terms, religious faith stands, the very sun of this interior world, motionless in the depths of the spirit; and all that lives in this interior world revolves around that single sun alone, so that it may receive light and warmth from it on all sides.

In the course of these conversations, evening had begun to fall. It was a source of joyful elation for me to see any treasured religious conviction secured from danger in such a simple and convicing fashion. These reflections seemed to save religious conviction from unbelief and scepticism in the simplest way. The dry clarity of this teaching itself, which never falls under the suspicion of wishing to seduce feeling or imagination, offers the most plausible defence against unbelief and scepticism. Both the boastful and the timid attitude to unbelief and scepticism are persuasively presented as puerile.

Furthermore, I was equally convinced by the claim that the pure expression of this holy truth could only be discovered by seriously searching into one's own spirit, and through trust in the truth which dwells within.

Late as it had now grown, I nonetheless urged Evagoras to tell me how he thought the religious conviction should be correctly expressed.

Evagoras: Here, every truly living message is limited by metaphor. If the individual is to be powerfully affected by thoughts of devotion, and if the whole community is to be suffused with the pious motion of devotion, then the holy work of religious symbolism must penetrate the public life of the nation by means of language and religious practice.

But the important thing for us is to discuss, without any use of metaphor at all, the idea of the divine and the eternal upon which the metaphor rests. What we, with our scientific education, wish to learn is how wholly to avoid confusing metaphor and thing. In this case, the foundation of the metaphor is the belief which is common to all nations and peoples, and which is expressed by everybody in metaphorical form — most people confusing the metaphor which is embodied in symbol and myth with the thing itself.

If we wished to draw a precise distinction between the thing and the metaphor, our discussion would be very protracted, for there is nothing positive which we can say about the thing under consideration here. We can only contrast the higher eternal truth with what appears to man's senses, can only contrast what is perfect, free, eternal and independent with what is imperfect, temporal and dependent, by using negative expressions. Permit me to mention one major idea. All the explanations which I could so readily give you about my expression of faith would be fairly obscure. So, just consider this one point for a moment.

Man is acquainted both with the bodies which surround him in the world and with the mind which is within him. Relatively to the being of things, the physical and the spiritual interpretations present themselves to man as being, so to speak, in conflict with each other. In its initial attempts to develop, the understanding gives priority to the physical interpretation of things. The understanding regards that interpretation as being immediately certain, and it aims to protect the spirit indirectly, by its means. It attempts to do this in a variety of ways, twisting and turning its thoughts, now in one direction, now in another. But the nature of the physical world is unwilling to yield any certain evidence of spirit. The hopes of the understanding are dashed over and over again. And the basic error consists in attributing priority to the physical interpretation of things. Spirit ought on its own account to be allowed a validity purely its own. If you make the spirit the interpreter both of your own life and of the world, you will see the moral ideals of life and religious truth suffused with a bright light. What was it that we learned earlier? That there is an impregnable truth concealed in the innermost part of the spirit, which is inaccessible to the language of the understanding. You asked about the person who wished to attack this truth itself, and my reply was simply that such a person had failed to acknowledge his own trust in the independence of the spirit. As for insight by itself and all its impulses — we could play indefinitely with delusion, madness and dream. But insight only has the role of servant in our spirit. What is important is the moral significance of life and its inner power. But this moral power belongs to the self-reliance of the spirit, and it is this same moral power which settles the present dispute in virtue of the perfection of its own power.

The idea of spiritual independence is none other than the idea of faith in the eternal life of my spirit. And the ideas of God and eternal life are valid for me with the same conviction as this self-reliance itself.

For someone who can say to himself, in the innermost recesses of his spirit, that he does not possess this self-reliance — for such a person, religious truth must be meaningless, and God and eternal life but empty words.

But human reason is endowed with this self-reliance. It is in virtue of that self-reliance that the infinite beauty of nature manifests itself to us, it is in virtue of it that the higher ideals of honour and justice, love and friendship, make their appearance in our life, and along with them there appears faith in eternal life and omnipotence, holy and infinitely good. Self-reliance and independence of spirit, as the animating ideas of our entire action and belief, must be the beginning and the end, the very echo of all human wisdom.". . .

Julius: Here I see and hear the deep meaning of what you have said. These mountain masses, these simple peasants — they all declare spiritual self-reliance, do they not?

Evagoras: You have, indeed, hit upon my best thought! Honour and justice — when will their pure and simple maxim eventually be acknowledged by a civilised nation? Dear friend, how simple and clear it all is, and yet how difficult it is to realise and preserve it. We shall soon be in agreement about these matters. What else, then, is duty, what else, then, moral truth, than trusting in the inner worth of one's own spirit, than feeling the inner nobility of the spirit and giving it effect? What else is it that man wills and seeks with purity in the depths of his heart, what else is the furtherance of duty, justice and virtue than this one thing: that the pure appearance of spiritual nobility and beauty should take form in human life? The preservation of one's own honour, and the acknowledgement, in justice, of the worth of the other person, and that for the sake of spiritual nobility and beauty — this is the fulfilment of the sum of all moral commands.

What makes our ordinary behaviour and affairs so pititful is the fact that we have grown accustomed, as a result of a foolish misunderstanding of religious humility, to a morality of cowardliness and mistrust. No one publicly advocates robustness of behaviour or resoluteness of character. No one has praise for anything but compliancy and passivity. Patience and peaceability are, doubtless, noble virtues. But it is also possible to be too patient and too peaceable. Do but consider: whatever would become of someone who in all honesty said to himself that he was thoroughly worthless? Outside help is of no use to someone who cannot help himself. It is indeed true that when someone is dead and honourably buried, he is of no further concern to any living soul. And that is just it! Scribblers in their books and preachers in their pulpits with their whining piety — they are afraid of life. Their wish is to help people at least to sleep, if not actually to death. They are too timorous to adopt a healthy, vigorous and courageous life.

Certainly, I commend peacefulness to you, provided that it serves justice. But I commend the love of combat to you just as much, provided that it serves the cause of honour. I commend to you the man of peace, who neither seeks nor starts a quarrel. But the man who cannot, or dare not, take up the challenge of a quarrel started by someone else and then pursue it to its conclusion is a pathetic wretch. Brave self-reliance is the only moral principle of life for man!

And for this reason, take special note of what honour demands: nobility and beauty of spirit, with its development of healthy power, makes its pure appearance in the just and honour-loving character alone. The chief command of morality is this: the avoidance, on the one hand, of the false arrogance which refuses to acknowledge that others have the same rights as oneself, and the defence, on the other hand, of one's own rights, which are recognised to be equal to the rights of others. What is important here is recognising the spirit of this teaching. Above all, distinguish the worth of the person from the subordinate worth of his position in society. In the context of everyday affairs, who will refuse to obey the orders of his superiors, or who will refuse to issue orders to his subordinates? But behind all these relations there stands the pure personality of man in its freedom. And here honour and justice apply equally to everybody — here it is the duty of everybody to defend their own honour. . . .

Julius: Honour and justice — when will their time come?

Evagoras: My ideals are the ideals of the great life of the nations. The person who is unable to further that cause is of no help at all. Those who are filled with the spirit of God, those who are able to light the flame of patriotism, those who can ignite the fires of religion — they alone can fight for this victory. The sacrificial flames must burn on the altars of the God of justice. And these sacrificial flames must burn in the life of entire nations, nations inspired with enthusiasm for religion and filled with fervour for patriotic honour!

We were silent for a while. I then said to Evagoras: "Ah, your beautiful dreams! If only they could be more than dreams."

Evagoras: Dear friend! The spirit of man receives all its good gifts from the hand of angels in a dream; and the memory of that dream ought to be preserved in the waking hours. May there be many, very many, and ever more people to dream this dream of ours. The truth which lives in that dream will awaken within them. And fortified to insight, it will also eventually summon action into existence. — What, then, do we really lack? I shall tell you. The great objective in the public life of our peoples — what else is it for the most part than a patchwork of individual lives forming the gigantic mask of a carnival-fool. How do the great men of our country show their greatness, how do they display their superiority? In ridiculous self-complacency, with absurd trifles and tasteless display, and by preparing huge quantities of food and drink sufficient to satiate thousands. And then there is the trumpery nonsense of their liveries, their stables, and all the rest.

Do you think that recognising these stupidities for what they are is wisdom of such difficulty and profundity? Could not this same pride and self-importance manifest itself far more robustly and far better if, instead of making a show of themselves to the people with these absurdities, they displayed themselves with the building of temples, public works of art, public institutions of education and benevolence of every kind? And just consider what a huge difference that would make.

My dear Eugene, was not Evagoras right in this? Would it not be easy enough to give all this a practical application?

DIALOGUE V

Julius to Eugene

I already find myself under Italian skies. Far away to the north, I can see the gleaming mountain ranges of the Alps. The serene evening pours out its rosy shimmer over their peaks, until they yield it back again to the sky above them, and sink into the night with a pale blue light. From here, in Milan, the end of my Alpine journey, I wish once more to send you a detailed account of my doings. . . .

I experienced all these things in the company and under the guidance of Evagoras. I could tell you a great deal about my conversations with him, but I shall limit myself to describing merely a part of what we said to each other.

We were seated at the craggy edge of Mont Brevan, high above the vegetation-line, in the open air. Before us lay the snow-covered mountains and glaciers, and the needle-sharp crags of Mont Blanc and its sea of ice.

Julius: It is strange that the first impression of the sublime in the beauty of nature differs so often and so completely from subsequent impressions. Something which, when seen for the first time, makes an overwhelming impression of sublimity upon us, will shortly afterwards merely present the appearance of serene greatness and pleasant beauty. . . .

Evagoras: The example of the sublime in the natural objects before us makes plain that all that is significant in human life receives its force simply from the idea of the independence of the spiritual power within us. It is not the external object which is the sublime. The sublimity is to be found within you alone. The object arouses your feeling of independence.

Julius: But surely that would detract from the sublime in nature.

Evagoras: A very dry computation will determine in advance what produces a permanent impression of the sublime in nature around us, and what does not. You will then, probably, agree that I am right. The magnitude of an object which is colourless, dark, and possessed of a specific proportioned form, will repeatedly make a sublime impression on you. By contrast, an object which is far larger and far more magnificent, and which, by virtue of its illumination and the splendour of its colours, reveals a greater richness of forms, will present itself to your unaccustomed gaze as something sublime. But, once you have grown accustomed to its appearance, what will remain will be serene beauty, whereas the overwhelming feeling of sublimity will have vanished. . . .

And why is this so? The reason is this: the feelings of the sublime simply apprehend the language of the memory of your higher origin in the divine life. You praise the beautiful for its own sake, giving it, so to speak, a share in the inner worth of the spiritual life. On the other hand, in the present case of the sublime in nature, you are simply searching for a symbol of the eternal ideas within you.

The intuition of external objects will constantly arouse within you the feeling of the sublime under two forms, and in each case you will find confirmation of what I am here saying, namely, that what produces the impression is merely a subjective relation to your spiritual activity.

To take the first point: How does that which is seemingly the most meaningless — the grey open sea, the pyramids, mountain crags — have such a powerful effect? Simply by giving your spirit what it seeks: a symbol of the eternal. And this only occurs according to your imagination's measure of comprehension. The individual object, as it were, is for you an image of the infinite whole of the universe. Intuited in its undivided unity, the individual object achieves the most which your gaze can grasp at one go. It is simply the limit of the power of your imagination which provides the measure and produces the effect.

The second factor, however, is the power in nature, which seems to constitute an insuperable threat to your own power — the thunder and lightning of the storm, the wild agitation of the sea, the roar of the waterfall. What is important here is clearly this: your physical powerlessness creates an awareness of your inner spiritual power. This awareness results from the contrast between the two. The power of phenomena presents itself to you as an insuperable physical threat. But within you is the free spirit's sense of independence, and that is invulnerable to any physical threat.

Thus, whenever we have the feeling of the sublime external nature simply offers us images for inner contemplation. If you wish to know what such an image means, you will only find it in the spirit itself. For this reason, the mind will be moved by sublime feelings in a manner different and in ways of greater diversity, once the spirit and its appearance are to be found in life itself.

Consider the highest ideals of literature, and especially the high ideals of tragedy and lyric poetry. Here, the mystery of the sublime manifests itself, so to speak, in the ideals of moral power, heroic greatness, and the religious ideas of the divine and the eternal. You will see true sublimity making its appearance in art, when, in lyric poetry, devotion is animated by the idea of eternal life, omnipotence, and holy goodness, and when, in tragedy, the power of art presents the moral energy of the human spirit for our contemplation in order to arouse our enthusiasm. But in all this, it is the spirit itself which alone counts. That this is so is most clearly apparent from the fact that it is not merely the conquering power which raises us to the sublime. The supreme ideal is the tragic ideal of self-sacrifice — the power of the vanquished spirit has its own intrinsic value, too.

Let me convince you. The gentleness of the elegiac moods has, of course, corrupted the ideals of epic and tragic poetry in modern art in a great many ways, and it has done so by offering us nothing but gentle sentiments instead of the ideal of greatness of soul. I refer you to the purest ideals of Aeschylus and Sophocles. The imitation of these ideals has never matched and could never match the original. In this connection, a future genius will first have to create our ideals for us. For the representation of greatness of soul we lack both the bearing and the background to the picture. Such a bearing and such a background is something with which no individual poet can provide himself. It is only creative nations which can produce these things. Since the time of Aeschylus and Sophocles, our nations have been uncreative. We lack the world of heroes! We lack mythology! We lack, as is often said, the Fate of the Greeks. It is only this inanimate omnipotence, before which even the gods themselves bow down, which the power of the spirit can stubbornly resist and to which, without being impaired, it can unyieldingly succumb. Before the living God, the human spirit cannot vaunt its strength; it can but bring the sacrifice of pious humility. The natural philosophy of antiquity gave the ancients the ideas of Fate. — May the Socratic-Christian philosophy give us the pure idea of spiritual power as an ideal, for conversion by a future creative genius into art. This pure idea is the idea of self-sacrifice for the sake of honour and justice. It is an idea which is aware that happiness and life are nothing in comparison to the power of the eternal ideas. The genius who seizes this idea will give us a modern poetic creation of true sublimity and true originality.

In this connection, consider the best of modern literature, that of the two German writers, Goethe and Schiller. Goethe's incomparable descriptions have a pleasing beauty, but it is a beauty which never rises to originality or tragic sublimity. Schiller lacks Goethe's perfected power of description, but the ideals, which are the object of my search, revealed themselves to him when he was composing *Don Carlos*. Unfortunately, he later showed that he had not understood himself, for he went on to philosophise about the possibility of reconciling the Greeks and Shakespeare. But let a youthful genius, endowed with a newly awakened and sound taste, develop in accordance with these models, and you will see the ideals of my hopes make their appearance.

We often reverted to reflections such as these. One of the most beautiful expeditions of our journey was the trip on the Lake of Vevey to Geneva. The panoramic views of lower Wallis, which we were just leaving, and the brilliant beauties of the area around Lake Leman, led us back once more to the same idea.

Julius: What you have shown me vividly reminds me of your frequently reiterated assertion that piety and taste, religion and beauty enjoy the same rights, and occupy the same territory, in the life of our spirit. What you have just said has made the truth of this assertion that much clearer to me. The self-reliance of the spirit and the pure idea of spiritual power are, indeed, the fundamental ideas animating moral and religious feeling. And here, once more, the fact is manifest that, in all the feelings of the sublime, it is solely the idea of the dignity of the spiritual life which makes its voice heard.

Evagoras: You will hear exactly the same answer if you ask yourself about the nature of beauty. What is the beautiful? Why do we call that which is beautiful, beautiful? Because it is pure spiritual power, or because it is held to be worthy of comparison with it. You will see the spirit of beauty in nature transforming itself in a thousand different ways into a diversity of forms. And yet the spirit of beauty is everywhere the same, for that which it has formed is pleasing simply in itself and on its own account alone. The mighty being which subjects all things to metamorphosis is not willing to submit to any kind of service; nor does it wish to arrogate to itself any dominion. To each thing it allows its own free atmosphere, its own life. Someone whose love merely drives him to take possession of the beautiful — such a person should be bluntly informed that he is not inspired by the pure love of the beautiful at all.

Run your eyes over all the forms of the beautiful, and ask yourself the question: What is it which pleases us, purely in itself? The answer is: Spirit and life. All the magnificence of light and sound in nature — what is it which invests it with nameless beauty other than the mysterious word of the spirit, echoing in the life of nature, half perceived but not at all understood by us. Ever nearer and ever higher, the ideals of beauty present themselves to us all the more purely and all the more securely, the more purely the essence of the spirit manifests itself to us. Ever further from the free play of forms and ever nearer to the spirit, the beauty of the human body excels all other beauty in external form. Beauty of expression in deportment, countenance and gesture of every kind, in their turn, excel every other beauty of the human form, until, eventually, you are able to apprehend the high ideal of beauty in the beautiful soul alone. That beauty emanates from the moral power of the spirit. Virtue and character are its names. Here, once more, ask of the ideals of art: in what do they serve the divinity? Ask them, what is the nature of their pride? What is the character of their claim to superiority over all common manual work? And the answer you will receive will be: the ideals of the spiritual power are alone important; all else is incidental.

Julius: Yes, indeed! The examination of any product of any art confirms what you say.

The sacred seriousness of enthusiasm transcends any kind of free play whose object is mere amusement. Its ideals, expressed in heroic greatness or the tenderest image of love, are simply the ideals of the inner beauty of the spirit. This is clearly evident when one considers the ideals of sculpture. Here, no beauty has any claim upon this art lower than the beauty of the human form. And even here, sculpture seeks heroic and godlike ideals. Furthermore, if one considers painting, the infinite wealth of subordinate beautiful forms, in which the life of nature is manifest, are easily separated from the single ideal of enthusiasm, which here too seeks its ideals in the beauty of the human form alone, in greatness of soul, piety and love. And likewise, again, poetry: its concerns climb ever higher from the lightest, charming toying with forms to sacred seriousness itself. And when its ideals are attained in epic and dramatic form, all that counts is beauty of soul, beauty in the inner life of the spirit.

Evagoras: From what I have just said, I can acquaint you with the distinctive spirit of the teaching which I regard as the correct one. For it is precisely these assertions about the significance of the feeling of beauty which are the most important of our convictions.

Compare the results of our observations. What is the essence of moral ideas? Pure power of the spirit. What is the idea of truth? Self-reliance of the spirit. What is the idea which is fundamental to our religious feelings? Independence of the human spirit. What, finally, is the sublime? Greatness of soul. — And what is the beautiful? The pure appearance of the spiritual life.

You will, therefore, see that the essence of the true, the beautiful and the good is for us one and the same. Its most perfect interpretation is manifest to us through the ideas of strength of soul and its virtue. It is only because of the needs of man's finite life and the requirements of man's finite knowledge that the ideas of the true, the beautiful and the good, come to be distinguished at all. In their essence they ought never to be separated.

If, starting from just this common essence of all ideas, our concern is to validate the rights of the individual forms of the true, the beautiful and the good relatively to each other, then we must, in particular, pay attention to the claims of the beautiful.

The human spirit is easily moved by the ideas of the beautiful, and everybody is happy to yield to their power. But what, fundamentally, is our interest in them? What is their significance for human life? As the matter ordinarily appears in life, the answer is easy: they are used to provide for our entertainment in the evenings, to provide for the adornment of our dwellings, to provide the rich and the aristocratic with the means of display. We, however, say: the power of beauty in the life of man ought to awaken our intuitive awareness of the ideas of the eternally true essence of things, an intuitive awareness or presentiment which animates faith within the sphere of human knowledge.

In addition to the ordinary view of things, which is based on understanding, there is, within our spirit, yet another view of the world — a higher and a transfigured view of the world, which belongs to religion and beauty. This transfigured view of the world has, in the ideas of beauty, its own higher right to truth, so to speak. This truth is distinct from the truth of the understanding, which dominates the sciences. The truth of beauty is the torch which lights the man inspired with enthusiasm, is the torch which lights the man of devotion, and all those who dedicate, or strive to make a sacrifice of, their temporal existence to eternal ideas.

We are all acquainted with this light of beauty, for it has penetrated to the innermost parts of our spirit. We find it everywhere present in the life of those who are cultured. Follow the whims of the poetry of the sentiments, and see how it toys with laughter and tears. The dreams of such poetry awaken the sorrow of an infinite yearning in the heart of man, a sorrow which may also be aroused by that which is the most joyful. But these very same dreams can also in their turn make everything in human life, including that which is the most serious, assume the appearance of the comic. And yet there is a deep significance in these dreams, and that significance is the truth of beauty. Similarly, in every elevated emotional mood which is the product of conscience or piety, you are rendering hommage to that same truth of beauty.

I am saying that this view of the world, which is based on feeling, is very different from the usual view of things, which is based on understanding. Because of this difference, it is generally regarded merely as the prophet of the dreaming and poetic imagination; and as such it is proclaimed to be made for the play of amusement and its delusions. People wish to deprive it of its truth, supposing that it belongs to the world of dreams, to the meaningless. But such is not the case. On the contrary, in so far as beauty inhabits these dreams and dwells within the poetic creations of the imagination, so too does sacred seriousness have its habitation there as well. This view of the world has not been devised as a mere plaything. Indeed, it has not been invented by man at all. It rather belongs, as the truest of truths, to the deepest and the firmest fundamental form of man's spirit. That other truth, the truth of the sciences, the truth which is based on the understanding, is and remains nothing but life's mediator in the service of work. — This holy truth, on the other hand, is our spirit's first legislator, which controls work in so far as it specifies the objectives of work.

By drawing comparisons, it is possible to recognise the truth of my present claims in ordinary, everyday things which are near to hand. Man's judgement of the nature of things is entirely different from the calculations performed by the understanding in relation to the business of life and the means employed there. Reckoning the yield of a field, calculating the amount of water flowing from a stream on to a mill-wheel — that is one thing. Contemplating the life and motion in a stream's blossom-nourishing play of waves, or in the germinating, budding, maturing grain — that is quite another thing! You can trace this contrast for yourself through all your knowledge, from the smallest of things to the greatest. The same is true of the relation between the feeling, with which you apprehend the sublimity of the star-studded heavens, and the art of the calculating astronomers, which tells you the magnitude of the stars and the laws of their motions. Or do you want a comparison drawn from life itself? Your assessment of someone's usefulness or skill is the product of a calculation; but the character which commands your respect, or a person's amiability, affects your feeling in quite a different fashion.

When the understanding is concerned to regulate or control the whole business and machinery of human life, it holds a thoughtful dialogue with nature, reflectively attending to its replies. But it is in silence that feeling and taste listen to nature's own language, the language of the gods, the language with which every blossom flowering in the light and the entire splendour of the beauty of nature around us perceptibly addresses us.

For someone in search of spiritual development, there are two things of importance relating to this contrast between the intellectual, scientific view of the world and the view of the world which is based on taste and the feeling of beauty. Firstly, we must neither use feeling to fashion science, nor may we aim to subject the view of the world which is based on taste to science, nor strive to convert it into a science of the beautiful. Each of these views of the world has its own distinct and separate rights, of which neither may be deprived. Secondly, the sphere of taste ought to be guaranteed its full rights. The truth of the beautiful ought, in its full significance, to be affirmed.

Anybody who is free from prejudice will readily concede this first point, namely, that a separation between taste and understanding, between the life of the feeling of beauty and the life of science, belongs to the health of the human spirit. However, a fuller justification of the definition and determination of the boundary between taste and understanding requires fuller investigation. My present concern, however, is the second point: the full guaranteeing of the rights of the realm of taste.

You have seen that this view of the world, based on the feeling of beauty, is to be found in the seriousness within our lives — but it is not fully recognised for what it is and for what it ought to be. On the contrary, all too often we entertain the suspicion that it ought merely to serve the illusory and idle play of amusement. And what is the source of this error? The mistake arises, I think, from the fact that this more vital view of the world has become alienated from the circumstances of our national life. . . .

Certainly, everybody lays claim to know the truth of virtue, justice and religion. But virtue, justice and religion are not themselves truths — they are action and feeling. Beware of the naked truth, lest it drive out action and feeling. Is not the most strenuous reflection necessary in order to produce a genuinely original advance in one's understanding of such things? What is the advantage of spreading so-called correct convictions, if you do not at the same time impart an understanding of them. What is to be gained by patching up the common man's catechism, if his understanding of the new one is no greater than his understanding of the old, if he recites the modern version with as little comprehension as he does the traditional? If one introduces an education which one is unable to bring to completion, the excessive preoccupation with the enlightenment of the common people about religious concepts will have a positively deleterious effect on the moral enlightenment of the people. A person who does not think feels himself bound, at this humbler level of spiritual development, by conscience; feeling will not lead him astray. The moral convictions of the man who starts to think inevitably begin to falter. And when that happens, independent thought must be highly developed, if it is to attain that degree of clarity about our relations to a higher world-order which will permit our old moral beliefs to be founded upon our new understanding. The man who half-thinks will only seek his own advantage, and try to free himself from the seemingly burdensome precepts of morality.

Admittedly, the loss of this or that particular image of this or that specific religious practice is a loss of no great consequence. But let him who robs the people of these images beware that he does not, at the same time, also deprive them of the life of faith as well — the life of faith of which these images are the symbols. Let him beware lest, instead of producing healthy clarity of conscience, he introduce moral scepticism, and thus end up corrupting and profaning both church and state.

You will now understand me. The one-sidedness of the conceptual, scientific culture of our day must be resisted. Warmth of spirit must once more be won for the life of the nation. The enthusiasm of patriotism and religion must be used to breathe the breath of life into the commonwealth of church and state.

The question which is, therefore, important above all things is: Who will once more bestow the warmth of life on the holy symbols of our people?

Heavens above! That is the achievement which our age needs and which must come — the acceptance of the consecration of religious symbols, with clear and honest thought; the bestowal of the living warmth of religious devotion and enthusiasm upon the strong and healthy life of the peoples, free from affected cant and all its wiles.

DIALOGUE VI

Providence

The following account was written to Julius by Eugene.

I remember Christmas with particular vividness. We were all gathered together at home, for Amalia was the queen of the festivities. Among all the children's splendid gifts was my present to Dora's little Philanthes, my favourite. It was a fantastic costume, with a bow and arrow. It was this which gave him the greatest pleasure -- and put us all in the greatest peril! Clarissa said to the lad: "All you need now to play the role of Cupid is a pair of bright wings." But he playfully threatened us with his bow and arrows, which seemed to be the exact opposite of Cupid's shafts. I replied: "You are giving him too pretty a role; there are, I imagine, other gods apart from Amoretto who are equipped with bow and arrow." Clarissa replied with the question: "What are you thinking about, you who dream of war? We are dealing with Apollo, the dragon slayer." Evagoras interrupted: "You want to be such good Christians, and here you are saying that, of all the gods, the god of love is to be despised. Are you not aware that Hesiod sings the praises of Eros, describing him as the strongest, the mightiest and the most ancient of the gods? Are you not aware that he celebrates love as the creator of the world? And ought we not to worship God as love? Is not the idea that love created the world, the most beautiful idea of which the human spirit is capable?"

The numerous little candles vanished with the disappearance of the children to bed. Left to our own conversation, concern for Julius returned to the mind of each one of us. That same day we had received letters from him in which he described how he was hard pressed in the battle and how the army was short of everything. In a situation like this, the members of a family are mutually moved by emotions deeper than usual. Everybody feels closer to each other. But no one is willing to suggest a common theme of conversation, and everybody soon falls silent.

And so it was with us. We were sitting together in silence when

Clarissa had the happy idea of calling Evagoras to account for what he had said earlier. She remarked: "In your opinion, the idea that love is the creator of the world is the most beautiful idea of all. Why, in that case, do you always withdraw when, in good faith, I express the hope that the Divine Love will lead us to a happy goal?"

Evagoras: You know how punctilious I am by nature, Clarissa. I must draw your attention to the incorrectness of what you have just said. As long as you do not question me, I shall not criticise you. But if you attack me, I shall have to defend myself.

Clarissa: Let us share your justice, as well. Give us, once and for all, a clear statement of your view of Providence and the divine governance of the world.

Evagoras: I could express my opinion in a few brief words, and you would then have no hesitation in agreeing with what I said. But that would be of no great help to any of us. In these matters, the prevention of error is always the most difficult task, and it is one which can only be performed by the understanding. For the pure feeling of religious awareness dwells in every human breast in the same fashion. For this reason, therefore, if you wish to hear me, I must crave your patience.

Eugene: Tell us your opinion in whatever way you wish. You know that we are always happy to listen to what you have to say.

Evagoras: Well, then, Clarissa, let me address myself to you with an assertion, the truth of which can easily be established. Man does not understand, nor can he understand, the purpose of the world. Let us consider this claim for a moment.

We generally imagine that we have a fair idea of what we want in this life. Whence and how we have entered this life is a question which may, if necessary, be ignored. But, to pursue the matter further: what will be the outcome of this life? What is the nature of the future life? Religious hopes and expectations relating to the future give our question about the purpose of the world, and all similar questions, its great interest. Anyone who has been educated to the level of religion will find these questions interesting. And then, too, there is the craving for knowledge, which wants to understand the past. You will agree that your question about Providence and the divine governance of events is the same as the question how the fate of everything harmonises with the one divine purpose, to which everything which happens in the world is subject. You will also agree that the true interest of this question is religious in character, and that its interest is the same as the interest of those other questions — what can I expect beyond the limits of this temporal existence, beyond the limits of the cradle and the grave? For man becomes quickly aware of the fact that *one* dominant power holds together and absolutely rules the whole universe, which appears to him under the order of natural laws. Thus, whether my question concerns the petty fate of my own life, or whether it relates to the fate of the greatest events in the world, the person who owes me an answer is always the person who claims to understand the idea of all things being omnipotently controlled.

To all these questions I must, I think, first reply: it is only because of the finite character of our sensibly stimulated life that human knowledge has to construe the essence of things as existing in infinite space and infinite time. The true and eternal being of things knows neither space nor time. Man's conviction, however, only touches this true essence of things with the living belief of all reason: the belief, namely, that eternal goodness is the archetypal Being, in virtue of which all things exist. But this belief cannot be captured in the concepts of any science or of any intellectual discipline. Properly understood, it belongs to the idea of the beautiful and the sublime alone, by means of which human feeling grasps life in nature.

In this way, therefore, I oppose concept and taste, the realm of scientific understanding and the realm of pure feeling within our spirit. I would now say: all the ideas of religious exaltation, enthusiasm, piety and devotion are to be found in this pure feeling; they are, of necessity, alien to science.

Clarissa: I am quite ready to admit that. But consider! Whom does that help — you or me?

Evagoras: Did I not say that the preliminaries would quickly be completed? But you will soon be disappointed by them. I am now already in a position to maintain that we do not, and cannot, understand the purpose of the world, for that denial is involved in what I have just said. The idea of the purpose of the world belongs to faith and feeling alone. However, in order to avoid any subsequent misunderstanding, I shall try to make this idea still more precise.

Consider, for one moment, the following point. If, even in the case of the tiniest of things, we are to understand the purposefulness of a thing, our insight into the nature of that thing must always be first imbued with a certain perfection. For example, let us get someone to show us the mechanisms of a variety of clock-movements or machines. It will not be difficult to understand the difference between spring-operated and pendulum clocks, between wind- and water-mills, between spinning- and weaving-machines, and so on. But it does not occur to you to enquire more closely into the purposefulness of the individual mechanisms. To do this, you would have to examine in detail how all the parts of the machine were interconnected with each other, you would have to follow the mathematician in his calculations, you would have to examine how the forces operated relatively to each other in accordance with those calculations, and how that harmonised with the prescribed purpose.

Understanding the purpose of a thing is always what one arrives at last of all. The fullest understanding of the nature of a thing presupposes an understanding of its purpose.

If you now proceed from the tiny mechanisms of human art to the whole of nature, you will quickly come to realise that you do not have full knowledge even of yourself. As a consequence, not even your own purpose can be entirely clear to you. And what do you know of the world? What you know is so little, so scattered and so incomplete that it could not occur to you to investigate the meaning of the whole. In order to attain agreement about the final purpose of the universe, we should of necessity have to have a comprehensive view of the whole history of the universe, for only the spirit of the whole could be its purpose. But man's view apprehends only a tiny point out of a limitless infinitude, and even that tiny point cannot be completely understood. Our knowledge of this particular instant of terrestrial life bears no relation at all to the infinite existence of the whole heavens.

What, then, can man know? Begin by turning your gaze upon the infinite space of the sky. See how all the motions of the constellations are measured by simple cosmic laws. Then come closer to our solar system, and finally fix your attention on the earth within the solar system. The light of the sun is the source of its life; its axial rotation measures the successive periods of the day; the oblique inclination of its axis determines the alternation of the seasons. Light, through the interaction of the atmosphere and water, generates plant and animal life on the earth's surface.

There was no trace of organic life during the most ancient period of the earth's history, when the mountains were being formed. Gradually, zoophytes and acquatic animals made their appearance, and then land animals emerged, albeit animals of species which are now extinct. Only at the very end did the human species first make its appearance.

The history of man goes back to those periods of antiquity when the hereditary distinction between the races began to take form. The nature of the peoples and the manner of their lives varied a very great deal. Understanding awoke to spontaneous activity only in a few nations.

With this spontaneous activity of the human understanding the history of man really began for the first time on a large scale. It manifested itself in the passing down and growth of intellectual culture among particular nations. The greatest history known to us of this kind is the Asiatic-European culture which came from the Orient to the Mediterranean, and thence to German Christendom. The story of this culture is called *world history*.

With this thread to guide us, we shall be able to assemble a really entertaining compilation. But notice how small man's greatest achievements appear in the nature of things, and how small what we call world history is.

From all the millions of suns down to our own, and from this down to the tiny earth whose surface alone we can observe; how immeasurably great is the history of the surface of the earth in comparison with the history of man; and how great, in its turn, is the whole history of man in comparison with Asiatic cultural history, of which alone we have greater knowledge.

This is the reason why even the question about purposes in the world can be asked only relatively to the petty circumstances of human life: relatively to the great totality of nature, even the very question itself is meaningless. The spontaneously active understanding imposes on itself the task of its own development in national life. The question which we address to world history is how the nations, from which we have inherited our culture, gradually advanced culturally. And in raising this question, we keep our eye focussed, not on God's purpose for the universe itself, but on man's own achievement.

Clarissa: Permit me to interrupt you. What you have said is well and good. I have no objections to what you are saying, but it sounds much too artificial and much too diffuse to me. My view is much simpler and much shorter. Is it not a beautiful thought that God cares for all living things, that he created them for his own delight, and that he wishes the happiness of them all? Can I not call these things the purpose of the world?

Evagoras: That seems impossible to me. There are many people, of course, who will find it agreeable to human wishes that God should have set himself such a purpose. But he certainly does not have such a purpose. There is much to be said in this connection. Simply consider, for example, the following point. If the Lord of the earth had willed that human beings should live together in happiness and pleasure, then his power must indeed have been small to have left this burning uninhabitable desert and this wide expanse of ocean where there could have been laughing fields. In the north, on the other hand, it is only with difficulty that man can protect himself from the bitter north wind, which has been the premature death of so many. Still more, he ought to have prevented people, so many of them, from delighting in the misery and suffering of others, for it is infinitely less painful to suffer at the hand of Fate than through the malice of someone who is stronger than oneself and against whom one is too weak to take vengeance. Is it not pity alone which is often sufficient to incite an impartial observer to wreak wild vengeance on the proud criminal who tortures the innocent to death? And yet, the gods permit such wickedness, allowing the sun to rise, now as in the past, on the just and the unjust alike.

Clarissa: You are obviously contradicting yourself. You yourself said at the beginning that we could not understand the purpose of the world. But now you wish to criticise the dispensations of Providence. In saying that, are you not placing too much confidence in the correctness of your insight? Do you know, then, what is necessary to a person's true happiness? Do you know to what end this or that suffering is beneficial to a person?

Evagoras: Did I not predict that we should soon be disagreeing about the application of that first idea? I would simply turn your reproach against yourself. It is you, not I, who have spoken with presumption. I said, and you agreed with me, that the concepts of the human understanding were incapable of grasping the purpose of the world. You objected that the happiness of all living creatures was the purpose of the world. By thus appealing to the understanding you are contradicting what had been said before. Happiness and pleasure are human ideas. The purpose of the world, however, is a divine idea, which our understanding is incapable of grasping. I am not criticising Providence. Trusting in its omnipotence, I am merely saying that happiness and pleasure are not its purposes; if they were, there could be no suffering or unhappiness. Certainly, pain and suffering and unhappiness of every kind are beneficial to man in many respects — but they do not immediately produce pleasure and happiness, for they are, of course, their opposites. I am all too familiar with the pious pretence which appeals to our ignorance. You made use of it yourself in your reply to me, for your advice to the unhappy man was that he should seek consolation in his ignorance of the purpose of this or that suffering.

If you wish to insist on this idea, then you must withdraw what you said to start with. Happiness is a human concept, and for that reason alone, you must not elevate it to the status of God's purpose.

Clarissa: Fair enough! Happiness may not be the right word. But you have not refuted my idea.

Eugene: It looks to me as if you are already starting a cautious retreat.

Clarissa: I am not sure about that yet. Give me leave to develop my idea. I am taking the matter quite simply. We believe that God has made everything well. Our more cultivated understanding of nature corresponds to this belief. Consider all the wonderful dispensations which occur in the life of man. These dispensations look as if they were accidental, but the pious man still thankfully recognises them as the gifts of divine goodness, and their contemplation disposes him to devotion and edifies him.

Furthermore, consider all the infinite art in the mechanisms of nature. You will never succeed in explaining that art, but it will afford rich material for pious contemplation. I am fully aware that Evagoras treats me ironically on account of my observation concerning the divine governance of nature and its purposefulness. No matter how much you manage to explain with your laws of gravitation, I shall not be diverted from my admiration of nature's infinite wealth of beauty and art, or the delightful profusion of its life. I shall not mention all the delicacy and splendour of plant and animal life which the microscope reveals to us. I shall merely draw your attention to the following phenomena, about which I have recently been reading: the wonderful intercourse of insects and flowers; the way in which the bloom of the aristolochia traps a fly until it has pollinated the stigma, and then releases it; or the way in which dates and figs are fertilised, and so many other similar phenomena. Where are your explanations of them?

Evagoras: Excellent! I am not going to attempt to explain these things here. I share your delight in the observation of nature. I look on the infinite beauty of flower-life with as much delight as I do on the pleasure of children at play. But what is it which delights us here? I would merely say: the phenomenon of spiritual life here makes its appearance through physical forms, and mysteriously manifests itself to our feelings. It is your feeling alone which senses, in the beauty of living nature, the eternal truth which dwells within our spirit. It is affinity of spirit which here delights us. But it is not our wish to furnish the understanding with proof positive of its concepts. You will never demonstrate to the understanding that nature operates purposefully. You will never do so because you refuse to measure these observations against concepts. You do not wish to offer explanations. Simply because we cannot name any valid purpose of nature, the understanding has no business here.

Let me offer you a simple comparison. You wind a thread round a child's finger in a tangle, and then, with a secret pull, you undo it. You arouse the curiosity of the child who wants to know how the trick is done, just as we wish to understand how the conjuror performs his sleight of hand. Now, is there any affinity here between our curiosity to understand nature's purposefulness and our interest in contemplating nature? Do you wish to divine nature's trick in the same way?

My answer is negative. That is exactly what you do not wish. It is precisely the inexplicability which you value. For that reason, be loyal to this way of looking at things. Do not confuse the observation of feeling with the interest of the interpretative understanding. The understanding is incapable of grasping nature's purposefulness at all. That this is the case becomes evident whenever the understanding is misguidedly employed in feeling's contemplation of nature.

It is no easy matter for a philosophical observation, like this of the purposefulness of nature, to remain in a childlike state for such a long time. The distinctive feature of man's achievement is the progress towards a goodness which is not yet in his power. It is in this way that man orders his affairs. It is in accordance with this law that the supreme task of history, the independent development of the human understanding, is to be executed. The purposefulness which is the concern of the understanding is this: a good purpose is finally to be realised by the skilful deployment of a small amount of energy in the battle against numerous impediments, the ultimate objective being eventually attained by a large number of indirect means. But what relevance is this supposed to have for divine purposes, for the purposes of the Almighty? God creates goodness in perfect purity, immediately and in himself. God does not create goodness by a gradual process of improvement, or with only partial success.

If we wanted to interpret the purposes of the world in terms of the concepts of our understanding, we should have to be satisfied if nature only sometimes achieved the purposes we attributed to her. You will admit that if we had really discovered even a single divine purpose, then everything would have to subserve that purpose in the most minute respects and without exception. Many people excuse God by saying that he subordinates and sacrifices lower purposes to higher ones. But, if these purposes were really God's purposes, then they would certainly all be fully and simultaneously achieved, and with equal ease.

Man, in his machine-like doings and dealings, subordinates means to ends; and he is pleased with the effort and labour, which are in themselves without significance, provided only that they eventually achieve their purpose. Gradual development to what is better is a source of pleasure to man. The following are examples of such gradual development and improvement: the seed grows into a plant, and the plant produces flowers and bears fruit; the family develops from the child to manly independence; finally, one's own spirit develops from the first stimulus of sensation to intelligent self-consciousness and its spiritual life-work.

But how is this supposed to apply to the purpose of nature? The idea of becoming better has no application to the world; the only idea which is applicable is that of being perfectly good.

Cecilia: It also follows from what you say that the idea of man's divine education — an idea which appears so plausible in many accounts — must be completely rejected. If I rightly understand you, you will disallow everything that Clarissa argued earlier — special dispensations of Providence for the individual, and, on a larger scale, the interventions of Providence in guiding history to what is better. Tell us more clearly what you think about this matter.

Evagoras: I have no original opinions on it. Judge for yourselves. The unexpected dispensations of history which produce improvements, or the unexpected dispensations in the life of individuals, are easy invitations to devout reflection. If it is true of our own life that unexpected good fortune is dispensed to us by the hand of Fate, then our devotion is forcibly constrained to gratitude to the higher Giver.

But take care that your cleverness and alleged wisdom do not attempt to show off with this observation. Do not convert it into a doctrine of divine guidance — but rather leave to feeling what belongs to feeling.

Otherwise you will be disturbed again and again by the nonsense to which we have already alluded. The unexpected accident and the blind hand of Fate can just as frequently advance the power of evil, or hasten the decline of goodness, as it can favour and further the cause of goodness itself. The wish to describe the whole strenuous business of improvement as divine is always evidence of a childish lack of reflection.

Vivid accounts of man's divine education will, it is true, seem beautiful to the unsuspecting mind. But once the error has been pointed out, this childish belief inevitably provokes irony. How comic is Lessing's view that God chose the Jews as his people and his instrument simply on account of their primitive character and their ugliness.

No, this cannot be called the work of the Almighty. The above objection applies even more strongly to a belief which was prevalent in the uninformed times of antiquity. According to this belief, the spirit of goodness is fighting a strenuous and difficult battle against the spirit of evil. This latter is, in fact, the true master of the world which will first have to be won back to goodness with the passage of time. Unless you oppose this refractory power of evil to God, the whole doctrine lacks inner coherency. The divine cannot, properly speaking, become better; it must be good from the start.

It was for this reason that I initially drew your attention to the subordinate position of so-called world-history in nature. The constantly blossoming life of the human spirit is man's own responsibility. His understanding should learn to help itself, should learn to establish, maintain and extend the power of the spirit in the life of man. But do not tell me that this work of man is the work of God.

Emphasising what is spiritually most pure, giving prominence to the power which furthers the spirit as it really appeared, so that others may contemplate it, admire it and take it as their paradigm — this may be the finest thing in the account of human history. What another was able to do, is given to me too as an objective for which to strive.

To man is given the task of helping himself. From Fate we have nothing to hope. With blind power it brings prosperity and ruin, growth and destruction, sometimes in the furtherance of goodness, sometimes to the advancement of evil.

Cecilia: That is a comfortless doctrine. Man feels that he is dependent in a thousand ways, feels that he is entirely at the mercy of irresistible superior forces. What would happen if we were not able in thought to approach these powers with trust?

Evagoras: Dear friend! If I had to say that we could not approach these superior powers with trust, then, certainly, the severest censure would apply to all the doctrines I am expressing. But the comfortless doctrine does not need to be the worst doctrine. The securest man is the man who needs no consolation. He is comfortless, not because he lacks the comfort he needs, but because he needs no comfort at all.

This is what I was warning you about in connection with the mistaken idea about Providence. It is with instinctive thankfulness that the pious man raises his eyes to heaven for the good fortune he has received. But he should not seek good fortune from above. He should tell himself that the cruelest fate may befall him as easily as it befalls anybody else. He ought not to transfer to God the responsibility of advancing his own interest, nor ought he to wish to preserve himself from misfortune by means of the magic of devotional formulae.

Just think of all the dreadful suffering which can befall man: one person has to languish away half his life in a dungeon because of a tyrant's wrath; not you, but one of your nearest and dearest — a husband, say, or a wife, or a child — falls prey to madness; a highly educated and cultivated man, through some minor fault of his own, drags out his existence in extreme poverty, fighting against every privation, tortured for many years by a cancer from which he eventually dies.

Dora: Do not paint any more of these dreadful and unnecessary pictures.

Evagoras: Hear me out, my dear. It might well be of profit to us. Would you, through your prayers, expect Providence to spare you such horrors? I say, "No!" The sun rises on the just and the unjust alike. Your only consolation is the probability that you will indeed be spared, for such extreme catastrophes only befall a few.

Clarissa: You see! There is that tone again, which I dislike hearing. I trust in the goodness of God. You do not really believe in Providence at all. For me, the consolation for all unhappiness is the fact that we shall receive an eternal recompense.

Evagoras: No, I do not believe in Providence as you describe it. It is precisely this Providence, of which I have no need. Nor — to put it bluntly — do I like it either. The only thing which ought to count is, as Cecilia said, that man can look up in trust to the higher powers, believing that the limitless power of love created the world and that every being has received the breath of life from the spirit of eternal beauty alone — for all the healthy life of nature and the deepest recesses of man's own spirit proclaims this truth to him.

Clarissa: Now you are talking quite differently and really well. My own thoughts expressed in other words.

Evagoras: Perhaps, indeed, more correct words for your less correct ones.

Cecilia: Let me try to mediate between you. In intention you seem to me to be in agreement. But I realise that in these things a great deal depends on the education which one's judgement underwent in youth, and on the imaginative mood which was given with that education. Once one has acquired a favourite dream of religious consolation, it is difficult to free oneself from it and to change one's mind again. The same is true of the tone of pious contemplation, and the habits of prayer.

Clarissa: Certainly! And then again, in these matters of feeling, very little depends on dry, intellectual correctness of expression. Is it not in hallowed images alone that this feeling and devotion dwells, growing and flourishing in one way for one person, and in another for another person?

Evagoras: Indeed, I would not encroach upon the rights of these hallowed images. Without them, no devotion would be expressed among men. But consider how far this goes. The high seriousness of moral ideas, which expresses itself not in images but in naked truth, interferes with this symbolic language of retribution. The important thing is to preserve the clarity and purity of these moral ideas.

For this very reason, any mistake here is hateful to the man who understands these things. Your view of Providence, and your trust in it, always conceals that idle pride which proclaims itself a child of the light, a chosen one, beloved of God, set apart from his fellow-men, who are hated by God, who are the heretics. Unless you had this pride, you could never come to have the confidence that the benevolence and providence of God would certainly protect you from misfortune — but not your neighbour! What happens to others may, with exactly the same justice, happen to you as well.

Hence, entirely different reflections are necessary if we are to rise to the level of genuine trust in the holy Providence which rules the world. Honest and healthy devotion is to be found in the ideas of submission. Consciousness of the independent character of our spiritual life is the decisive factor in the full awareness of our religious feeling, and with this the sense of being superior to all the vicissitudes of joy and suffering is also decisive. According to Christian teaching, our conversion is in heaven. The value of life resides in the inner beauty of life's spiritual development alone. Whether the circumstances of my finite existence are radiant with happiness, or whether they display the deepest misery, is not what is important. Only the inner beauty of the spirit has significance. All the hope and fear which accompany the vicissitudes of finite happiness and unhappiness, disappear in the face of the sublime thought of death. It is this thought which leads me back to the original source of light, back to holy love.

Clarissa: You have persuaded me. Yes, what you have just said is the same as what you have told us before. For man, true value resides in the inner beauty of the spiritual life alone. Today you have fully convinced me. I do not think that I shall disagree with you on these matters again.

The peace of God in one's own heart, the firm inner tranquillity of trust in eternal Love have, indeed, nothing to do with this play of joy and suffering, or with their vicissitudes. On the contrary, it entirely raises one above them, and enables one to attain to a genuine devotional self-understanding in the feeling of the inner sublimity of the spirit.

Evagoras: We are agreed. So just one more remark to keep us in agreement. You see how the business of the concept and that of feeling are distinct, and how it is only the latter, with its animation of feeling, which can be of service to devotion. But, in the educated spirit, the understanding also wants, by means of concepts, to assist the life of feeling, the intuition of what is beautiful in nature. We want, so to speak, to make a regulated business of it.

Among much else, you will here discover why we are attracted by the idea of man's divine education, even though all historical research is forced to reject the notion.

An unprejudiced person who is unconversant with the matter says: the only mainstay of our faith is the hope that things will gradually improve with man. But he fails to take into account the fact that all strict historical research is constrained coldly to contradict him: the same laws of recovery and decline regulate the whole course of the world from the beginning. Nor does he take into consideration the fact that such consolation in fact benefits no one. I should have thought that, if between birth and death, I can be satisfied with the world as it is today, then my children may be satisfied as well. What help is it to me if, after thousands of years, other nations, wholly foreign to me, should improve a little as a result of my slight labour? If this improvement is to help me, then it must, I suppose, occur in the place to which I shall go when I die.

It thus once more clearly emerges that, if my life has value, that value must reside exclusively in the inner beauty of the spiritual power itself, independently of all success.

What, now, is the point of interest in our observation on the progress of the human spirit in history?

The image of the good in nature, the appearance of the holy spirit in the transformations of nature, is, for man, connected with the development of life. It is thus that we regard the flowers of the meadows, it is thus that we regard the growth of the spirit in the child — and it is thus, finally, that we regard the growth of the understanding in the history of the nations.

The thing which interests us most here is this. When the explanatory understanding is occupied, it constantly stimulates feeling as well. You may, for example, enjoy studying botany, or some of you may even perhaps amuse yourselves with Greek. To take the case of botany: other people, who are not fools, probably attach no importance to the numerous names and their many subtle distinctions. But, over and above this study, there is always the beauty of plant-life itself before one's eyes.

Now, the same is the case with history as well. If you say nothing about the inner value of human life, if you are silent about the good and the bad which is to be found in it, if you only speak of the stages of spiritual development, you will certainly find in history, to the extent that it is history and not, say, a mere catalogue of tyrants, killing and being killed — you will, I say, find in history a clear and regular progress from ancient Asia, with its religions and its priests educating and ruling, to the freedom and beauty of the Greeks, to the world dominion of the Romans, to Christianity, and on to modern Europe. It is the tree of knowledge which you see germinating, growing, spreading its branches ever wider. It is only with the explanatory understanding that we can trace its history. But, in doing so, we also focus our attention on all the beauty and sublimity of spiritual power in history. In this way, scientific and intellectual progress once again operates as a stimulus to feeling as well.

In my opinion, all mistakes about Providence spring from two errors. The first consists in confusing the purpose of the world with man's earthly destiny, with the task which has been given to man in this life. The second error consists in misunderstanding the nature of man's earthly destiny itself.

As soon as we have recognised that the entire value of this earthly life consists in the development of spiritual beauty alone — spiritual beauty as it exists in the history of man in all the development of his inner spiritual life, and especially in the ideals of honour, justice, love, friendship and devotion — as soon as we recognise this, we shall affirm the ideal of tranquil self-understanding.

The person who is clear about this will demand nothing of Providence in what relates to the succession of joy and suffering, happiness and unhappiness. He will quietly and humbly accept what Providence bestows upon him. We shall be satisfied with each of its gifts, for we live joyfully believing in the eternal beauty of the heavenly life, in the holy love which creates the world.

How do we, so to speak, come to have dealings with this belief? To do so, we need explicit word and image. But do not over-estimate the image either. Only in the splendour of the self-sacrificing spiritual power of the whole nation can sacred significance continue to live for the dream of religious literature.

Our Christian piety, and yours in particular, is poor in images. You are not interested in the image of the divine conqueror, who ordering things for the best, overcomes giants, monsters, and evil spirits. Indeed, you will have nothing to do with the image of the avenger, whose look of fire sees to the bottom of all hearts, and who will return to judge the world. — The only image which is of importance to you is the image of the Comforter, Holy Love. Your only concern is the Divine Love, which is the eye, the light and the sun of the spiritual world.

Clarissa nodded friendly approval to Evagoras and said: it looks to me as if you could charm my feelings as well, if you wanted to.

DIALOGUE VII

Religious Practice

Woldemar: At the public ceremonies of our nation, we often recall your father's teaching that piety and taste belong to the same element of our spiritual life, that the ideas of religion and the ideas of the beautiful and the sublime have sprung from a single source.

Admittedly, the treatment of the freedom of the will, the immortality of the soul, and the unity and omnipotence of God, in our religious teaching, together with the use of imagery and its interpretation, disturb, it seems to me, the harmony between religious conviction and the feelings for the beautiful and the sublime. Merely consider what piety may mean to the cultivated spirit who loves beauty. Or consider the harmonious character of the enthusiasm of our nation at our sublime public rites. Everybody will feel that this enthusiasm, along with devotion, flows from a single source of life, and that all significant feeling for the beautiful and the sublime serves the same emotions.

But it will be especially apparent to anybody who looks at history that every great creation in the arts has been produced in the service of religion. Religion taught the Indians, the Egyptians, the Greeks, the Moors and the Germans to build their great architectural monuments, it taught sculpture to the Egyptians and the Greeks, it gave the Greeks the invention of drama, and it gave music and painting to the Greeks and Germans. All great literature has sprung from sacred literature.

Otto: By means of the understanding, we initially interpret the higher truth with the ideas of faith, with the ideas of spiritual independence and freedom, with the ideas of the eternal life of all spirits, with the ideas of the living divinity and the holy origin of all things. But if we ask: what is the real significance of these religious ideas for human life? — if we ask: how does man, how does the man of culture, live with them? — if we ask these questions, the reply we shall hear will be this: these religious ideas are not meant to produce insight in the understanding, they are not meant to effect the prudent organisation of our affairs for our benefit and profit. It is, at best, foolish superstition which has that need of them. For the man of culture, these ideas possess validity only through and in feeling.

We see the serious basic moods of religious feeling manifest themselves in human life in three forms, which can be called enthusiasm, sacrifice and devotion. But it is precisely these basic moods which are most intimately connected with the feelings of the beautiful and the sublime. It is they, indeed, which prescribe the highest ideals to epic, dramatic and lyrical literature.

Consciousness of guilt in one's own breast bestows upon one the virtue of pious humility before the eternal, pure and original source of justice and love. With the introduction of this humility into the spiritual life of man, there is also introduced the destiny that sacrifice, that death suffered for the sake of the victory of the good, become the supreme moral and aesthetic ideals.

Enthusiasm is the true source of life in the moral life of man. To that enthusiasm there belongs energy and vitality in adopting the good. The importance of enthusiasm is thus to be found in the ideals of love and friendship, in zeal for the spirit's progress to art and science, and, finally, in the higher ideals of the unified life of the nation: patriotic love and religious enthusiasm.

Devotion in the pure thought of God is the most distinctive emotion of religion. At the same time, it is the thought which is fundamental to all our feelings of the sublime. Devotion in prayer is man's most powerful guide to the good. It is also the most powerful means of effecting the spiritual synthesis of the nation's thought and life into a living organic whole, for, from the idea of the equality of us all in the eyes of God, it generates humble brotherly love, the fundamental idea of the Christian faith. Devotion is the vital power of piety and of religious virtue: its pure and simple guidance of feeling, through the most powerful and the most sublime idea, is best able to resist the headstrong drives of the emotions. This is why religion must lend all man's moral development its innermost power. Where this is not the case, how easily can man, in moments of misfortune, fall into inner confusion through the violence of his sensual desires. Only devotion is capable of thoroughly purifying us. In this is to be found the whole importance of religion.

Philanthes: Excellent! You have shown us the whole form of our religious life. In each individual form, we shall notice how religion is connected with the power of our moral life, in our striving after honour, justice and friendship. We shall further notice how, on every occasion, religious feeling inwardly stimulates the moral life and attempts to be of service to it.

Nonetheless, we can still separate the interest of conscience and its moral demands within us, so to speak, from the interest of religious faith, which is grounded, as it were, more deeply within our spiritual life than conscience itself. What, do you suppose, is the distinctive nature of our religious convictions when they are viewed in separation from the demands of conscience?

Arthur: Let me try to express the matter. One of our leading teachers says: all religion springs from man's feeling of dependency. Moral ideals belong to the life of action. Conscience decides what we ought to do. But in the life of action, man feels limited on all sides. Within, man is limited in respect of energy and vitality. Man is also limited in every intervention in the external world, without which no activity is possible at all. He thus feels himself, in all his action, dependent upon a higher power. Hence it is that man's idea of the active life withdraws into the interior of contemplative feeling, and the ideals of religion and beauty appear to it. The need arises within us for greater harmony with ourselves and with the world. It fills us with a yearning for peace of soul and contentment — questions of religious conviction. Faith answers with the idea of higher expectations, of eternal hope. Our feeling of dependency leads our thought upwards to the original source of all things. In this elevation of feeling, our inner confidence of spirit comes to life in belief in the eternal love of the All-merciful. This love remedies our inner inadequacy, and establishes the world-dominion of eternal goodness.

Thus, our spirit's profoundest thought of truth is the belief in Eternal Love, the Creator of the world. This belief is acknowledged, in life, by the feelings of intuitive awareness, in which the whole of nature's life addresses us with beauty or sublimity.

Philanthes: From what you have yourselves just now said it is easy to see that three elements are, so to speak, united in our religious convictions. The first and most essential element is the emotion of enthusiasm, submission to God, and the devotion in which piety consists. In virtue of the emotion of enthusiasm there is in each person a *religion of the heart*, the most inward part of our *moral* life. This moral-religious feeling is served, in the knowledge of man, by the supreme idea of eternal truth: the belief in the divine governance of the world, the eternal destiny of man, and the eternal purification and sanctification of his will. In virtue of this, the *doctrine of faith* is the second element in the religious life.

The third element of religious life consists in the fact that the truths of faith spring from the innermost part of our spirit. None of our senses, no intuition, can bear testimony of them to us. Faith comes to life for us in the aesthetic view of things, in all the most serious feelings of the beautiful and the sublime. But these feelings can only become the communicable possession of a complete human society by means of *metaphorical language* and *metaphorical symbols*. Thus, the third, aesthetic element of religion manifests itself in consecrated metaphorical language and consecrated rites.

Thus, the interest of the moral element of religion, or piety, is that man should be or become *good*. The task of piety is that of the moral education of the spirit. The interest of the doctrine of faith is that man should learn to recognise and express eternal truth with ever greater correctness. The task of the doctrine of faith is thus directed to human knowledge. But the aesthetic interest of religion is that man should learn to recognise all serious beauty and sublimity with ever greater purity and power. This yields the task of the development of taste and the feeling of beauty.

Let us now compare what we have discovered with the development of public life in the nation. And let us raise the following question: what distinctively religious institutions can there be in the state?

Otto: Good! This reflection will lead us to the nature of positive religion, and that, of course, is what we are really concerned about.
Philanthes: Are you opposing positive religion to another sort of religion? What do you really mean?
Otto: I shall try to explain my view.

To begin with: In the sciences, in which we are supposed to recognise laws, we oppose things of *positive determination* to things of *natural determination*. Laws are of natural determination, namely, when they are laws of which the truth or suitability is to be determined by us according to our own insight and by means of our own judgement. Of positive determination, on the other hand, is everything which is valid in virtue of arbitrary agreement, or in virtue of an authoritative decree made by someone else. In the case of such positive determinations, one cannot use one's own judgement to test the assertions in respect of their truth or suitability. They must rather be accepted, as they are given to us, on the authority of someone else.

Thus, all the laws of natural science, mathematics and philosophy are of natural determination. By contrast, what the words in a particular language mean must be positively determined. The laws regulating trade in the state, the laws regulating the institution of legal proceedings against someone, and such like — these things must be positively determined. Also of positive determination are a nation's customs and practices in matters relating, say, to marriage, the birth of a child, the death of a relative, and so on. And this is also true of religious practices, as well.

In all matters where man depends on nature or even his own will, his judgement is of natural determination. The origin of all that is positive is to be found, by contrast, in the dependency of one man upon another, in the laws of the union of the state, according to which someone must obey the command of the government, or must adapt himself to the customs of his country, and through which the social order exists and is maintained. All positive determinations are based upon the way in which government activity and practice establishes social forms in the life of the state.

Arthur: That seems strange, indeed! Do you wish to reduce all positive determinations to affairs of state? For example, language? Is the state, then, in addition to regulating judicial practice, also to order linguistic usage? Would that not be a very foolish sort of despotism?

Otto: The latter would certainly be so. But what do you think? A government could always exercise such a despotism, of course, through its academic specialists.

Arthur: Yes, certainly!

Otto: We should merely advise the government not to meddle either in this or any similar matters.

My opinion is that we must make a distinction here between state concerns and government concerns. It seems to me that every matter of public life is a state concern. Many of them would, however, be better left to the free play of forces in the nation, rather than being the subject of immediate government intervention. An example would be language. What, then, is your opinion? Do we wish to make the distinction in such a way that we regard all the positive forms in life as the concerns of the state, in each case, however, further enquiring whether it would not be better to leave it to the free play of forces in the nation, or whether it would not be better to make it a concern of the government?

Arthur: Here, I can happily yield to your opinion.

Philanthes: And I am completely crossing over to Otto's side — namely, in what relates to religion. You will find that the wisest of the ancients, Plato and Aristotle, have no hesitation in regarding matters of positive religion as belonging to the concerns of the government, and having them ordered by the legislator. In our country, for reasons which we shall examine later, that would be ill-advised.

Nonetheless, we must still save ourselves from the opposite error. The attempt is often made to bring the state and church into opposition with each other, the opinion being held that the state should interfere as little as possible in church affairs. But this view is merely the product of the contingent circumstances of our history. Our ecclesiastical constitutions have been ordered by priestly power in conflict with military power, whereas all the other parts of the state constitution and legislation were introduced by military power, or that of the princes. But this independence of the ecclesiastical state has merely arisen as a result of the superstition of remote antiquity, and in part as a consequence of need. We do not at all favour this split in the government. We merely ask to what extent the concerns of positive religion are to be made concerns of the government, and to what extent they are to be left to the free play of forces in the nation and to the choice of individual communities.

Are you in agreement with that, Arthur?

Arthur: Yes, you seem to me to be right.

Philanthes: Good! Then let us now look back at what we agreed upon in connection with the three elements of religion. Let us ask which of the three elements is fitted, and in what manner fitted, to become a positive institution in the state. Let us first consider the doctrine of faith.

Arthur: No, the doctrine of faith must not be the work of positive determination. The truths of faith and of our heavenly expectations are eternal truths, immutably the same for all nations and all time. Such truths belong to world-religion, and cannot be subject to either national or ecclesiastical modification. In this connection, the human understanding may concern itself with no more than the gradual correction of the expression of these truths. This is obviously a task which belongs to a particular branch of knowledge and which is of an entirely natural determination.

Philanthes: And now? What is the situation with respect to the moral element, with respect to piety itself?

Arthur: That, too, cannot possibly be of positive determination. Man is pious only in the inner recesses of his soul. What true piety is, and what the pious man ought to do — that is something which his moral feeling tells him; and it does so on the basis of an appeal to the moral truth, which is common to all people. And with respect to that moral truth, the understanding has the task of gradually acquiring clearer insight into such matters. Moral philosophy, on the one hand, and the doctrine of faith, on the other, are two branches of knowledge of entirely natural determination.

Philanthes: There is, accordingly, nothing left for positive treatment apart, I suppose, from the aesthetic element of religion.

Arthur: So it seems. The reasons, it would appear, can easily be given. Consecrated rites and consecrated metaphorical language are of human ordering. The institutions by means of which the attempt is made, in this place or that, to give communal stimulation to pious feelings, and lend life to the truths of faith, admit of very great diversity according to the nature of the nation and the period of history concerned. Images and practices, provided that they are not indirectly involved in error concerning morality or faith, are, for the most part, of arbitrary determination. Their suitability is determined not by a branch of knowledge but only by taste and by the sense of beauty and sublimity.

Philanthes: Here you see what view is to be taken of the development of positive religions if, with the development of our public life, we are to progress towards a certain perfection. But you will also readily concede that, among our peoples, the circumstances are radically different.

The teachings of faith and love, the teachings of eternal truth and of what is good in itself for man, ought to be common to all languages and all times. In this context, there is only one truth, and it it always the same. But ranged alongside it, and developing simultaneously with it in the history of mankind, are all the positive institutions and forms of public life. These latter, insofar as they are of positive institution, are also, without exception, of arbitrary ordering. They can equally well assume one form in one place, and quite a different form in another.

In so far as these positive institutions can be ordered in the state according to exact rules, they include positive rights and laws, which have been formed by the gradual operation of habit and the institutions of the legislators. They shade into the less determinate forms of moral practices and custom, and through them, into the positive views of religion. For to positive religion there really belongs all the symbolism of feeling, which is fixed in public life, but which can no longer be measured by specific legal rules.

In this connection you presumably know how difficult it often is correctly to combine the general theory of the good and the true purpose of human existence with positive legal theory. In this area, the state legislature can easily introduce real reforms, once the problem is clearly perceived. Far more difficult, on the other hand, is the relationship of the doctrine of faith and virtue to moral practices and religious usages and all positive matters of religion, for their importance is to be found in the feeling of the whole nation — and they are supposed to be the nation's symbols of that feeling. The legislature can impose order upon them, what it cannot do is directly create them. And thus it is that in the history of the nations we frequently come across ceremonial ritual, which has become fixed by custom and law, but which is merely the corpse of a past national spirit. With its rigid forms, it simply constitutes an impediment to new life. This is the reason why all religious reformers are hostile to such defunct ceremonial ritual. In these matters, there is not a great deal which can be reformed in a peaceful fashion, unless the re-fashioning of life issues from the enthusiasm of the nation itself.

The great difficulties of a gently progressing reform of religion in public life thus consists in the following fact. In national life, the elements of morality, doctrine and symbolism, which are so heterogeneous, can only develop in vital union with each other. In the process, scientifically acknowledged error in the doctrines of faith and morals can long be protected in popular feeling by an established symbolism. And here, the state legislature has little power, of a peaceful kind, to reform the symbolism.

Otto: And what, in your opinion, ought to be done under the circumstances?

Philanthes: We must now proceed with circumspection. Let us pause for a moment to consider the following point. The doctrines of faith and morals must develop as branches of knowledge. But in the real life of the nation this development only occurs in combination with the metaphorical language and the sacred practices of its positive religion. I wish to call the combination of this metaphorical language, of these religious myths or sagas, with sacred practices: the religious symbolism of a nation.

A nation's religious symbolism, depending on its level of development as a nation, must be connected with its needs if it is to be contented with its fate and with itself. At the stage of earliest barbarity, man's wishes are simply directed outwards. The sense of dependency is only awakened in him when, in his struggle against hunger, sickness and weather, he is overcome by higher powers. Thus, imagination moved by fear is the first inventor of mythologies about the gods and of rituals for their service. Earliest barbarity merely seeks to flatter or bribe the higher powers with sacrificial offerings, in the hope of persuading them to treat men with gentleness. When, however, those who are more cultivated turn their attention to these higher beings, moral ideas awake within them. To the feeling of external dependency there is now joined the feeling of inner inadequacy. The reproaches of conscience stir, and they awaken a yearning for the expiation of guilt. There thus arises belief in divine retribution for all wicked deeds. The reconciliation of man and divine justice, which is effected by such retribution, is the fundamental idea of the more civilised positive religions, in spite of the varied nature of the succession of images and sacred practices expressing that idea.

Finally, we think that these images of punishment and retribution are not the best fitted to express man's yearning for a return to eternal purity. Believing in the world-dominion of eternal goodness, we interpret our feelings of outer and inner dependency in terms of confidence in the freedom and independence of the spirit. This confidence becomes for us the healthy fundamental idea of religious contemplation, for it raises us, in our submission to the supreme and sacred will, above all the vicissitudes of Fate, and thus above all the sufferings of our earthly existence, as well. In spite of all our feelings of inadequacy, it makes clear to us that beauty of soul is the only good known to man which has an existence in its own right.

With the gradual advancement of the truth of morality and faith, the foundations of all religious symbolism are naturally also transformed. It will be our wish to see all error and immorality eradicated from these foundations.

Metaphorical language (religious mythology) and symbols in consecrated rites are, in themselves, of course, neither true nor false. But they are, nonetheless, still symbols and similes for morality and faith. For this reason, they fall into error indirectly as a result of defects in the doctrines of virtue and faith. The most important thing is that the image and the symbol should not any longer be superstitiously confused with the sacred and moral truths themselves. The chief thing for the true and beautiful advancement of positive religion is that, in public life, image and symbol should no longer be confused with eternal truth. Each should be correctly distinguished from the other.

But even if religious symbolism should be completely purged of all error, it is not to be supposed that all educated people would have to agree on the same images and symbols. The nature of our aesthetic convictions in no wise corresponds to that expectation. The oak which grows beside the tulip tree and the passion flower, the tiny flower blooming in the grass beside the palm tree — each of them is beautiful in its own fashion. Likewise, there is a great diversity in the moods of the sense of beauty itself, and a still greater variety in the images expressing that sense of beauty. One person is moved by the power of the heroic epic, another by the friendly charm of the pastoral play; one person is moved by jesting, another by yearning, and a third by the overwhelming and the tragic. And even with songs, one person is more moved by the sublime, while another is more attracted to the serene and the mild. And so emotion, image and symbol will assume very different forms in religious symbolism, where it is national life itself which produces these forms. Every family of nations will love and esteem the images and symbols with which the religious feeling of their youth grew up.

We must now seek to apply all these principles, in their interconnections with each other, to real life. I should like to begin by attempting to offer you a general application to the Christian faith.

Although most teachers still seek the essence of Christianity in certain myths, I am forced to maintain that true Christianity is not a positive religion but the world-religion. Its eternal truth is expressed in the doctrines of faith, love and hope, which were first taught to our ancestors through the Gospels and by the Apostle Paul. These three teachings are the same for all time and for all languages.

The truly Christian consecrated rites are very simple. All Christians have baptism and communion. That is to say: whereas the heathens believed in several national gods, the Christians believe in one God only, the holy Origin of all things. Accordingly, the Christians believe in an invisible community of saints, to which all men are called, and which all men can enter during their life on earth, provided only that they embrace each other with equal and humble brotherly love. The real union of mankind through the spirit of this humble brotherly love, that is to say, the founding of the Kingdom of God on earth, is the one great Christian ideal. The pure light of that ideal has shon through all the darkness and mists of superstition, during the various transformations of the European churches. And it will continue to shine, fashioning the life of the nation to ever greater beauty.

And with respect to all the other traditions of the European priestly hierarchy and its rites: no nation should be spared or indulged any part of those traditions once they have ceased to be subject to the peace and brotherly love of all mankind, once they have ceased to be subject to the spirit of truth and beauty.

When the Christian cult was first introduced into the Roman Empire as the religion of the court and state, the higher clergy were already involved in a blood-thirsty dispute about their metaphysical mythology. We shall no longer be obliged to seek the truth from the interpretation of those dreams. But these European churches have borrowed the greatest part of their cult, along with a great deal of superstition, from the more ancient religions of Buddha in Tibet and China. Probably earlier than the Roman church, there was to be found in these countries the same priestly rule, based on a monastic economy, and the same superstitious belief in an infallible human head. There was also to be found a similar reverence for the mother of God and the images of the saints, the same altar robes, the same singing of choirs in a language unintelligible to the people, the same rosary, the same incomprehending recitation of forms of prayer accompanied by the telling of beads, and many other things, too. The only difference was that, thanks to the Gospels, the mythology of the Roman church became simpler, and, thanks to the Greek arts, the Roman worship of images became less tasteless.

Certainly, the true nature of Christianity was first recognised when it freed itself from this Buddhism.

If I am now to turn our attention to matters of greater detail, then let us first focus our attention on the interests of the doctrines of faith and virtue.

Just as faith and virtue develop historically in union with religious symbolism, so likewise, there must develop, parallel to positive religious practices and religious literature, positive doctrines of faith and morals. The positive element of religious symbolism is always mistaken when it interferes in the doctrine of faith, for image and symbol are then always confused with eternal truth. This positive doctrine of faith is, in fact, always heathen in origin, for the object of its worship is not God, but merely a national spirit who affords protection. Those who subscribe to such a doctrine regard themselves as the chosen people of the god in question; other people are held to be heretics, and, if they are not actually persecuted, they are held in contempt or, at least, regarded as inferior.

The situation in respect of positive ethics is quite different. The positive element in the doctrine of ethics consists, apart from the legal code, in moral practices and customs, the observation of which is expected of every member of our nation who has enjoyed a good upbringing and has a decent character, that is to say, of anyone who is well-bred. Now, you will readily appreciate that it is good education alone which can effect the virtuous development both of the individual and of the nation. But education is habituation. The virtuous development both of the individual and of the nation depends upon our being led, from youth upwards, to the choice of good habits, and our growing up in good habits. Now, in addition to the legal code, moral practices and customs are the forms of this habituation as they have taken shape in public life. With respect to those views of life which are based more on feeling, the moral education of a nation, in addition to depending on the legal code, also depends upon good moral practices and good customs. These are the means necessary to acquiring the secure development of a beautiful family life, and public esteem for valour, honesty, honour and the love of truth and beauty.

But it is precisely this positive element in moral practices and customs which blends most intimately with positive religious symbolism. Piety is the virtue of feeling, and, at the same time, the spirit of the religious life. Piety is protected in public life and animated by communal devotion, in other words, by consecrated rites and metaphorical language. Piety must, in its turn, cause the moral practices and customs of our nation to be held sacred in the love of the fatherland which is, at the same time, religion itself.

We thus see that the interests of positive religion are most intimately connected with the interests of the morality of the people. Every advancement of positive religions has, at the same time, been the advancement of positive morality. And, just as the Christian teaching progressed from separate national religions to a world-religion, so, likewise, it has progressed from merely regarding external rites as sacred to the inner life of the soul. It rejects dead works, and honours only what happens in faith and love.

Now, although the healthy life of a nation will always need such a positive doctrine of morals and its consecration through its connection with positive religion, we can nonetheless easily isolate the pure doctrine of virtue which is connected with the doctrine of faith. Neither of them is of positive determination; they are both of them of purely natural and intellectual determination. It is here desirable to eliminate the confusion of image and thing. It is also to be desired that conviction should become clearly articulated truth, and that, in this form, it should become the property of the nation. The objection will, of course, be raised: do you want to turn every peasant in the land into a philosopher? Our reply will be: do you want to call every schoolboy who knows his multiplication table a mathematician? The philosophy of faith and love is far more apparent to human feeling than it is to the art of calculation. Incidentally, the important thing here is not that each of our fellow-citizens should advance from living feeling to thorough understanding. What is important is that the public life of the nation should be endowed with the truth in clarity and purity.

The achievement of this objective requires two things. The first requirement is this. It should be the responsibility of the intellectually cultivated conviction to ensure that the doctrines of faith and conscience, publicly acknowledged in the nation, should express nothing but the pure truth. Accordingly, the educated part of the nation should, as a rule, not merely be persuaded of, it should be convinced by, the truth. The second requirement is this: public life, in its forms of class distinction, should recognise this pure truth.

The first of these requirements is more easily assessed. The second, on the other hand, involves great difficulties, in that religious symbolism is here connected with the development of conviction, and it drives its roots into the innermost parts of civil life and its forms.

The introduction of the doctrines of faith and morals into public life depends entirely upon the solemnity and dignity of the doctrines relating to the religious initiation of the youth. This solemn and dignified initiation will awaken devotion and reverence throughout the whole nation down to the least educated of its citizens. For the common masses, the credentials of the doctrines are merely the customary forms of religious worship. Most people know the doctrines of faith and morals off by heart. And most people believe them, at best, for the sake of devotion, and otherwise merely as a matter of habit. The hereditary habituation of a whole nation, or society of families, has protected, founded and sustained every positive religion and the positive doctrines of faith and morality found therein. Habit caused the Persian to bend the knee to Hom, the Indian to Aoum. Habit elevated the *Kyrie eleison* to the status of an inspiring battle cry for the Christians, and the *Illah Allah* likewise for the Mohammedans — and it will submit more easily to pure truth than to error.

No nation needed *reasons* for holy truths apart from us modern Christians. Our restless understanding created difficulties for itself, because it was no longer willing to surrender itself to custom without question.

If reasons do have to be given to the person who has started the search for reasons, then, it seems to me, that the right answer — the answer given in terms of love and faith, the answer which makes immediate appeal to sound feeling and common sense — can be much more generally understood than any of the alleged justifications which appeal to history. And another thing — it is truth alone which cannot be made ridiculous.

The common prejudice that proofs which rely on tradition and history are far more intelligible to the people is based on the simple fact that we are accustomed to that approach and that those who favour this method confuse image and symbol with the thing itself.

If someone is asked, "How do you know that?" he will reply: Several thousand years ago, God himself communicated this fact to certain pious people, who then passed it on to others; eventually some of them committed it to writing in foreign tongues, other people then translating it into our own language. Look! Here is the Book — it is simply called the Book. All the catechisms, hymnals and sermons derive from this one book. Generally, those who have, from youth upwards, been accustomed to catechisms, prayer books and sermons, will be filled with reverence for the Book by what they have been told. But most of them will have no clearer idea about the matter than they do about any other doctrine learnt parrot-fashion. And what does this way of arguing really establish? Vedah and Koran also mean quite simply the Book, just like the Bible. And the same explanations are given in their case, as are given in the case of the Bible. And if we could give no better reasons than these, the Bible would be worthless to us.

Anybody who starts to think for himself about these explanations will inevitably ask: has it been correctly translated? Did the alleged authors really write the original text? Were the accounts given to them accurate? Did the first account really come from God himself? — But there is no satisfactory answer to any of these questions. In contrast to this, I commend the truth which is immediate, pure and unalloyed. Its message is simple and always the same: this you understand! This is what your own sound feeling tells you!

Certainly, if we elevate the public doctrine to the status of pure and impartial truth, then many people will learn that off by heart as well. But if the people of better education themselves start to reflect, then they will perceive within the doctrine an inner light which will reconcile them with each other. Traditionally, by contrast, a person's so-called own reason was often told to remain silent, for it was felt that reflection might well generate scepticism, but that it could scarcely produce conviction.

A nation, it seems to me, has achieved religious peace once the public expression of faith satisfies each person in his own way, the one with liveliness of feeling, the other with clarity and certainty of insight.

Arthur: In saying this you seem to be granting that the friends of natural religion and the so-called rationalists are right. But are they not criticised on the grounds that their religious teaching is too cold, too dessicated and too abstract? Is it not objected against them that the common masses, who are still at the sensuous level, need a sensuous foil to set off their ideas of faith, need sensible images in order to achieve piety?

Philanthes: It is, indeed, true that a religious teaching is cold if it makes no appeal to the feelings, is desiccated and abstract if it permits no place beside it to the images and pictures of religious symbolism. We shall strive to keep ourselves free from these two errors. But as far as the sensible foil and the sensible images are concerned: their defenders are, in most cases, in error because they confuse feeling and intuitive awareness with sensibility.

Among our peoples, the so-called educated people are frequently as sensuous as many of the less instructed classes. But that is not what is important to us here.

Golden altars and embroidered robes, great processions with resonant music, icons and banners certainly serve the idle curiosity of the common masses. But whether they are of service to piety is very dubious. If a priestly conqueror, sword in hand, wishes to force a new religious practice upon the peoples, he can easily win the masses to his cause by means of such gorgeous display. He will not, however, succeed in spreading piety by this device alone. The so-called sensuous splendour of sacred rites only has inner value when it is animated by a pious and pure sense of beauty, and then it can be extremely important to public life.

But such display is not necessary in order to introduce religion to the sensuously primitive and wild human spirit. All that is important is the awakening of piety. Its life is of quite a different kind: it exists inwardly, in moral feeling. The famous heroes of the faith, the peaceful converters of the heathen, the missionaries who brought words of peace, and with them, piety, to the wild hoard of mankind, proceeded quite differently. They did not need the worship of images, nor gorgeous outward display. The only thing they needed was the inner peace within their own hearts. It is the misfortune of the sensuous savage that, when his sensual appetites are stimulated and his emotions aroused, it is the passion of ill-humour, displeasure and anger which is far more easily and far more powerfully excited than the passion of love and cheerfulness. It can thus easily happen that the life of the primitive and uncontrolled man is one of displeasure and interior agitation, which is a source of displeasure to the man himself. Now, if our savage sees the messenger of peace approach, and if he sees him making self-sacrifices, manifesting no self-interest, harbouring no suspicions, expressing constant tranquillity of spirit and cheerfulness of heart, the contrast to himself will speedily awaken within him the yearning for inner peace. And any teaching which fills his heart with peace and his soul with piety — any such teaching will exercise an attraction over his spirit.

This is how we ought to judge the intellectual development of the doctrines of faith and virtue. But we have previously seen that, in order to secure these correct convictions for public life, a further particular influence, that of the forms of distinction between the estates of society, is required. The pure truth must be acknowledged in those forms of distinction in civil life itself.

Arthur: What do you mean by this notion of the influence of the estates in civil life on religious conviction?

Woldemar: In general, I understand you very well. Every positive religious opinion is the hereditary property of families. Every ecclesiastical constitution in the state will, on account of the state, favour certain positive religious views. The influence of the church will be especially important on the academic world in public life.

Philanthes: Quite right! We must pay closer attention to the influence of these forms of life. The forms of class distinction in family institutions, sectarian spirit, church constitution, and clergy and constituent parts of the state and its civil life. The legislature can intervene here, but it will only achieve something, if it is permitted to do so by religious symbolism, by faith in that symbolism, and by public opinion in the nation. Without such support nothing can be achieved, for, in these matters of feeling and conviction, the good can only be attained for public life by the nation's communal spirit. As I have said, the power of the rulers can effect but little in these matters by peaceful means. This judgement brings us to a well known maxim of criminal law. The question is asked: if you wish to prevent something, ought it to be severely punished? Prudence gives an affirmative answer in the case of actions which are performed from fear (say, of scandal) or avarice, or on account of some basic physical need. But in the case of actions issuing from the passions of enthusiasm, fanaticism or zealousness, prudence gives a negative reply to the above question. And the reason that it does so is that these passions are much more powerful than the love of life itself, particularly when they spring from religious ideas. In this context, violence only makes martyrs of the adherents of the outlook or doctrine. Their examples merely serve to fan the flames of religious enthusiasm, whether it be the enthusiasm of patient surrender or the enthusiasm of fierce resistance.

The sanctum of family life, so to speak, protects every hereditary superstition, with all its ugliness and immorality, much as sanctuary protects the criminal. Children acquire, even in the most deformed images, symbols of self-sacrifice and devotion. How is this situation to be remedied? Certainly, never by means of direct intervention in family life by the legislators. Persecution only has the effect of inflaming superstition the more violently; it never secures the victory for truth. But family life can gradually be reformed by public opinion in the state, if only we can fashion such a public opinion. Our attention is thus led to the positive ecclesiastical institutions of the state, and here the legislature can powerfully intervene once it harmonises with public opinion in the nation.

Among uncivilised people, power can be gained either by military means, through the force of arms, or by priestly means, through the superstitious fear of invisible higher powers. Thus, in despotic states, priestly rule has often protected the spirit, in its emotional and intellectual development, against naked military power. In civilised nations, just as military power has been converted into peaceful legislation, relying on the power of justice, so priestly rule has been converted into an educational force, exercising an influence on faith, and trusting in the power of truth.

All priestly rule is a dominion, based on superstition, of the learned estate. Its members claim, in one way or another, to be theosophists or theurgists. That is to say, they claim to stand in a more intimate relation to the gods or God than other people, and, as a result, to be able to secure what is best for man.

Now, the chief task of the learned estate in civil life is threefold: legislation and justice; the healing of the sick; and the education of the youth and the people. If we look at history, we shall see that, in the theocratic states of antiquity, the government, along with the above-mentioned threefold task of the learned estate, was in the hands of the priests or clergy. They are the regents, for they regard themselves as, and proclaim themselves to be, more especially sons of the gods than the rest of the nation. They are responsible for the legislation because they are supposed to have received the laws directly from the gods. They heal the sick by invoking the aid of good spirits and by driving out the evil ones.

But, as the level of spiritual education rose, the power of this superstition steadily declined. The power of the rulers is given a natural foundation, and the learned estate is increasingly thrown open to sound reason.

How far, do you suppose, have our state institutions advanced in this liberation of the spirit from superstition? Our physicians and sanitary establishments already seem to rely on sound reason alone, even though, in respect of positive religion, certain of our fellow-citizens are nonetheless of the opinion that men of piety used once to heal the sick by means of demonic assistance and by the banishing of evil spirits. Were a physician to accept this view nowadays and attempt to heal the sick in the corresponding fashion, he would, I suppose, be declared mad. But I am not a physician myself, of course.

To turn to the second point: How, do you suppose, do the legislators act? In respect of positive religion, again, certain of our fellow citizens may think what they please about what the Lord said to Moses or Zoroaster, or about how Urim and Thumim acted. Our legislators act as if they believed that true life is to be found in the rational spirit (logos), which was with God from the beginning, and that this spirit was the incarnate messenger of God, who dwelt among men. It is to sound reason alone to which our legislators appeal, in order to discover just and good legislation and to establish the just judicial verdict.

To take up the third point — what about the educator? Yes, indeed! Who are the educators, then? They have, in part, I suppose, separated themselves as a school from the church, but for the most part they still either consist of the clergy or are at least subordinate to it. Are we not to say that here a part of ancient superstition has lingered on? How people are to be educated and instructed, that, too, is a matter for scientific investigation to be decided by sound reason alone. It is by reference to sound reason alone that the legislators determine the choice of law, and that the physicians specify what medicaments are to be prescribed. Similarly with the class of teachers. Teachers, too, ought to be referred to scientifically formed reason alone for their specifications as to how they are to teach and instruct — not to mere oral traditions, once regarded as holy, nor to the traditional formulae of faith.

It is to this point, in my opinion, that the attention of those who are seriously concerned about the progress and reform of man ought to be directed. Public institutions for the education of the youth and the people are purely a concern of the state. Such a state institution of public education ought to be independent of all superstition deriving from the various positive religious views. Its only hommage should be payed to knowledge and sound reason.

Woldemar: Why do you accuse all our positive religious views of being superstitious? Are none of them, then, supposed to be wholly loyal to the truth?

Philanthes: In describing every state where freedom of belief is recognised, as it is in ours, I have, at least, chosen the most polite expression. It is true that, among Roman Catholic and Greek Orthodox Christians, among the Lutherans and the Zwinglians, there are some who regard their belief as the only source of salvation, and others who think that their belief is the only correct one. Although such disputes do arise between the members of the different branches of Christendom, nonetheless the relations of conflict are not what they are really supposed to be in positive religions. Here, one party, at the most, can be right, and the rest must be wrong. It would obviously be fairer to say: we all of us err, each in his own way.

The true doctrines of faith and virtue are neither Roman nor Greek, neither Lutheran nor Zwinglian. The intellectual development of the spirit ought to lead us to the point where the Roman, Greek, Lutheran and Zwinglian Christians, along with all the other sects of what name soever, all, with increasing unanimity, acknowledge the same eternal truth, ceasing to accuse each other of error concerning that truth, but rather seeing that the difference of their religious symbolism consists merely in a difference of image and symbol, a difference to which each religious family has grown attached as a result of education.

If that happened, things would be quite different. In the space of a short time they would find themselves in peaceful competition to see whose consecrated rites were the more beautiful, the more noble, and the more full of spirit.

This finally leads us to look at the matter from the other side, from the point of view of the positive interest of religious symbolism itself. In this connection, you will now find that civilised countries have very different state institutions. In many states you will find that there is a single predominant religion, a so-called state religion, a specific type of religious practice, which enjoys the protection and favour of the rulers and many state institutions, whereas other kinds of religious practice are either totally forbidden or, at least, very limited.

In other states, on the other hand, the toleration of different religious practices, or freedom of belief, is prescribed by law. The state favours no one kind of religious practice, but leaves the choice to the free discretion and pleasure of the citizens. The only condition is that in this, as in all other things, they obey the laws.

It is easy to see how history has led us to these latter institutions. The bitter experiences of the bloody wars of religion must eventually have made civilised people feel that in these things it is only the peaceful reconciliation of the factions which benefits belief, and that violence only dishonours the would-be proselytiser. This choice of tolerant legislation also harmonises with the correct view of the nature of positive religions. According to this view, positive religions do not really differ in respect of truth or error, but only in respect of the images and symbols which they employ in their consecrated rites. On the other hand, intolerance is inevitable in someone who is convinced that he and his sectarian fellows alone possess the ceremonial rites which bring salvation. But in most cases it will be found that, on the whole, the practice of religion has a livelier and deeper importance for the people in those states where a state religion is still acknowledged and sustained by force.

Which system are we now to declare the better? Ought the government wholly to refrain from interfering in the positive institutions of religion as such, leaving it to the congregations, or the religious families within the congregations, to order their religious practices as they see fit? Or ought the government to order the matter itself, according to the predominant view of the nation?

The answer we shall in general receive is this: just as people need language to express their thoughts, so also do they need metaphorical images and symbols and, through them, religious language, in order to communicate their religious ideas to each other. And just as nations leave each other in the peaceful possession of their own respective languages, or ought to do so, so too ought religious communities to leave each other in the peaceful and unviolated possession of their own respective consecrated rites, eager, indeed, in their opposition to the error of superstition, but unconcerned about the choice of symbols. On the other hand, the following point is not to be forgotten, either. The understanding would make no progress if each tiny society had its own language, and if communities of nations had no single common written language to link them together. Similarly, the development of feeling and the social education of people to piety, love and beauty, could not make any healthy or vigorous progress, if each tiny religious community stubbornly clung together around its own symbols, leaving the nation as a whole with no symbolism of religious practice.

This consideration quickly leads to the conclusion that, in matters of religion, the attitude of governments must vary according to the varying levels of development in different states.

If, in a given nation, there is a strong superstitious belief that a particular ceremonial rite is alone pleasing to God, then the government will share much the same opinion. It will neither wish, nor be able, to escape maintaining this cult as the state religion. In such a nation, there will not be many who do not share this outlook. If, however, sound reason begins to triumph over superstition, then individual judgements on matters of faith will gradually grow more free. A diversity of opinions will emerge, though these opinions will not completely rise above superstition. Many different factions will evolve and exist alongside each other. In this situation, the wisdom of the government will gradually and increasingly come to recognise the necessity of tolerance and freedom of belief, if the mutual hatred of the factions is to be replaced by their peaceful coexistence, and if the true power of peaceful instruction is to be guaranteed over belief.

But even this is evidently but a temporary and provisional expedient. Where a still higher level of development has been reached, a wise government will not want to protect any superstition connected with theosophy, or theurgy, magicians or witches. Indeed, it will not be able to tolerate either immoral superstition, or religious factions whose moral practices conflict with those of the nation. It will also have to be very much on its guard against any hierarchic superstition, which would keep its own subjects in a state of dependency upon so-called spiritual superiors abroad. In general, we may say that the whole institution of a diversity of religious practices scattered throughout the nation is simply a necessary expedient for the indulgence of superstition, which contradicts the true purposes of all positive religions.

Only when the whole nation is united around the same practices can the metaphorical language and consecrated rites of positive religion acquire true vitality and power over the people. Religious symbolism ought to guarantee the vital spiritual union of the whole nation in public life. That same religious symbolism ought, by means of its consecrated symbols, to encourage each person in his pious and loving attachment to the fatherland and the moral practices of his country, for in the past nation and home were as each of us is today.

You will also find that, once superstition has been completely banished, it will be easy to establish such a unity of national and consecrated practices. It was in this unity that the beauty of our nation found its existence and our art discovered its great and noble objectives. You will further find that the ordering of the matter can easily be left to the wisdom of the legislators. For, once people are clearly convinced that there is no disagreement about sacred truth, but only a diversity of opinion relating to the choice of suitable images and symbols, then every good citizen will happily make a concession to his neighbour, for the sake of patriotic love. And this will continue until the living warmth of common consecrated rites suffuses them all with the feeling of brotherly love, the divine truth of which the dying Jesus announced to our ancestors.

However, the church and religion ought not to be a particular state institution merely existing at the side of the others. Religion ought, rather, to touch the perfection of public life in all its forms and vital motions, in the way that beauty touches the flower!

Otto: You are, it would seem, speaking of distant times.

Philanthes: That may be! But what I have here said could, perhaps, also indicate an objective for us, albeit a distant one.

Woldemar: Venerable Philanthes, do but explain to me how you can expect so much of religious symbolism, when you have, so to speak, forcibly separated its development from the doctrines of faith and virtue. If faith and conscience no longer live in these images and symbols, will the latter still retain their solemnity and their profound importance? Will they not then, at best, be reduced to the level of cold and intellectual allegories?

Philanthes: Faith and conscience will not be separated from the living image and symbol, provided that the doctrines of faith and virtue are developed purely as branches of knowledge.

Certainly, no positive religious opinion will survive without a literature which is couched in the language of imagery and is concerned with the transcendental. Moses derived all his images from his own people; but they soon borrowed others from the Persians, and we have inherited those borrowings as well. In this connection, you are entirely right. All religious symbolism is aimed directly at feeling, and that is as true of religious literature as it is of every other religious symbolism. Where the meaning of this metaphorical literature, instead of being grasped by feeling, is understood as the interpretation of an allegory, it is reduced to an insipid and impoverished performance lacking in both warmth and life.

It is precisely this which we must examine more closely. How can life and vigour be preserved in these symbols alongside the thoroughly clear concepts of faith and virtue? How, in other words, are they to be kept free from all superstition?

Woldemar: I am eager to hear what you have to say.

Philanthes: This can easily be explained by reference to a variety of aesthetic symbols. What do you think? Have you ever heard that, when an army confronts the enemy and the martial music sounds out, the leaders must first approach the soldiers and tell them: "Pay attention now — when the drum rolls or the horns sound, it means that you are to be courageous, and that you are to march with a firm step towards the enemy! Ponder this well, and stir your courage with considerations such as these!" — Or do you think it would be of advantage to the courage of the new recruits, if they were to be instructed about the purpose of the martial music on their first exercises?

Woldemar: The first would be ridiculous, and the second superfluous. The meaning of the military music communicates itself, of itself, to the feelings of all the marching soldiers, without the need of reflection.

Philanthes: Did you ever hear of a pupil of the art of dancing who was unable to understand what the relation of the music to the dancing was?

Woldemar: No, indeed not! What I have frequently noticed, however, is that young people, as soon as the dance music strikes up, have difficulty staying still and involuntarily beat time to the music.

Philanthes: You will also, presumably, admit that, in church before the music starts, we do not need someone to come forward to explain to the congregation that the music is intended to awaken devotion.

Woldemar: Certainly not! As soon as the sound of the organ thunders through the cathedral everyone with ears to hear will feel the effect within his own heart.

Philanthes: In many symbols, you will, accordingly, recognise the operation on feeling of a power which is free, independent of concepts, and consequently distinct from superstition. Think of sublime ecclesiastical architecture, or great church music. A thrill of devotion at the deep stillness beneath the vaults of the cathedral seizes hold of us as we enter; and church music easily moves us to devotion. But whoever was guilty of confusing image and symbol with the thing itself, in this context? Whoever mistook the masonry of the church for God himself? Or the music for religious truth? In examples such as these, you can easily recognise the power of intuitive awareness and the feelings associated therewith.

Woldemar: Excellent! I am beginning to understand you. But is that supposed to suffice? Even if we wanted to spurn the help of painting and sculpture in religious practice, what about literature? Does not understanding have claims here as good as those which it has in science? How will you effect a complete separation between the literature of imagery and truth?

Philanthes: I have no wish to do so. Nor, indeed, could I so so, even if I were so inclined. What I do wish is this. The practice of religion should be served, not only by religious literature, but also by painting and sculpture. But it is also my wish that the image should never be confused with the thing itself.

I have learned how that objective is to be attained from Plato's account of the constitution of the ideal state.

Woldemar: What, then, is your opinion?

Philanthes: My dear fellow! By means of children's fairy stories!

Woldemar: Are you jesting? I do not understand you.

Philanthes: No, I am not jesting! Pay attention and I shall explain. To begin with, the situation with respect to many ideals of literature and the plastic arts is exactly the same as with music and architecture. In these arts, too, image and symbol are often meaningful and intelligible to all cultivated feeling, though far more so to the cultivated feeling of our own nation.

The songs of lyrical poetry are intelligible to everybody without their conflicting with faith or superstition. You will have no fear of being abused as a Parsee heathen if, in a hymn, you address God as the Light of the World, or as the Friend of Man. In particular, however, pay attention to the lyrical meaning of the ancient word of memory, of the consecrated utterance of our ancestral tradition. When the whole people sink to their knees in prayer as the organ plays "Oh Lord God, merciful and gracious!" — is it not easy to see how meaningless the criticism is? The consecrated utterance is, for one thing, the old familiar symbol of devotion, by means of which we are all led, with the greatest force, to the same devotion, in the deep recollection of that mysterious, invisible spiritual community, in which we all, as the children of God, stand linked with each other and with our ancestors.

But the situation is different in the case of that representative, epic and dramatic art, which is richest in forms. Here too we shall be able, by means of words and colours, and even stone, to represent intelligibly to each other devotion and rapture, love and gentleness, courage, charm and joy, and so much else that is similar. But here the image, unless it is associated with a particular and familiar story, only has the significance of a cold allegory; and the image is still less rich in meaning for us so long as the story has not acquired a significance of its own for us.

This reminds me of what Plato says about the songs of Homer and Hesiod. He criticises them as national myths and children's fairy stories. He subjects them to severe censure because they contain such unworthy and immoral accounts of the gods. But, at the same time, he remarks on how important such myths are for the education of the nation. We could add that they are important, not only for the education of youth, but also for the education of the whole aesthetic public life of a nation. It is only on the foundation of a distinctive, patriotically cultivated, rich, great and beautiful cycle of myths that new and powerful creations in the spheres of painting, sculpture, and all epic and dramatic literature, can grow and flourish with luxuriance and with true significance for the history of a nation.

Now, what is your opinion, dear friend? Is it not possible for us to continue to cherish our quite fantastic and beautiful national myths and fairy stories without becoming superstitious and erroneously supposing that such stories are actually true?

Woldemar: Why not! Even children do not take even the most attractive fairy tales for true stories, though no one has gone to the trouble of enlightening them on the matter.

Philanthes: How would it be, then, if we suggested to the nation that it should no longer permit the nurses of our children to invent our fairy stories and myths, but that, like the Greeks, we should entrust our poets with the unique and great task of creating for us a great cycle of myths, myths about angels and spirits for the women and children, myths about heroes and demigods for the boys, and historical myths for the youths approaching manhood?

Woldemar: What a great and splendid achievement that would be! I clearly see how the arts would then affect the whole of public life. Public life would be entwined around with their flowery tendrils, perfumed with their fragrance, and inspired by their vital freshness. I see an aesthetic public life, such as history has never yet seen, emerging from the union of the pure truth of faith and love with the power of poetry. And I distinctly feel that there is no danger of image and symbol, with all their splendour, encroaching upon the rights of truth.

Philanthes: Excellent, dear Woldemar! I see that our hopes harmonise with each other.

Arthur: Let us linger over this idea. Explain to me more clearly how such a rich and highly valued national myth could so much advance life in the arts?

Philanthes: All the elements of the artistic life benefit from such a myth. The enthusiasm and eagerness of the artist will be intensified. The efforts of many will be powerfully focused on a single task. Invention will be animated by a higher interest. And representation will be able to achieve perfect tranquillity and clarity, which would otherwise be impossible.

If the art of a nation is not rooted in a widely known and well loved national myth, each artist will find himself abandoned to his own individual efforts. The artists will scatter in the pursuit of varied and differing interests and soon find themselves devoted to providing amusements of a superficial and diversified character. On the other hand, a serious and noble myth which is loved by the people intensifies the interest and transfixes emulous invention within its magic circle. But above all, such a myth is the source of the perfected tranquillity and clarity of representation. This tranquillity and clarity is the foundation of all that is great in the arts — it is the very quintessence of what we understand by the classical. This is true even of sculptors and painters. No true artist will be satisfied with the treatment of vague allegories. A picture of which the meaning must first be explained in writing on a plaque beneath cannot make any great impression. True representation here requires a myth which is already widely known and loved. But this is even more true of representational literature. Epic poetry can never have more than a slight interest if it does not sing the living national myth. Finally, it is this national myth which must first prepare the foundations of tragic literature. The greatness, the tranquillity and clarity of the art of Aeschylus and Sophocles can here only be attained when the people are already familiar with and interested in the story and its heroes — when, in other words, the artist has no need to introduce his characters by means of artificial and incidental arrangements; he can concentrate all his energies on the presentation of the action.

Arthur: Certainly. The spirit of the whole people in this way moves its literature itself. It must endow it with a higher dignity, a deeper seriousness and a greater power, than when literature only exists in the narrow sphere of private entertainment.

Philanthes: This affords great prospects for the future. But, lively as our hopes may be, you will readily appreciate that there is little good advice that we can give our legislators for the realisation of these aspirations in our public life.

The hereditary prejudices of family life and education impede our path, and they will probably not permit any immediate major changes.

Looking at history, it is not difficult to give instances of greatness either from the past or from elsewhere at the present time. It is not even difficult to create new literature with the imagination. But this is of no help unless the spirit in the people draws near to such instances of greatness and displays a decisive public opinion. My father and Crates were successful in heeding this warning. Any such instance of greatness which is suggested will be greeted with either mocking laughter or open hostility, unless public opinion is already in harmonious agreement with the suggestion. In these matters, it is with enthusiasm that everything must be taken up, with enthusiasm that everything must be held fast and defended.

If you wished to arrange new political or religious festivals and celebrations for a nation which was lacking in enthusiasm, most of the educated classes, with their airs of intellectual superiority, would greet the proposals with sardonic laughter. They would say: "The fools! The fanatics! Yes, the common people do probably have to be hoodwinked if they are to be kept amused: *panem et circenses* said the Roman, *sussita* said the Greeks!"

None of this can help unless it first existed in the communal spirit of the people before it assumed specific form.

There is this further point to add. The half-formed understanding, no matter what airs it may give itself, still plays with symbols even in its scientific and intellectual pursuits — symbols which it takes for the thing itself. Now, as long as one's faith in the mystery of the symbol remains unshaken, one continues to be impressed by what is ancient, not venturing to initiate any change. But if that faith should gradually disappear, one then thinks that one understands the matter, and one will venture to consider changes and improvements. But on what changes and improvements is one to agree? Everybody will have his own suggestion, and the very variety itself will be a source of pleasure. The general symbolism will disintegrate into the less significant symbolism of tiny scattered factions. And here only the seriousness of a deeply experienced enthusiasm, felt by the whole people, could generate a worthy and permanent union of the nation as a whole, and produce the common observation of the same consecrated rites.

DIALOGUE VIII

Eternal Truth

A few days later Otto renewed his visit to the old man, this time asking him for enlightenment on the chief questions of religious instruction. Philanthes replied: "Some while ago I sketched a continuation of Cecilia's papers. Come and join me with my family. You and Theone shall take turns reading aloud from what I wrote, and we can then discuss what has been read." Otto followed him and the old man gave Theone the following conversation to read aloud.

The philosophical conversations, in which Cecilia participated and which were her favourite amusement, continued in the family after her death. With the little Eugene growing up, Amalia often steered the conversation round to the topic of education. It was in this way, on one occasion, that the following conversation took place. It was the result of a question which had been raised in relation to the issue of religious instruction. Amalia invited Evagoras to express his opinion about the correct instruction for the development of religious convictions.

Evagoras: I can easily tell you my opinion. But do not expect a doctor's prescription, which you simply send to the apothecary, who then gives you a potion, upon which all you need is a clean spoon to administer the medicine. I shall tell you my opinion, but you must then extract what may be of use to you. The child must learn religion, not at school, but in life itself.

Amalia: I have often had to dispute this matter with Clarissa in a curious way. I took myself to be supporting your views, and she to be opposing them. More specifically, I sought, in your name, to champion the cause of feeling, though not with complete success, while Clarissa defended the cause of proof.

Clarissa: Yes, that is how it was. Of course, I know as well as you that the life of religious convictions can only exist in feeling, once it has been aroused and developed. There I have no need of your help. However, once we have the feeling, it will still be necessary for the educated man to give an account of the foundations of faith, hope and charity. The reflective understanding must confirm that these convictions of feeling possess truth, and are not merely dreams or fantasies.

Evagoras: Good! So far we are agreed. I share your opinion. If you do not need my help, then let me go.

Amalia: Our agreement will soon be at an end. Clarissa now goes on to say that she often likes your argument in support of feeling, and that there were a number of things there which could have been expressed more clearly and vigorously. But how would it help? Everything depended on the philosophical observations which came afterwards. Clarissa's complaint is that once you had arrived at that point you became unintelligible to her and seemed to her to be guilty of sophistry. On the other hand, she commends the understandable clarity of the ordinary natural teaching of religion, where the existence of God and the immortality of the soul are proved from necessary truths, nature and human existence. Clarissa, however, is not willing to get involved in your sophistries, as she puts it.

If, on the other hand, I accept the conclusions of Cecilia's papers and our previous conversations, then it is clear that those proofs are delusions or, rather, errors of expression. I appreciate that we are here concerned with the convictions which are to be found, simply and immediately, in our feelings, and which cannot initially be presented in such an artificial and disursive manner. What Julius says, echoing your words, about the futility of proofs in these matters, and the necessity of immediate belief in the spirit; what Cecilia says, also accepting your opinions, about the uselessness of the usual calculations of natural purposes in connection with Providence — all that is so clear to me that I am convinced that we must accept it, and, when necessary, modify our other opinions accordingly. But if Clarissa were to ask: How are you going to guarantee the reflective understanding its rights and secure feeling its defence? — I should not know how to give a clear or satisfactory answer. To say that these feelings need no defence is, from one point of view, correct, I suppose. But it is not the last word on the matter. We must, after all, also inform the reflective understanding about these feelings.

Evagoras: Yes, dear Amalia, I understand your disagreement very well. But to resolve it would involve difficulties as much for me as for you. If Clarissa will condescend to listen to us, then she must concede that it is not possible to assist the truth of our convictions in matters of conscience, faith or intuitive awareness with demonstrations at all, for it is these convictions which show us first truths in our spirit; they do not shine with borrowed light.

Man does not need to learn these truths in the first place, as he does in the case of the experiences of life or the insights of mathematics. He has them in his possession from the very start. Here our only care is to ensure that the spirit is illuminated within so that it can become aware of that of which it is certain in itself.

Here, every stimulating doctrine or speech helps. It is not on account of their truth that those teachings are so dear to Clarissa. As with the unintelligible formulae of the catechism, the only important thing here is the truth of those feelings and their occurrence in the mind. If the pupil says: "I do not understand this or that particular thing in the catechism" then the teacher is at liberty to reply: "Dear child, these are sacred mysteries!" Custom acknowledges the symbols, and it is thus difficult to quarrel with them. Even if they contain doctrinal errors, they nonetheless stimulate consciousness of the holy truth, if the mind is accustomed to them. Accordingly, I think it best not to argue with Clarissa about these things. I shall merely express my view with the following warning. A certain striking strangeness of certain assertions is not to be used as an objection against them, for that strangeness is nothing but the *unusualness* of the expression. Every catechism contains assertions which are to a far greater degree unintelligible. But someone who has known them off by heart for so long will simply fail to notice them.

Clarissa: Today I am going to be very modest. I am going to start by making a concession even before I have been attacked. The only thoughts I have are other people's thoughts, which I have come to accept and grown to love. Accordingly, Evagoras, tell us your opinions.

Evagoras: Let us begin by using the idea you have yourselves expressed. All religious convictions are matters of feeling. All religious convictions exist in feeling. But faith and feeling are an original possession of the human spirit. Faith is older than and exists prior to doubt and disbelief. But as soon as man's reflective understanding grows in strength, as soon as it learns to feel its own power and becomes aware of its right to sift errors and prejudices (produced by habit) — as soon as that happens, doubt and disbelief must arise in these matters too.

The understanding, once it is in a position to convict error of its mistakes and is capable of ordering human affairs, learns to operate a certain standard against error both in the context of experience and in the sphere of proof. But if it applies this standard to religious convictions it fails him. No experience truly supports such convictions, and every attempt to prove them theoretically gradually falls under the suspicion of deception and surreption.

Here, at any rate, we must praise every pure stimulation of feeling as a sweet and nourishing milk for children and common people who cannot think for themselves, and also for those women who are unwilling to do so. But we need more than this for the independent energy of the spirit. We must be able to reply to the doubt and disbelief both of others and of ourselves, not by subjecting those first truths of feeling to deductions and proofs, but alone by justifying the valid claims of those feelings to the understanding. There is, it seems to me, an old error, and if one is guilty of it one will never quite be able to extricate oneself, with complete certainty, from the vexatiousness of doubt and disbelief. The mistake consists in attempting, with a view to granting the reflective understanding its right, to establish the truths of conscience and faith, not only with feeling, but also with the auxiliary means of deductions, proofs and definitions of terms. This procedure is adopted as an alternative to accepting the truths of conscience and belief directly from faith and conscience, merely granting understanding its right by proving to it the validity of the testimony which faith and conscience afford.

Amalia: Thus, we ought not to attempt to justify faith and conscience by trying to prove the truth of their assertions by appealing to other sources, as is usually done. We ought not to address ourselves, in this attempted justification, to what is believed. We ought, rather, to concentrate our attention on faith and conscience themselves, and simply show that they are loyal and truthful witnesses. But would you venture to carry out this programme in a fashion which was generally appealing and commonly intelligible? In order to establish the claims of faith and feeling against those of deduction and proof, will it not be necessary to presuppose a prior and all too scientific foundation — the theory of the faculties of human knowledge (if that is the correct designation)?

Evagoras: My view is that language is certainly capable of being gradually developed in a commonly intelligible fashion in this branch of self-knowledge. On the other hand, I am ready to concede the difficulties. But my present purpose lies in quite a different direction, and I fear the contradiction of neither you nor Clarissa. It seems to me that what is necessary first of all is that the independence of man's spiritual and moral life should not only be proved to him, but that it should become clear within him.

Disbelief in and scepticism about religious and moral truth arise in two ways. The one is calm and cold disbelief, which despises faith because it thinks it can see the lack of foundation. This disbelief is frequently combined with a deformation of the spirit in the direction of crude immorality and a contempt for all moral ideals. Frequently, however, it is also more nobly motivated by hatred of superstition and of the fury of religious enthusiasm. Through the latter motive alone it has secured for itself a place in the history of the progress of the human spirit.

The other type of scepticism is the disbelief of despair. It yearns for faith but it cannot find it. In the destinies of human life it detects, not the longed for divine Providence, but only the rule of naked violence and blind necessity. For that reason, it despairs of Providence.

But both types of disbelief are based upon the same error: failure to recognise the independence of man's spiritual life. Cold and contemptuous disbelief can only result from the understanding losing itself in a one-sided contemplation devoted, in part, to the clear necessity of the laws of nature which regulate the physical world and, in part, to the sensible limitation of human life, and, consequently, failing to find the ideas of the independence of the spirit. The disbelief of despair, by contrast, arises in the unfortunate person who over-estimates this earthly life with its misfortunes, and is unable to acknowledge the single law of the good and the beautiful in spiritual beauty and sublimity.

Both forms of disbelief disappear when confronted by the idea of inner spiritual dignity, and by the peace of God, which accompanies that idea. The person, for whom the ideals of spiritual beauty and sublimity have become living ideals, already, with his reasonable view of life, stands on the foundation of faith, without having first to fight a long battle against scepticism in order to win his way through to faith.

More powerful than all sceptical contradiction is the inner certainty of the spirit in all the emotions of the moral life itself. The life of friendship and love, enthusiasm for honour and justice, admiration for some achievement of spiritual beauty — each of these things has its value in itself. And then there is the triumphant idea of sublime patience in devotion, which transcends joy and suffering and rises above all the vicissitudes of happiness and misery.

No one who trusts only what is sensible will have heard this pure voice within himself. No one who only finds firm support for man's convictions in physical knowledge of the world will have heard this pure voice — this pure voice which, in joy and suffering, leaves no one comfortless this side of the grave — this voice which awakens love and hope in everyone.

Pure love is the first witness of faith!

The most important thing for faith, therefore, is that an awareness of the independence of moral ideals should be produced in life, and that they should be then justified by teaching.

Now, there are some so-called philosophical doctrines which are opposed to this pure spiritual message of self-reliance. But it is easy to show that they all arise from a misinterpretation of the sensible dependency of man's spiritual life.

It will, for example, be objected: who guarantees that your moral ideals are anything more than the gentle dreams of your imagination? Justice, friendship and love — what else gives them force than sympathy with others? But the source of that sympathy is, of course, in the end, nothing but the self-interest of each person, variously guided by habit and imagination. Is it not, then, quite easy to explain the mechanism of all our desire? The sensible dependency of your life must generate within you the instinct of self-preservation, and it is this which stimulates the whole of your will in your thinking spirit. Habit and imagination generate sympathy, together with the subtler delights of sympathy, where each person, in the last analysis, loves no one but himself. Even your ideal of spiritual independence — what else is that than the fantastic wish, generated by the instinct of self-preservation, to live for ever?

Whatever words these philosophers may choose, their empirical interpretation of all our willing is accompanied by that whole train of sceptical thought which seeks to destroy the independence of the spiritual life.

For this reason, our reply is easy.

You orators, who foolishly affect superior airs, learn to look more deeply within yourselves. Your life, which is supposed to be sense, is nonsense. Sense is but the stimulus of life. Sense presupposes a vital activity which is receptive to stimulation and which derives from some source other than sense. Subject your will to closer questioning about the object of its striving. Two requirements for the achievement of contentment will then reveal themselves to you, side by side. According to the one requirement, you merely seek contentment *with your situation*, contentment with your external circumstances, contentment which results from their corresponding to your needs and serving your interest. Here we are only talking about your power, and what is commended is commended only in so far as it loyally serves your purposes. Your instinct of self-preservation may certainly provide an adequate explanation here. But according to the second requirement, you seek contentment *with yourself*. In many respects you are satisfied with yourself, but in others you are not. In this way, we subject ourselves to the demands of duty and to all the requirements of beauty of soul.

Let us now see how these requirements of contentment decide our dispute. Our disagreement is this. You say: the sensible drives of our appetites are the primary drives, and they alone are immediate in character. The moral drives result from them only indirectly through the mediation of imagination. — We, in contrast, say: the pure moral drives of spiritual independence are the original drives. Now, who is right?

Do you not yourselves say: the sensible stimuli of our lives immediately yield one instinct alone, the instinct of self-preservation, in which we love ourselves and which drives us to defend our life against whomsoever it may be. Now, if this were our heart's only drive, it would follow that physical self-preservation would have to seem to us to be the most important thing in the world; to it all else would be subservient. But that is not how the heart of the civilised man speaks. He makes demands upon himself which subject him to the higher command of the good and the beautiful. And those demands which he makes upon himself cannot flow from the desire for physical self-preservation. That instinct cannot explain how man came to censure himself when he failed to comply with duty or obey spiritual beauty. These higher requirements, in which I issue commands to myself, and to which I demand obedience from myself, can only emanate immediately from the independent life of the spirit. The opponents of this view were sometimes, it must be admitted, wont to reply: the ideal of contentment with ourselves also arises from the interests of egoism. They say: we blame ourselves if we have lived in such a way as to damage our physical or spiritual health — in other words, if we have been disloyal to the demands of self-preservation.

But the real requirements of self-contentment contradict this alleged explanation in the case of every civilised person. Cowardice and baseness would frequently be a far more effective means of self-preservation than valour or the love of honour — except that cowardice and baseness contain within themselves an unconditional negative value, just as valour and love of honour possess an unconditional positive value. The unconditional negative value of vice, and the unconditional positive value of moral virtue, are clear to us from the ideas of the independence of the spirit alone; they cannot be of sensible origin.

But this polemical instruction, which seeks to save practical philosophy from error, is, for my present purpose, of subordinate character. What is of concern to us here is life itself, and the awakening of moral feeling within it. The first thing which we ought to further is the *animation* of conscience, so that conscience, in its turn, should animate faith. We must bring the moral development of the spirit to people, so that they should have an immediate vision of the fire, the light and the life of the spiritual world. All else will then happen of its own accord.

I do not here need to describe to you in greater detail the ideals of honour and justice, friendship and love, enthusiasm, humility and devotion. It will be your duty to initiate the youthful spirit into the pure life of those ideals, while at the same time warding off the prevalent sensuality and blind banausic activity.

Amalia: You say that love is the witness of faith. Faith and religious truth can only become clear to the man of truly moral development. Moral indifference must arise among people of education when they are merely taught the observance and pursuit of custom, propriety, fashion, skilfulness and aptitude — in short, things relating to prudence — instead of the acknowledgement of the cause of wisdom, the beauty of their own spiritual lives and pure love. With the growth of this moral indifference, faith also grows indifferent. By contrast, when the pious spirit acknowledges the pure beauty of the soul, it therewith acquires security of faith, as well.

Evagoras: That is my opinion. Love is the witness of faith. Once pure moral feeling has been stimulated, we have acquired the firm and fundamental conviction of all life in feeling. And this, in all its richness, we must continue to heed. Alongside moral development, the second thing which is important for me, both for individuals and for entire nations, is the serious development of the sense of beauty, of pure taste.

In the development of the sense of beauty we make the acquaintance, intuitively, so to speak, of the world of faith through its presentiments. We have before our eye that other element of our convictions which can never become a matter of concepts or of conceptual knowledge. That non-conceptual element of our convictions will never, therefore, be exposed to the one-sidednesses of disbelief and scepticism, all of which derive from a misplaced confidence in the omnipotence of science and knowledge. But here, with the sense of beauty, we, so to speak, contemplate the world of the good and the beautiful, and its eternal truth.

There is no thought in the human spirit which possesses greater purity, no thought which is more fully consecrated to that which is holy, than these light and luminous fantasies, with which the beauty of nature enriches us. The sight of the first fresh green of spring, the glowing colours of the autumnal foliage, the tree-tops swaying in the wind, the meadows rich with flowers, the calyx of the lily — do they not make us aware, in the innermost recesses of our moved spirits, of those Platonic recollections of an earlier divine existence — do they not arouse within us, quite independently of language and concepts, intimations of a higher existence? And it is not just the superficial play of poetry which is to be found in these higher feelings; it is the sacred solemnity of pure truth. This higher feeling, entertained in the candid contemplation of natural beauty, is furthest removed from all self-interest, all self-concern, all selfish aspirations. But there is an intimate link between these luminous fantasies and all the ideas of artistic beauty, whether they be gentle or mighty, all the feelings in the pure apprehension of the moral life and piety, for they are all suffused with the same vital warmth of eternal truth.

Julius: Yes, indeed! Individual luminous moments glow in life with the pure radiance of these deep and living intimations. I recall the morning after Cecilia died. I rode out before the town. The morning light illuminated the craggy slopes of the mountains. From among their fresh green foliage, the peach trees were forcing their scarlet blossoms among the white shimmer of the flowering fruit trees. How clear, how deeply calming was the feeling which grew from that contemplation.

Evagoras: No sensible desire is aroused in these luminous fantasies of natural beauty, nor any moral drive to action, as in the feelings, say, of honour or love. Such contemplation is quite purely the sublime intimation of the higher spiritual destiny which holds sway throughout the universe. You see, dear Clarissa, this, in my opinion, is also the spirit in your symbolism, which reverences the divinity as the architect of nature. I would merely give you a warning: never seek understanding in these realms where the rights of the sense of beauty alone have validity; for here all deductions, with their ever so precise concepts, can be reduced to shame.

But the flowers and the stars speak of eternal truth to the sense of beauty.

Clarissa: Ah! You are almost growing sentimental, Evagoras!

Evagoras: Quite right! People of moral education are all of them sentimental, each in his own particular way. Many of them do not wish to appear so — but then in that they often act very properly, as well. I do not speak to the flowers or stars, because I cannot speak their wordless language, though I can listen to it. But they speak to me!

But, of course, all this fantasy grows silly as soon as it is transformed into an allegory which can be grasped by the understanding, and still more so if you reduce it to the plaything, or the decorative embellishment, of conversation.

Such fantasy only has value for each person, individually, like prayer.

Clarissa: Very good! I have nothing to say by way of objection.

Evagoras: What I have set out to do is to remind you of the serious life in feeling, looking at it from the side which was most removed from the moral will. Its demands grow more important when, in friendship and devotion, it is more intimately connected with the will. With respect to the pure religious education of the entire nation, we must recognise the rights of the sense of beauty alongside and, indeed, above those of conceptual education. In this pure development of taste alone lies the effective defence of the nation's life against mysticism and the sectarian spirit, and, for that very reason, against disbelief, as well. Higher intellectual culture can never be a matter for everybody, whereas the pure development of the sense of beauty can. Now, if that sense of beauty is lacking, then fanatics, taking advantage of the nation's primitive taste and deploying a fantastic play of images, will easily make themselves popular and repeatedly succeed in introducing into polite society ghosts, witches and the rest of the riff-raff of hell.

Julius: Absolutely right! We should shout with joy if the nation, with great expenditure of effort, wished to light the flames of memory, if the nation were to erect mighty temples and achieve distinctions of every kind in the cause of the consecrated symbols of the peace and presence of God. But the people who are engaged in trade and commerce simply laugh at us enthusiasts, because such undertakings produce nothing tangible in the way of profit, yield no financial gain. And there are others, of a wise and serious turn of mind, who severely censure us because such things neither feed nor clothe the poor.

But I agree with you that such critics are deficient in one part of the healthy development of the spirit. The people engaged in trade and commerce, whom we have just mentioned, only know life from the point of view of their own business. The other class of critics, while acknowledging the commands of the higher moral life, only have an imperfect understanding of the nature and manner of the moral education of the people. They mistakenly hope that they, who possess no developed sense of beauty themselves, will be able to develop the people's sense of beauty and make them pious.

Amalia: We shall not quarrel with you on this issue. We sympathise with what you say. The *serenity* of pious feelings, the *purity* of all those tender and sincere moral emotions (which are the seat of morality in everyday life, with all its petty events) wholly depend upon the pure and subtle development of taste. These emotions are so intimately fused with the sense of beauty that the one cannot flourish without the other. They are the leaves, the flowers and the fruit of one stem. For that reason, you say that if someone's moral feeling and sense of beauty have been properly developed, then that person makes the acquaintance of the world of faith and intuitive awareness. He doubts as little of its being and nature, as he does of the sun's existence in the sky. He needs no proof that there is a doctrine of faith. His only question is: what is the correct expression of that doctrine? Tell us now, how would you present it to the understanding?

Evagoras: You will easily discover what must be the fundamental and introductory doctrine. The world of faith and the world of intuitive awareness reveal themselves to us if we oppose to the conceptual truth of knowledge the convictions which live in feeling and for pure taste alone. The question which we shall pose the understanding is, therefore, as follows. How and why do knowledge and feeling, concept and taste, differ from each other relatively to human insight, or, as I wish to express the matter, how and why do the different laws of *finite* and *eternal truth* co-exist alongside each other in our spirit? In this connection, specific instruction will be required. Here, we are concerned with a truth which is of such obviousness and simplicity. And yet we are also concerned here with a doctrine which, because of the unaccustomed character of its expression, can only be rendered generally intelligible with difficulty. I shall attempt to present the matter in its simplest form. Let me address myself to you, Amalia.

Do you take yourself, or any other person, to be omniscient?

Amalia: No! In my opinion, neither I nor anyone else is omniscient.

Evagoras: Can you tell me why that is your opinion?

Amalia: I shall try to explain. Someone who is omniscient has perfect knowledge of all things. He must not only know all things; he must also know each thing through and through. Human beings are lacking in both respects. We know of an unlimited past, but we are acquainted with but very little of what has happened in that past. Again, we know that a future is coming, but we know very little of what will happen in it. And then again, we know how space extends to infinity, but we are only acquainted with a little of what actually exists in that space. And, if we do know a thing, whether it be a body or a mind, we cannot understand any individual thing through and through.

Evagoras: Man is, thus aware that his knowledge of things is limited and conditioned. He contrasts this knowledge with the perfection of omniscience. Now, I would ask you to pay attention to the following point. You say: we become aware of our own ignorance because we discover that we neither know all things nor do we know any one thing through and through. What, then, is the source of our knowledge that there are more things and other things than those which, on any given occasion, we know? What is the source of our knowledge that in a single thing there is more than we actually find in it? We should not be able to arrive at this idea if we only knew things immediately, and did not also know the universal and necessary conditions, which are different from the existence of these things themselves, and upon which the mode of their existence depends.

Amalia: You are beginning to talk in riddles.

Evagoras: Be but patient with me! You have, after all, already yourself told me what I have just been saying. Time and space, for example, are such universal conditions. You know very well that there is a past, a present and a future in time. You know that there is a space which extends outwards in all directions. You thus know the place where and the time when things must be. But the things themselves which are, which were and which will be at this point in time and space — these things you do not, for the most part, know. This knowledge of the Where and the When, without the things belonging thereto, is really the knowledge by means of which you arrive at the awareness that you by no means know everything.

Amalia: Now I understand you. Little as I may know, I would not know whether the little I knew was not everything or whether there was not more, unless I also knew these universal and necessary conditions — that was how you expressed it! — as well. By their means I know that there is yet more, without actually knowing this more myself.

Evagoras: We have made a start. The way in which we know things as subject to these universal and necessary conditions constrains us to say that it is only a limited and finite truth which belongs to human knowledge. But we somehow have, in addition, the idea of the complete and perfect knowledge of an omniscient Being, who possesses eternal and divine truth. This divine truth is inaccessible to the concepts of man and his *knowledge*, and yet we possess the ideas of that divine truth in *belief*.

And with that, the whole task of the doctrine of religion is specified. Instruction has here to show the subordination of knowledge and its concepts to the ideas of faith. It has the further obligation of making this doctrine so clear that we do not, subsequently, confuse knowledge and faith, or conflate the ideas of eternal truth with the finite concepts of the laws of nature. Let us see how we can extend our agreement further.

What reason would you give me, do you suppose, for saying that man only possesses finite knowledge?

Amalia: I think I can answer your question easily. Rationality is what we call the noble disposition of the human mind, in virtue of which he attaches himself to the higher spirits and raises himself above the animals. Sensibility, on the other hand, is a lower disposition, which he shares with the other animals. Sensibility presumably contains the ground of the finitude of our knowledge.

Evagoras: What do you understand by this sensibility?

Amalia: The spirit of man is a living being. Its life consists in knowing, thinking, feeling pleasure, acting voluntarily. However, we only come to the activities of our lives through the mediation of sensations. These sensations must first be excited in our spirit by means of something else, by means of something other than itself, just as our knowledge is mediated by the stimulus of eye and ear, our desire by hunger and thirst. This dependence of our spirit upon external stimuli is called its sensibility.

Evagoras: Good! But in what respect do you raise man above the animals?

Amalia: Man alone can think. Man acts with free will, the animal only from instinct. Hence, man is capable of judging things according to concepts and universal rules. He does not merely know individual things in space and time; he also knows the necessary laws of nature, in accordance with which these individual things can be judged. Furthermore, man alone possesses the ideas of the supra-sensible and the divine, the ideas of morality and beauty.

Evagoras: Let me put it to you like this. Man not only knows individual things, he is also capable of apprehending the universal and necessary conditions of the true, the beautiful and the good. And he is capable of this in virtue of reason and the ability to think. Thought, namely, consists in the capacity of our understanding to guide and direct our thoughts with freely exercised attention. In this we possess a rationality which has arrived at the higher level of intelligent self-consciousness, and which is aware of the universal and necessary conditions of the true, the good and the beautiful.

The life of the human spirit is, accordingly, a sensible-rational life. In respect of its sensibility, it is limited, for, in order to exist, it needs external stimuli. In respect of its reason, it possesses an independent inner disposition to knowledge.

At this juncture let us consider the following question: What, do you suppose, is the nature of the fundamental form of knowledge, which must be sensibly stimulated?

Amalia: I cannot answer that question.

Evagoras: Let me explain. Suppose that a knowing spirit had its life wholly from and in itself. Whether its knowledge was great or small, it would be self-sufficient, would be dependent on no other thing, and could have no feeling of lack within itself. Its knowledge would constitute a whole, closed within itself and complete. In such a being, knowledge of things would not be distinct from their universal and necessary conditions. This spirit would not have to represent to itself any empty Where and When: every place in space and every moment in time which it knew would be occupied.

Let us now, by contrast, consider a sensible reason. In such a reason there is to be found the fundamental conditions of the only possibility of its knowledge. But it cannot itself determine *what* it knows, for it is dependent on sensible stimuli. There will thus arise in such reason, when it arrives at self-knowledge, a feeling of lack; and its knowledge must have the distinctive and fundamental form *that it can never become a closed whole*. The conditions of stimulation are not to be found within itself. It is, thus, never determined within itself whether there could not always be further stimuli.

Amalia: I understand you very well. Certainly, since our senses make us dependent upon something which is alien and unknown, and by means of which we on any given occasion first learn what things exist, it follows that we must always be anticipating possible new experiences. We can never, in this sensible fashion, arrive at the representation of a completed whole.

Evagoras: Excellent! All sensible reason must, therefore, once it has arrived at self-consciousness, apprehend its own knowledge as *defective* and *absolutely incapable of completion*. That this is so is plain from all our representations of space and time, number and magnitude. Time overruns every limit, space extends beyond every boundary, no number is the last, or the greatest, or the smallest — the whole of space cannot be completed, nor the whole of time, nor the series of numbers.

That is involved in the nature of sensibility. But, in addition to that, human reason is still capable of arriving at the idea of omniscience. In disposition it arrives at self-consciousness of its independence, even though, in execution, it always remains limited. Irrespective, therefore, of the fact that human knowledge is not the knowledge of an omniscient being, we can, notwithstanding, compare our imperfect knowledge with omniscient knowledge. In this way, we contrast the finite truth of a sensibly initiated human knowledge with the eternal truth which belongs to the knowledge of an omniscient being.

Now, how will the essence of things itself be constituted, then? As an omniscient being sees it? Or as man's spirit apprehends it?

Amalia: We can only assume that the true essence of things is as the omniscient being sees it. Man can only know it in so far as his convictions harmonise with the eternal truth of the omniscient being.

Evagoras: Let us pay closer attention to the difference between finite human truth and eternal truth.

To the omniscient being we must attribute perfect knowledge of the essence of all things. Our knowledge, by contrast, remains incomplete, though not incomplete in the sense that we have to reject it as invalid. In virtue of the independence of rational life we are confident in ourselves, are certain in ourselves, that we possess true, even if only limited, knowledge.

But this limited human knowledge — and consider this point well! — must differ from that of an omniscient being, not simply because it constitutes merely a part of the knowledge of an omniscient being; it is wholly different *in kind*.

We only know a part of things, and each individual thing we only know imperfectly. It is impossible to convert these parts, by addition, into a perfect whole, in order to arrive at the knowledge of an omniscient being. For what constitutes the distinctive character of human knowledge is the very fact that, sensible in origin, it never admits a whole, that it is *incapable of completion*. There is no part of things which we know as it is constituted in itself. Each thing which we know is known in a human and limited fashion, distinct from the true essence of the thing. Finite human knowledge cannot be completed so as to become knowledge of an omniscient being. We must rather contrast finite human knowledge, in its incompletability, with the knowledge which possesses eternal truth. And we must do so, by construing this knowledge of an omniscient being as freed from all the limitations of our knowledge.

It is thus that we distinguish, therefore, the manner in which things *appear* to man from the true essence of things themselves. Man is capable of acknowledging his own limitations as such. He says to himself: eternal truth belongs to the unlimited knowledge of the omniscient being alone. Eternal truth is only to be found in the way things appear to man in so far as we imagine the *limits* of human knowledge as *cancelled*.

On this basis, we can now make clear the fundamental characteristics of human knowledge. The spirit of man, in the self-confidence born of the feeling of its own independence, takes its knowledge simply to be truth. But it only fully counts as *eternal truth* in the *feelings of intuitive awareness*. Such feelings of intuitive awareness differ from knowledge and belief in virtue of the distinction between finite and eternal truth.

It is just because we are bound to sensible stimuli that we can grasp only finite truth immediately. Knowledge and concepts only serve to clarify the limited knowledge of man with its finite truth. But eternal truth presents itself to us, through the mediation of finite truth, in a fashion which is both less open and inaccessible to concepts. The language of the heart refers in feeling to eternal truth. For us eternal truth lives in these feelings; to them belong religious feeling and the feeling of beauty; out of them our whole world-view of the good and the beautiful developes. The fundamental convictions embodied in these feelings of intuitive awareness can, however, be expressed by the reflective understanding in the *ideas of faith* as the ideas of eternal truth.

Amalia: How do we come to acquire these ideas since we are unable to reach eternal truth?

Evagoras: In the same way as we come to acquire the idea of an omniscient being — through the self-knowledge of our own limits. All our positive conceptual knowledge is bound to the finite. But we ourselves say: *finite truth contains within itself eternal significance; all that is necessary is that the limits of finite truth should be thought of as cancelled*. We say: it is merely the limited character of human knowledge which does not hold of eternal truth. The ideas of faith are our representations of the fact that the limited character of our mode of construing things, with all its consequences, cannot hold for the essence of things itself.

You will find what I say confirmed in all our religious convictions. In so far as these convictions are expressed conceptually in faith they merely contain expressions which *negate limitations*. These expressions assert: you must think away the limitations of the human view of things from your finite knowledge; you then interpret them with reference to eternal truth.

For this reason, we reject the physical nature of things in respect of eternal truth, and believe only in a world of spiritual life, the higher order of which we acknowledge in the moral laws of virtue and justice.

With this religious view of the spiritual world, our rational existence is raised above bodies and relations of magnitude. The fundamental ideas of eternal truth become eternal life or the immortality of the soul, and the freedom of the will.

But in these two ideas we are simply raising the eternally true nature of the independent spirit above the limitations of our knowledge of it. When we describe the soul as immortal and speak of its eternal life, we are denying that the soul is limited by physical form, or by space and time. When we call the will free, we are denying that the active power of the will is limited.

We say of our life that, contrary to appearances, it is not finite and mortal. We say of the life of the rational will that, contrary to appearances, it is not dependent upon nor subject to any alien power, but, from the point of view of eternal truth, free. The ideas of immortality and freedom, and, with them, all the ideas of faith, thus merely contain the idea of the cancelling of the limits of the faculty, by means of which we grasp eternal truth.

Amalia: That is completely clear, and I find it instructive for the chief ideas of the doctrine of faith, the ideas of the immortality of the soul and the freedom of the will. From the point of view of eternal truth, we must believe in immortality and freedom because, with immortality and freedom, we merely hint at the difference between perfect truth and our limited manner of representing things. But how does the first and the highest of all religious ideas, belief in God, harmonise with this doctrine? Are our ideas of God also merely expressions which negate limitations? This, at any rate, is not clear to me.

Evagoras: In order to reach clarity on that issue, we must look at the nature of human knowledge from another point of view. You will then certainly find that man can only express his belief in God by means of expressions which negate limitations.

We just now found that, in the dispositions of reason, the universal and necessary conditions of the true, the good, and the beautiful, are determined. We also found that it was only in accordance with those universal and necessary conditions that knowledge was possible for us. But our spirit is not capable of generating its own knowledge. It must first be led to it by the sensible stimuli of sensation.

In this way we are introduced into the world by means of the senses. But the senses permit us to distinguish body and soul, in respect of our own life, and the physical and the mental realms in respect of the world. — The Lord of them both is, we say, the omnipotence of God. But God is spirit.

But how, do you suppose, do we arrive at these relations in our knowledge? What is the source of this distinction between body and soul? I maintain: it is determined for man by the nature of his sensibility. The essence of things appears to us by means of two major kinds of sensible stimulus. By means of the outer senses, the organ of which is to be found in our body, we know things outside ourselves. By means of an inner sense, on the other hand, the physical organ of which we do not apprehend, we know our own spiritual life. The different senses speak, as it were, very different languages. Inner sense speaks only of my Self, of the I and its mental activities. The outer senses speak very different languages among themselves. They show us colours, sounds, smells and other things, but in the last analysis they all speak of the same physical existence of formed things in space. To these things in space the different senses merely attribute different characteristics. The first reason why man distinguishes body and soul, matter and mind, is to be found in the dispositions of our various senses. The question, therefore, remains: what meaning may this have for the essence of things. This distinction does not immediately affect eternal truth at all, for it is, of course, only determined by the particular characteristics of man's sensibly limited mode of construing them.

All that is involved here is the fact that things *appear* to man sometimes as body and sometimes as spirit. But we were agreed about this a moment ago, and it does not follow that things are truly the one or the other. On the contrary, if we wish to determine our representation of their true essence, then we must first compare our sensible knowledge with our idea of eternal truth, and see what part of sensible knowledge may survive the comparison.

Here we come upon the age-old but ever new doctrine of the nullity of the spatial and the temporal, the doctrine of the non-being of the physical world and the sole importance of the spiritual world alone — doctrines which the majority of people reject as empty sophistries or dismiss as plain foolishness, though others subject them to mystical distortions. In fact, correctly understood, these doctrines are part of holy truth.

We say that in the knowledge of an omniscient being there is no space, no time, no physical world. We also say that, from the point of view of the omniscient, the only part of human knowledge which can appropriately be interpreted as eternal truth is his knowledge of the spiritual life. This is a consequence of our earlier observations; it is simply an extrapolation of those ideas of faith which, with respect to eternal truth, repudiate all the limits of our mode of construing things.

The same things appear to us as bodies and mind. I appear to my outer sense as body; to my inner sense I appear as mind. I know other people as bodies, but I interpret this knowledge, through appeal to my own self-consciousness, as being at the same time knowledge of other minds and other mental lives. The whole of nature, which appears to me as a physical world, is also, construed in its beauty and sublimity, interpreted as spiritual life. The only difference is that no concept is adequate to the latter representation. Here my consciousness can only exist in feelings.

To consider the matter more exactly: we may not assume that there is a physical world and a mental world existing side by side with each other, as if there were two different worlds. We ought not to assume that there are bodies and minds existing alongside each other. That is not what our senses teach us. The senses call the same thing sometimes body and sometimes mind. Different languages, as it were, are speaking about the same thing. Physical language is the language of our outer senses; mental language is the language of our inner sense. Man uses these two languages, side by side, for without mental language he would not find himself, and without physical language he would not find the world or his position in it. But, to start with, both languages speak merely of appearances, not of eternal truth.

Amalia: In that case, we have another question: What is the application of what you are saying to eternal truth?

Evagoras: We shall have to look for the answer to your question in the following way. We shall think away from appearances all the limitations, which belong to the sensible way of construing things, and then see whether anything is left which survives confrontation with the ideas of the perfected and the independent.

We must, accordingly, first translate physical language into mental language. We must then affirm the requirements of perfection and the cancellation of all limits. The ideas of eternal truth will then show themselves in what is spiritual.

Now, what were the signs of lack in the human mode of representation which distinguished it from the omniscient mode?

Amalia: The distinctive difference was the fact that sensible knowledge was incapable of completion, and that we could never arrive at a completed whole in the case of magnitudes and numbers, space and time.

Evagoras: In other words, nothing which is subject to the law of incompletability can be an eternal truth. Everything which is subject to that law belongs to appearance alone. The eternal truth which inheres in appearances can first show itself when we have repudiated everything which is incapable of completion in appearances.

Now, if we consider our sensible knowledge, what immediately emerges is the fact that space and time, number and magnitude have no eternal truth in themselves; they are merely the conditions of the appearance of things for man. It follows from this that our knowledge of the physical world is not immediate knowledge of eternal truth. On the contrary, everything in the physical world reduces to appearance, for our representations of what is physical is entirely constituted by what is spatial and temporal, and by relations of magnitude. By contrast, in the case of our knowledge of mental life and of the things related thereto, the characteristics of things do not disappear even when I think away the incompletability of all magnitudes. There is here a reference to eternal truth.

As far as insight into these things is concerned, therefore, everything depends upon our acquaintance and familiarity with these views about the distinction between appearance and eternal truth. No matter how puzzled the layman may be by the strongly worded denial of the reality of space, time and the entire physical world, it can, nonetheless, be clearly shown that man, in his representations of the physical world, does not have knowledge of the true essence of things; he only has a *human view* of things.

This is especially apparent if one considers how everybody employs such different modes of representation alongside each other — modes of representation which would clearly contradict each other if they each claimed to show the true nature of things.

Let me present you with three different major views which, taking into account the limitations of our sensible knowledge, enjoy equal validity as *world-views* alongside each other.

The first and most important of these world-views arises from my sense of my own existence and from my consciousness of my own mental or spiritual life — it is the *spiritual world-view*. It contains self-knowledge, knowledge of the moral order of things, the whole world-view of the beautiful and the good.

The second world-view recognises the physical in relation to mind — it is the *outer sensible world-view*.

The third world-view is the perfected knowledge of the physical world — the *physical mathematical world-view*.

We know the things which are external to us by taste and smell, by colours and sounds, and by the other intimations of our outer senses. But as the philosophers of antiquity already taught, what we are dealing with here is not the essence of the thing itself, but merely an intimation of its existence which is given to the knowing mind. For by which eye and under which illumination is the true colour seen? By which ear and by which blow upon the resonant object is the true sound heard? — To these questions there is no reply. The real characteristics of bodies are not colours or sounds but merely the conditions of their stimulation in that which is illuminated or resonant. Accordingly, the first sensible view is repudiated, as far as the essence of things is concerned. It is merely the view of man, to whom things make their appearance.

Whither does that lead us? Apparently, to a certain mathematical and perfected knowledge of bodies. The stimulatory conditions for colour and sound, which we just mentioned, are motions in that which is struck and in the ray of light. In all sensible perceptions, we are thus referred to the motions of bodies. By their means colours, sounds, taste and smell, even the appearance of mind itself, receive their spatial and temporal determinations.

Intuition thus leads us into the world of motions. It is here that the things themselves must first be sought. It is here that bodies are known as they exist, so to speak, independently of mind, in relation to each other, moving alongside each other through time and in space, mutually repelling and attracting each other. This is the necessary, fixed and mathematical view of the external world. Leukippos already specified the fundamental ideas of that world: the full, the void, and the necessity of motion. Or, in other words: space and time, the mass of bodies located in and occupying space and time, and motion in accordance with necessary laws. The mass of bodies is, according to this view, their immutable essence. The only change which this mass undergoes is the change of location by movement. Colours, sounds, and the like, and even the appearance of mind itself, merely belong to the changing characteristics of that mass.

This is the world-view of the astronomers and of all practical people, which enables us to build, to order the affairs of civil life, and predict the course of the constellations. It impresses the understanding as the most certain world-view, for it arises from the most obvious assumptions, rests on necessary laws, and is best able to survive that strictest test of man's understanding — predicting the course of future events. But this world-view also knows nothing of mind or life, nothing of the beautiful or the good. It has, therefore, become the stumbling-block to practical wisdom. We must here combat the error of its presumptuous claims.

For that reason, I now maintain that this world-view, according to which the essence of things is supposed to consist of bodies in motion, is, like the first sensible view of things — indeed, more so! — a human view which merely shows us appearances, not the true essence of things.

Now Clarissa, you most enjoy arguing with me: I shall address myself to you. My intention is to show that there is no physical world at all.

Clarissa: Very well! Before me on the table there is a candle in a candlestick. Show me that neither candlestick, nor candle, nor table exist in the world.

Evagoras: Stop! I must be careful with my words. What I am saying is this: the physical characteristics which we perceive in the candlestick, or the candle, or the table, or things generally, do not belong to the true being of these things. They only appear to human beings in this fashion. Of course, real things appear to me as candlesticks, or candles, or tables. But what they may be in themselves is for the most part unknown to man, for these physical characteristics do not belong to their real being.

Clarissa: Agreed! I am waiting for your proof.

Evagoras: A body, like your candlestick or candle, cannot possibly be something which exists in itself. I shall try to show that this is so from its divisibility.

The candlestick consists of metal. Before the metal was formed into the candlestick, it was a mass with quite a different form. The silversmith transformed it, and gave it the shape of a candlestick, and in that way the candlestick came into being. You will admit that it consists of the metal, from which the silversmith formed it, and that it only exists to the extent that the metal exists.

Clarissa: I am happy to make the concession.

Evagoras: The base of the candlestick is formed from one piece of metal, the middle section from another, and the upper part is formed from a third piece of metal. Your candlestick only exists to the extent that these pieces of silver also exist.

Clarissa: Right!

Evagoras: But the base of the candlestick itself consists, in its turn, of several parts. Above is one piece of silver, below another; there is one piece to the right, and another to the left. These parts are compounded together into a single whole, which has the specific form of the base. And the base of the candlestick only exists to the extent that these pieces of silver also exist.

Clarissa: Certainly!

Evagoras: But each specific part which you look at in its own right exists in its turn as a whole composed of parts, and it only exists to the extent that its parts exist. How does the process go on? How far can this division be thought of as continuing?

Clarissa: I do not know. You tell us.

Evagoras: Well, I say that it continues without end. No part can be the last; each part is, in its turn, compound. Suppose that you wished to specify a particular part as simple. That part would be in space. Its mass would occupy a space, and in this space it would be possible to distinguish an above and a below, a right and a left. But if every part in its turn is compound, then it does not exist in its own right, but only in virtue of its parts, which, in their turn, do not exist in their own right. In short: in this mass of silver, and consequently in your candlestick, you will find nothing existing in its own right, nothing which is really existent in itself.

Clarissa: Very cunning! I can also see that what you say about my candlestick is true of all bodies whatever. Every drop of water, no less than all the suns and stars, every crystal, and similarly all plants and animals, consist of some mass or other. That mass is infinitely divisible and has, accordingly, inspite of its immutability, no existence in itself.

Evagoras: I should like to show you another such feat. How big, do you suppose, is the table on which your candlestick stands?

Clarissa: It is circular and has a diameter of four feet. You can calculate for yourself what the surface area is by employing the Ludolphic number pi.

Evagoras: Enough of its diameter. It is four feet across. But how long is a foot?

Clarissa: You measure it as you wish. I measure it by the ell.

Evagoras: Good! I could, I suppose, say that a foot was half an ell, or twelve inches long. But then the question would arise, how long is an inch, an ell, a mile, and so on. Where do the questions stop? The answer will have to be given without the assistance of numbers. Number only measures by reference to a given mass as unity, and there the question is: *how large* is the unity? At this point our concepts are at an end, and we are helpless from that point onwards. The unity must be presented to intuition. But does this intuition of the table or the ell tell us anything? My opinion is that intuition leaves the matter, *how large* a thing is, quite indeterminate. And again, this question has no determinate meaning for the being of the thing. In itself it has no determinate magnitude. To start with I can only ask: how large does it seem to be? And the answer to that question depends upon its distance from the eye, upon the nature of the observation, and upon the imagination of the observer. In short: here too you will find that among all the relations, there is nothing which exists in itself. Who is supposed to have the right answer in this determination of the size of an object — the short-sighted or the long-sighted observer, spectacles or the naked eye?

Clarissa: That is also a very cunning argument!

Evagoras: From what I have said you will recognise the nullity of the physical world and its motions; it is nothing more than a compound of the parts in which no existence is to be found.

But I should like to perform the same feat with the world in space and time as well. Let us ask, namely, about its magnitude. The universe in space and time consists of nothing but magnitudes, and yet it cannot itself have a determinable magnitude, whether finite or infinite. If, namely, we ask whether the universe in space and time has a beginning and an end — we shall not be able to conceive either of the two possibilities. The universe is here taken to be the completed totality of all things. But such a totality in space and time can only be thought within specific limits as a finite totality, and that would not be the universe. Give the universe a beginning in time, early or late, as you will. Time itself runs backwards beyond that beginning, and the universe would then, in a contradictory fashion, consist partly of an empty time without beginning prior to the beginning of things, and partly of a filled time subsequent to the beginning of things.

Clarissa: I am beginning to like what you say! Who is there who does not sometimes sceptically amuse himself with the riddles of time. An infinite past — which has really flowed away and which is, nonetheless, without beginning. Reality only in the moment of the present; and this moment of the present already sunk in the nothingness of the past as soon as I even try to think it. The moment of the present alone real, and yet that same moment of the present is nothing in comparison with the shortest duration of an event occurring through time. Certainly, you are right! All this would be pure contradiction in relation to the being of things itself. But one can easily see how man's sensible way of construing things, which never attains to completion, must be bound to such modes of representation.

Evagoras: I knew that we should become friends again at this point!

The contemplation of the infinity of the future, the contemplation of the limits in space and the impossibility of limiting space itself, will yield the same results. The things which are present do, after all, exist. Now, how are we to take incompletable space, in which it is impossible to think any complete totality of what is present, any completed existence, any totality of things? Obviously, such incompletability contradicts the being in itself of things in space and time.

Clarissa: That is quite certain! Had you wished to show us the nullity of the physical world quite independently of anything else, I should not have understood you. But now that you have drawn our attention to the sensible limitedness of man, and the incompletability of human knowledge, your teaching is completely clear to me. To man, who is sensibly limited, the things which are external to him must appear as bodies. But what they may be in themselves is not thereby known.

And yet, having applauded you in this matter, I shall quickly withdraw behind my own frontiers again. What do you intend with all these arguments? You have given us the paradoxes of infinity, and one is happy to amuse oneself with them on occasion. But how holy truth is supposed to be found in them, I do not understand.

Evagoras: These riddles are, indeed, suited to become holy truth. Does not the Apostle Paul call all man's earthly knowledge merely an obscure riddle in just this fashion? In my opinion, we are in complete agreement.

If you supposed that space, time and the physical world belonged to the true being of things and that their representation was not merely the consequence of the necessary limitations of human knowledge, then the contradictions which commonly appear to inhere in the denial of the reality of the physical world would indeed arise. But if we look at the matter more precisely, if we start from the assumption that we can only talk, to start with, about the human mode of knowledge and its law, and not immediately about the true being of things, then it will become clear that, for a sensible mind, the incompletability of man's knowledge is a natural consequence of his limits, limits which can, indeed, have no meaning for the essence of things itself. Relatively to eternal truth, we must, therefore, imagine the cancellation of all the consequences of these limitations and, therewith, all the representations of the physical world. The denial of the reality of the physical world then stands connected with the doctrines of holy truth.

Let us see whither this present combination of ideas will lead us. Relatively to eternal truth, the greatest difficulty involved in the denial of the reality of the physical world consists in the fact that the developing understanding, when it seeks a firm support for the uncertain indications of sense, finds itself naturally referred, in the first instance, to mathematical certainty, so that subsequently when that certainty is repudiated, all truth seems lost for man. On the other hand, it is important to remember that this mathematical certainty is merely the outcome of a scientific artifice. The judgement of man's common sense in life by no means continues in agreement with the utterances of that scientific artifice. The mathematical certainty in our knowledge of nature belongs to that view of the world which I have called the world-view of astronomers and practical people. But do not suppose that this view of the world is the one which is the most natural to man. The astronomers and the practical people just mentioned say: the essence of things for the physical world consists in immutable mass. It is this which is the thing itself. All else is merely a relation, a quality, or a state of that mass, not the thing itself. It we adopt this way of talking then we shall say that a river, a plant, or an animal is not a thing but simply an event. The river has its existence only in virtue of the hourly changing water which flows along its bed. Here, therefore, the water would be the thing, whereas the river would merely be the form of certain changing things, a form which merely belonged to the state of those things. The same thing is true of plants and animals. In their growth and conservation, the juices and the other stuffs of which they are constituted are constantly changing and being renewed. They too do not remain the same for a single day.

But that is by no means how we take the matter in our everyday judgement of things. In the external world, which can be beautiful, it is precisely the animals, the plants and the rivers which are the things themselves. It is to them that we attribute qualities and states. This view would obviously contradict the previous one, if we wished to regard these things as the eternal and true being of things, and not merely appearances. You can thus see that the most common-or-garden judgements about external things which regards formations as things and which thus knows external things in their relation to the mind — such judgements presuppose, at the deepest level, the nullity of the physical world relatively to eternal truth.

Let us take it as established, therefore, that, relatively to eternal truth, all the physical determinations of things disappear. It follows that man can only consider the eternal true essence of things as spiritual. Our ideas of eternal truth must, therefore, issue from our knowledge of our own spirits, and can, in the interpretation of all things, only point to the spiritual life. He who correctly understands himself will also find that we have greater success with knowledge of the mind than we do with knowledge of the physical world. No matter how much every *appearance* of mental life may depend for man upon knowledge of the physical world and mutability in time, there is nothing which contradicts the thought that a mind or spirit is truly present. The essence of mind or spirit can be thought simply and independently. Its life can be thought of as being independent of time, and its knowledge, love and action can be thought of as being independent of space. It is here alone, therefore, that our faith, together with its eternal truth, joins appearances. Its world is the world of spirit.

It is true that, in so far as we know the life of our mind in time, we also only know an appearance of its activities from an imperfect perspective which is very much bound to the physical world. It is not, therefore, the temporal life of the spirit which is its eternally true essence. With respect to the ideas of eternal truth, we must first form the completed idea of the world of the spirit, by ignoring all the limitations of the human interpretation of things.

And now I shall be able to answer Amalia's question how it can be true of our belief in God, which is contained in the ideas of the independence of the spiritual world, that it too can only be expressed by means of statements which negate limitations.

Independence and freedom of the spirit, we have already said above, are, as the fundamental ideas of eternal truth, simply the assertion of the spirit's independence of the physical world and its laws. Now, since the physical was found to have no validity for the true essence of things, it follows that we must assume that the spirit is independent and free.

Furthermore, what other is that supreme idea of holy Omnipotence and the world-creating Love, which is the ultimate foundation of all things, what other that fundamental idea of devotion, of the all-ruling spirit of beauty and sublimity — what else are these ideas for the understanding than the perfecting idea of the eternal truth of the spiritual life, which eliminates all limitations? God is a spirit and the holy Lord of the spiritual world. We can only express this faith by declaring that the work and truth of the spirit is independent of all the limitations of appearances. These appearances only belong to man's imperfect representations; they derive, in particular, from the fact that man is constrained to represent all the things which exist outside himself as bodies, and that he cannot immediately know minds outside himself.

Amalia: Now I understand. The idea of God affords us, if we reject all that is physical, the supreme perfecting of the ideas of the independence of the spiritual world. We can only speak of these ideas by means of expressions which negate limitations.

Evagoras: Let us now summarise what we have established so far. Man is not omniscient: for him every representation of a whole is simply a limitation. It is for this reason that we cannot speak of the being of things absolutely. We can only speak of the way in which things appear to man, and of the limits of the knowledge which man possesses.

Man does not know things as they are *in and for themselves*, but only as they exist *for him*. It is thus that he knows bodies which neither exist in themselves nor — still less — for themselves. The only thing which exists for itself is the self-conscious mind, and, therefore, as far as we know, man himself with his endowment of understanding. All talk of the true essence of things really reduces, as a consequence, to mental or spiritual self-knowledge.

But for us the law of the spiritual is not only knowledge of the existence of things. The spirit really lives in the mind and the will. The spirit lives in the way it knows the value of things, and in the way in which, as a result of that knowledge, it is driven to voluntary action. For us, therefore, the law of the true essence of things is the *law of value*, the law of the good and the beautiful. The world of eternal truth is *the world of the good and the beautiful*.

Now, that which does not exist for itself, cannot have any value for itself either. As a result, there can be no question of bodies possessing inner independent value. Indeed, of all the beings which are accessible to our sensible knowledge, rational man is the only one which exists for himself. To him alone are we able to attribute an independent value in himself.

It is from this source that there develop the fundamental ideas of our *moral view of things*, in accordance with which we judge the spiritual activity of man. The man of understanding as *person* possesses in himself an independent value. He exists as an end or purpose, and is a being of unconditioned *personal dignity*. Everything else with which we are familiar is, as thing, subordinate to persons and may be used by persons according to inclination. But for persons there issue from the idea of personal dignity the distinctive laws of the world of the spirit. Persons in the community of action are subject to the laws of justice. Everything which is good and beautiful for man is determined by reference to this sense of his own dignity. And that same sense of dignity also animates every acknowledgement of the beautiful and the sublime in nature.

But in what way does this teaching that man alone exists for himself and alone possesses value for himself — in what way does this teaching have validity?

It obviously has no validity for appearances, or for the nature of things, or for their finite truth. Human life, like every other natural phenomenon, is destroyed in nature by the play of forms. Humanity may be the most powerful force, subject to organic laws, on the face of the earth. But all that belongs to humanity is frail and subject to destruction, like all other terrestrial phenomena. No notice is taken there of man's personal dignity; man does not appear there as an end in himself. The ideas of the world of the beautiful and the good are valid only for the eternally true essence of things itself. They are valid only in virtue of the idea of the holy, original foundation of all things, in virtue of the world-creating eternal goodness. And man only finds evidence of these ideas in his own heart. In his belief in eternal truth, man comes into possession of these ideas through the moral ideas of spiritual beauty and sublimity, which awaken in his conscience. And once he has discovered them, all the beauty and sublimity, to be found throughout the ever freshly youthful transformations of nature, become for him the holy symbol of the all-prevailing love.

Like moral taste, moral feeling also enters the feeling of beauty. To every feeling of beauty it lends a higher, purely spiritual significance. The feeling of beauty, which is bound to religious feeling, then harbours within itself presentiments of eternal truth. The spirit of man acknowledges, with intuitive awareness, the dominion of the ideas of faith over all the phenomena of nature.

Here we see but the shadow. Above us is the light! Faith lives in the yearning for the higher eternal home to which we humbly hope to return. But in our temporal life, as well, we believe in our own eternal destiny, and, in this belief, we subject ourselves to all the demands of the spiritual good and beautiful.

And so my last word is the same as my first. Pure love is the witness of faith, faith in love and love in faith. In conscience, man finds himself through love for the first time on the native soil of faith. But if man examines himself more closely, he will once more find that love is only awakened by faith, will find that love only lives in faith.

I recently spoke about this subject to the people. Let me repeat to you what I said to them.

Clarissa: Do that! We ask you to do so!

Evagoras: I began with the words of the Apostle Paul:

> For we know in part, and we prophesy in part. For when that which is perfect is come, then that which is in part shall be done away. For now we see through a glass darkly; but then face to face: now I know in part; but then shall I know even as also I am known. And now abideth faith, hope, charity, these three; but the greatest of these is charity. Follow after charity!
>
> Though I speak with the tongues of men and of angels, and have not charity, I am become as sounding brass, or a tinkling cymbal. And though I have the gift of prophecy, and understand all mysteries, and all knowledge; and though I have all faith, so that I could remove mountains, and have not charity, I am nothing. And though I bestow all my goods to feed the poor, and though I give my body to be burned, and have not charity, it profiteth me nothing.
>
> Charity never faileth; but whether there be prophecies, they shall fail; whether there be tongues, they shall cease; whether there be knowledge, it shall vanish away.

The Christian teaching has made man aware of the fact that human knowledge is a patchwork and a riddle, a dark mirror of the truth. It has made man aware that faith and hope live eternally in the man who has learnt to believe where he does not see. Truth is not to be found in the knowledge of our earthly shell. Truth is to be found in the perfection, that is to say, in the independence of the spirit alone. We ought to worship God in spirit and truth alone! Our citizenship is in heaven, but the kingdom of heaven is within us. For when it it said: God created man in his own image, that is not an assertion about our earthly shell. It is an assertion about the spirit within. The heart has but to reach within itself, and it will find that the spirit is the temple of God.

It is thus that we believe in the invisible kingdom of God, and it is thus that we entertain our hopes of it. Now, of what use is this belief to man?

If riches are the object of our search, or the explanation of nature and her secret forces, if we wish for advice about health, or skill, or any kind of earthly well-being — if these are the objects of our desire, will faith be of help to us? Are its expectations directed towards these earthly goods? — "No!" we shall each of us reply. The attainment of these earthly goods requires no more than human knowledge and human art. Human knowledge will have to help us here, not the gaze which is directed to the unfathomable, nor the hope which is focused on the invisible. You will not become a ruler, or a rich man, or a wise man through faith in the invisible. What, therefore, is the use of faith? It is of use inwardly to the spirit within us. It is of use to us in that it may afford us peace, the peace of God, in which alone we are the children of his kingdom.

This is what scripture says: "Peace I leave with you; my peace I give unto you. Not as the world giveth do I give unto you. Let not your heart be afraid, and fear ye not!"

Do not expect the kingdom of heaven to consist in the enjoyment of a fullness of peacefulness and joy on earth. Do not imagine that being the children of God consists in his storms blowing away above our heads and only affecting our God-forsaken neighbours. Do not suppose that being children of God means emancipation from the trials of this earthly life, being spared sickness, and epidemics, and the terrors of war. He makes his sun to rise on the unjust and the just alike! — The peace of God does not consist in earthly joy. Nor does its absence consist in earthly suffering. — God does not give as the world gives. True peace, which is alone the peace of God, dwells inwardly within us, inaccessible to all the earthly vicissitudes of light and darkness, joy and suffering. In sickness, anxiety and need, in all earthly sufferings, the heart is referred back to itself, and the immortal spirit within us is so reared that we come to possess the peace of God.

And this peace of God then generates in the heart of man hope and love: the hope that we shall live trustingly in God who is eternal love, and who will keep us in his truth and love; love that we shall, even in this earthly life, come to share in the fatherhood of God.

Whether we are rich and distinguished, or poor and despised, whether we are healthy or sick, whether we are powerful or powerless in this earthly life, whether warm sunshine smiles upon us or whether we are oppressed by dismal mists — all this is a matter of indifference to faith and its eternal truth. Provided only that love is active among us and constantly dwells within our hearts, the sick man is not sick, the poor man is not poor, the despised man not despised. For it is in love alone that each enjoys true health, genuine riches, the dignity which alone is real. But where love is lacking, there is no spiritual joy in happiness, no wealth in earthly glory, no power in boastful strength, and life — nothing at all! Love alone is the vanquisher!

And thus the happiest of men are those who glorify the eternal faith, who are the joyful witnesses of its spirit, its truth, those to whom it is given to surrender the joys of their earthly life and life itself to death, so that their brothers on earth should have peace — the true peace, the peace that belongs to God's brightest truth, the peace of his inner clarity of spirit, of his loving warmth of heart, which seeks nothing but the eternal beauty of the spirit.

"No man hath greater love than this, that he lay down his life for his friends." Such a man irradiates this earthly life with the dawn of God's eternal day. The courage of faith! And in the courage of faith, sacrifice for the sake of brotherly love, even unto death.

"Charity never faileth: but whether there be prophecies, they shall fail; whether there be tongues, they shall cease; whether there shall be knowledge, it shall vanish away." Heaven and earth shall pass away — but charity shall last for ever.

Amalia: Accept my thanks, dear Evagoras! You have made many things much easier for me to grasp. Every educated person is helped to faith when the superiority of faith and intuitive awareness over human knowledge is made clear to his understanding, and when the language of feeling in conscience, taste and religion is justified to him.

Evagoras: This, I say, must be made universally understood in our nation. The further developments of this doctrine can, for the most part, be left to the men of learning. What is important for the people is a way of speaking which stimulates enthusiasm, humility and devotion.

Amalia: We must let you go, for we have detained you far too long.

Evagoras: The friendly fashion in which you have listened to me will, surely, force me to stay, will it not?

DIALOGUE IX

Knowing and Knowledge

After the above dialogue had been read and the company had assembled again, Philanthes addressed himself to Otto, suggesting that they should discuss what had been read.

Otto: It seems to me that Evagoras' teachings show strong promise of effecting the reconciliation of the language of popular instruction and the teachings of the philosophical schools. I see you, as a result, better defending the fundamental teaching of the older Eleatics, which is so simple in character but which is so often misunderstood; and I see you, in particular, better defending the teachings of Plato, and then reconciling them with the teachings of the Apostle Paul. You defend Plato's theory that only a shadow of the true essence of things appears to man in the world of space, sight and touch; that man only raises himself to eternal truth by means of the invisible and intangible element of spiritual truth in pure thought and in the ideas of pure thought, not in sensations; and that the higher spirits to which this true essence of things is immediately clear, apprehend necessary truth and the spirit itself in its justness, moderation and all the other virtues, not viewing it, as man does, in physical form.

Plato, however, erroneously hoped to elevate himself to knowledge of eternal truth by means of the higher knowledge contained in pure thought. You, on the other hand, venerate the Christian teaching, which construes all knowledge as piecemeal and transient, and subordinates it to the eternal truth of faith and conviction in trust.

In this I see a doctrine which could make a major contribution to effecting the firm establishment of peace between school and life. So many of our teachers are still guilty of the mistake of wishing to elevate a would-be, higher knowledge above faith. They are unable to penetrate to the insight that it is precisely faith, as opposed to knowledge, which is the firmest conviction of human reason, and the foundation-stone and only support of all certainty for man. Knowledge is, of course, simply cognition which is originally empirical in character. Faith, on the other hand, is the original moral conviction, which issues from the self-reliance of the spirit. But, obviously, this conviction which arises from our confidence in reason, that it is receptive to the truth, is higher than any empirical instruction. For if reason were not in itself receptive to truth, how could it be led to the truth by the senses? For man, the first truth is to be found in that *of which the spirit is certain in itself*, in that which is self-evident to it. It is in virtue of this alone that it is also able to follow empirical instruction. Anybody who in any way gets involved in the dispute about truth and falsity, or truth and doubt, presupposes this truth in faith, this confidence that one is receptive to the truth. This is the foundation of all knowledge. Everybody is confident that he can judge, and this confidence determines the fundamental feeling of all certainty in our spirit.

Faith is thus superior to knowledge. But let us proceed. To knowledge you oppose not only faith, but also intuitive awareness, faith and intuitive awareness combined. In virtue of faith, eternal truth is supposed to enter our consciousness in feelings of intuitive awareness. In connection with this relation, I remember very well what your father said about the truth of beauty as opposed to the truth of knowledge, about the feeling of beauty as opposed to the concept. And yet this relation between faith and intuitive awareness is by no means so clear to me as that between knowledge and faith.

Philanthes: Let us subject the notions to a more precise examination, taking them one by one. We shall, I suppose, first have to consider more closely the nature of knowledge, in order to see how faith is opposed to it. Then the gap which faith leaves behind and which intuitive awareness fills in each civilised person, will more easily emerge.

Otto: Let us follow your lead.

Theone: Stop a moment, father! I insist on our right so speak as well. We — that is to say, mother and I — are very satisfied with what you said in connection with feeling and faith. And yet we are almost amazed at the way in which you men of learning, who make so much of intellectual education, still wish to speak in such a derogatory fashion of knowledge. Faith and feeling have a higher status for you than knowledge, and your truth is supposed to be independent of knowledge. Where then is the dignity, the great importance, of knowledge?

Philanthes: Ah! If you are so bold as to meddle in these matters of ours, so bold, indeed, as actually to criticise us, then we shall oblige you to defend our cause yourselves! You seem not unfamiliar with the great advantages which intellectual education affords. Let us hear what you have to say in this connection.

Theone: If it must be, then let me try. But you must help me on my way a little. However, starting is no difficulty: enlightenment of the spirit is in all things of use to man, and enlightenment is the result of intellectual education.

Philanthes: Good! You say that enlightenment is of use to us in all things. I should like to mention some of these things specifically. Which branch of knowledge, do you suppose, in trade and commerce, advances prosperity and comfort? Again, which branch of knowledge benefits state institutions? Thirdly, which branch of knowledge benefits virtue and piety? If you can commend to me knowledge for all these things, then I shall have to release you again.

Theone: You have helped me on my way. The first question is easy to answer. It is to the development of the natural sciences, through all the branches of natural philosophy, that we owe the art of trade and commerce, and all the conveniences of life arising from them. Horticulture and agriculture are instructed by natural history, and the other arts are instructed by chemistry and mechanics.

Philanthes: And state institutions?

Theone: You yourself mentioned the political sciences in that connection. Only with their development have people learnt to order the laws in such a way as to make secure and peaceful mutual assistance possible.

Philanthes: But virtue and religion?

Theone: Man does not acquire virtue and piety through knowledge. Virtue and piety live in feeling, and they can only be formed and protected by feeling. And yet, even here various branches of knowledge are very useful. Virtue must be formed by education. Now, it is true, education in life is far more than mere instruction at school, and only instruction belongs to knowledge. Nonetheless, this instruction is still a highly indispensable part of the whole, and without it no education will succeed.

This is even more true in the case of religion. Here scientific education fails to notice its most important benefit, the driving out of superstition. Scientific knowledge has driven out the fortune-tellers and magicians, the witches and ghosts. Scientific knowledge has started to drive out the superstitious hatred of heretics and unbelievers, has started to make man listen to the gentle admonitions to practise universal brotherly love.

Now, father, am I not talking like a book? You must now release me!

Philanthes: That seems doubtful to me. You will probably have to continue your resistance for a while. In the case of trade and commerce, and in the case of the state, you spoke favourably of scientific education. That much must be admitted. However — and do not be offended! — in the case of virtue and religion, precisely the most important cases, you do not seem to have been loyal to your resolution to defend knowledge.

Theone: But why do you say that? I commended it, after all, for its benefits to instruction and its hostility to superstition.

Philanthes: Yes, in that connection, you did eventually speak generously of knowledge, perhaps because you felt that you had just been disloyal to your protégé.

Theone: Was I disloyal to it, then?

Philanthes: Were not your first words: "virtue and piety live in feeling; they are not the work of knowledge"?

Theone: Ah! But I must remain loyal to the truth. But is there not enough left for the honour of knowledge?

Philanthes: I am right! You are caught prisoner, dear little Theone! When I maintained that feeling and faith have higher rights in our spirit than knowledge, you raised the objection that I was depriving knowledge of something which rightly belonged to it. And now you are saying the same as that for which you censured me.

Otto: Yes, dear Theone, you must concede the point.

Theone: Yes, I suppose I must. But show me now what the situation really is.

Philanthes: I must praise you now. The first thing you said characterised the matter well. Intellectual education is *of use* to all things. Of all things knowledge is the most useful. But tell me, is it also, do you suppose, the beautiful?

Theone: Virtue and piety are alone beautiful in the human spirit. Knowledge will only appear in a very subordinate position to the extent that virtue also has a share in it.

Philanthes: Excellent! Knowledge is the most important of all the implements which man needs. Every skill, every art, that is to say, every goal-directed human activity needs scientific education, and gains by the progress of knowledge.

Knowledge, indeed, develops man's finite truth, which he must follow in all his actions. Hence it is that knowledge *is of service* to every mediated activity, from the meanest to the noblest, from the humblest trade to virtue and piety. For it teaches religion which *expression* of faith is the correct one. It teaches virtue the direction in which the pious will should direct its efforts, teaches it the object for which the moral will should strive.

By contrast, the ideas of that which is the supremely beautiful, and which is, consequently, the purpose in that which is good in itself — these ideas are of eternal truth. Knowledge receives them from feeling, and must subordinate itself to them.

But here too the performances which are supposed to subordinate life itself to these ideas, belong to mediating activity and need knowledge. Feeling, left to itself, is dark and easily confused; the concept forms an alliance with feeling and gives it expression. And thus, here too, the need arises for the assistance of knowledge, not in order to generate or establish feeling or faith, but in order to serve them, and to effect their clear articulation.

Now, dear Theone, I shall let you go. You and mother should go and enjoy yourselves in whatever way you like. For now I have things which I wish to discuss with Otto, and they will probably not afford you much amusement.

Theone: We shall stay and listen as long as we find your discussion entertaining.

Philanthes: I address myself, then, once more to you, Otto. What would you say constituted the nature of scientific knowledge?

Otto: I should say nature herself. Knowledge, your father said, was knowledge of the things which we receive through intuition. Accordingly, we know about the existence of things in space and time. This knowledge becomes scientific when it is knowledge of the things of *nature*, that is to say, things subject to necessary laws. Mathematics, with respect to this science and, therefore, with respect to the nature of things, determines the necessary laws of magnitude and the constant connection of appearances. The philosophical doctrine of nature, on the other hand, determines the necessary connection in the existence of things, according to the laws of permanence, causation and interaction. The being of the things of the world is here founded in the immutable being of things. In virtue of the necessary law of the interaction of the forces of these beings, all change and alteration in appearance is also subject to necessity. The being of things is inaccessible to all change and destruction. The primary force inhering in them is immutably determined. Alteration only affects their states, their relations. But this alteration of their states is also bound to a necessary law of coming-to-be and passing-away, according to which every event issues from an antecedent event, just as the forces of the beings mutually interacting with each other cause them to issue from their interaction. This necessary subjection of appearances in space and time to law seems to me to constitute the scientific character of our knowledge, so that the purpose of science is, at all times, the ordering of appearances according to universal perspectives and the explaining of the course and connection of appearances in terms of universal laws.

Philanthes: Is it not true that anyone who, for a single moment of the past, the present, or the future, knew the state of each and every thing in the world under natural laws, and also knew what beings and forces existed, could also calculate from that knowledge the whole existence of the world and the whole course of events, showing how motion followed from motion, how life arose from life, how thought developed from thought, and that for the whole of present, past and future time?

Otto: Certainly!

Philanthes: Let me express it in an even more intuitive fashion. The necessity of the laws of nature determines that if a single breath of air were to move differently to the way in which it does move, if a single grain of sand were to lie differently to the way in which it does lie, if a single drop of water were to fall differently to the way in which it does fall, if the tiniest creature were just once to move differently to the way in which it does move, or if a single person were once to act differently in the least significant of his actions to the way in which he does act, then all this would have to take place in an entirely different universe. Indeed, the power of the necessity of nature is so great that it unfolds its necessity backwards, even beyond an alleged creation of the universe. If someone were to object to this entire argument: all this must have had a beginning sometime, then the reply could be made: is not the being of things firmly enough grounded in the immutability of its beings and their forces? Does not every event issue of necessity from some antecedent event? But if our objector were still to insist that all this motion had a beginning in immemorial antiquity, I could reply: the first day started yesterday morning. Yesterday morning, God the punisher created the entire universe around me out of nothing as my dungeon. If the other person were then to reply: Do I not myself remember the day before yesterday? — then we should retort: In exactly the same way, there is to be found, from time immemorial, in the existence of every moment of the universe the memory of a complete time which has lapsed and which had no beginning. Nature admits of no beginning; it merely manifests the developments from what has passed. It is, accordingly, completely self-sufficient in its permanent being, which has no beginning, and in the necessary law of its changing states. Beginning and creation must be sought outside nature. For nature herself these are ideas with no application.

The inviolable law-abidingness of the universe in space and time is extremely important to us here for two opposed reasons. The inviolable law-abidingness, for one thing, is the pride of man's thought. Although we can only observe a little of the confusion of changing events, and that little but disconnectedly, nonetheless, nature's regularity enables us with our knowledge of the laws of nature to guarantee, in universal perspectives, the unity of the universe. For that reason, it also enables us to know the past as far as it extends, though we have no experience of it, and to predict the future.

On the other hand, however, it is precisely the necessary law-abidingness of nature which contradicts the ideas of independence and freedom. The being of the world, subject to the laws of nature, is based, it would seem, on the beings and forces in the world, which have no beginning and are not subject to change. The states of these beings, however, are constantly changing, and, as a result of this constant change, each being is dependent on its relationship to all other beings. Furthermore, and this is of even greater importance, it is subject to its fate under the necessity of those laws. Accordingly, no being exists here freely for itself, as eternal truth requires. Each being only exists in virtue of its connection with other beings. Independence in this world is impossible, for each being depends upon the necessity of some law, though this law is not a being in itself, any more than empty space is. It is, therefore, precisely the scientific character or the law-abiding nature of our knowledge which distinguishes this knowledge, as a merely human view of things, from the true being of things.

We shall, accordingly, my dear Otto, have to examine the work of science more closely, both in respect of faith and also in respect of the claims made by the understanding to develop knowledge.

You are not unacquainted with the diverse character of the disputes between the supernaturalists and the naturalists in this connection. The dispute arises, in my opinion, as a result of the fact that the nature of faith and knowledge has not been correctly construed, and the two not correctly distinguished. If we wanted to defend the supernaturalists in this dispute, then we could commend them for speaking in favour of faith and eternal truth and opposing the false presumptions of knowledge. But we also hear them eagerly talking about miracles in nature. We hear that they, in part, equate faith with the acceptance of certain stories from history, and with the acceptance of certain historical traditions about our relationship to God and the higher spirits. For this reason, they generally seem to wish to help faith through superstition. That, certainly, is not becoming to men of scientific outlook. And since Theone has already said that we wish to be men of scientific outlook it follows that our secret preference for the rationalists is not difficult to divine. For the rationalists maintain the rights of knowledge, and, like us, assert that the only true faith is a purely rational conviction. Nonetheless, we must also say to them: Dear friends, beware of trying to find an explanation for everything in nature. Remember that nothing in nature can be explained in terms of purposes except the behaviour of man and the other animals, when they pursue their own purposes. For, unless we made this distinction, we should not be able to guarantee the rights of faith, and we should completely lose our intuitive awareness of the beautiful and the sublime, with all its higher significance. In order to clarify this matter, let us examine the tasks of knowledge more closely. You will easily be able to give a preliminary account of the matter in terms of the distinction which my father made when he differentiated man's three views of the world, as we heard in what we recently read.

Otto: Certainly! Under the laws of nature we see, so to speak, two worlds united into one — the physical world and the mental.

But for human knowledge and science, the physical world alone affords a firm foundation. In the appearances of bodies, mind or spirit merely manifest itself as a faint breath, like the flames which flicker around the sacred springs of the Parses, burning among the stones but not consuming them.

In developed knowledge of the physical world, bodies only appear through form and motion, so that the whole course of events in the physical world is, in the last analysis, understood in terms of the reciprocal relationship of action and reaction in the mutual motions of masses.

By contrast, it is first within ourselves that we come to know the mind in its successive activities. But we only succeed in determining those activities temporally by reference to physical activities. Our own mental existence appears to be bound to our bodies and dependent upon them. It is only by reference to physical forms that we can divine the existence of life outside ourselves. We each of us follow the analogy of the dependence of our own mind on our own body.

And yet we cannot know the physical world, either, independently of our inner life, even though, in our complete knowledge of the physical world, we know that its existence is self-sufficient and is in need of no principle outside itself, either from the point of view of its being, or from that of its alteration.

All knowledge of bodies, namely, is relative. We know them partly in the relation of bodies to bodies, and partly in the relation of that which is physical to me, that is to say, to mind. In the first relation, the body is nothing but a mobile mass in space with motive power. The only relationship between one body and another is the relation of these motions. But our knowledge of bodies does not start here. Initially, they appear to us endowed with the characteristics in which they manifest themselves to our sensibility. Colours, sounds, smells, tastes, and the manner in which the physical manifests itself to the general sense of touch and feeling, never belong to a body relatively to another body, but only relatively to me. The leaf is not green for the blossom, and the blossom does not display the splendour of its colours to the leaf. The leaf and the blossom only manifest these colours to me, the representing mind. The only relationship between leaf and blossom is the relation of motion and motive force. Light is neither bright nor dark for the body to which the light gives colour for me. In the interaction of bodies with my eye, there is only motion and that which is capable of motion, whereas light and colour only exist for me. In the same way, sounds, smells and tastes do not belong to one body relatively to another; they only belong to it relatively to spirit.

Philanthes: Good! That will do for the moment. I now go on to say: the knowledge of bodies, which you began by characterising in terms of form and motion alone, is the only knowledge which is completely scientific. To quote Pascal: "What surpasses geometry, surpasses science as well." In this knowledge of form and motion, explanation advances with sureness as far as explanation can advance at all. Here we find science in its fullest strength and here we also find the limits of science most clearly indicated.

We know this world of motions as a world for itself, so to speak, as a world of its own, as a world subject only to the laws of reciprocal causality. This reciprocal causality can be completely explained by us through the philosophical doctrine of nature and its mathematical laws. And this is so, even if, because of the complexity of the mathematical calculations, we have hitherto often been unable to extend the explanation in detail.

The laws of gravitation were first developed from the supreme principles of the inertia of masses and the equality of action and reaction. In the laws of gravitation we have the ultimate explanatory foundations for an account of the evolution of the heavenly bodies and the interacting motions of the suns, planets and moons.

The expansibility of gases, the expansion of liquids, and finally the expansion of solids — in other words, the appearance of masses under a variety of specific forms, as for example in crystallisation — are all explicable in terms of the supreme laws of gravitation, even if, hitherto, the explanation has not completely succeeded in understanding all the phenomena. Furthermore, we fully understand the mechanical laws in accordance with which masses move relatively to each other according to their specific gravity. In the relations of attractive and repulsive forces we also possess the supreme principles of explanation for the chemical phenomena of the penetration, composition and decomposition of various materials. We see the whole of chemistry, in its subordination to these supreme principles, entering into the mathematical doctrine of nature.

Finally, we understand why it is precisely the most expansible materials which must be the most powerful. This also leads us to the principles of explanation of those subtler phenomena, which bind everything together, and which we find subject to the laws of light, heat, fire, electricity and magnetism.

The concept of the mathematical doctrine of nature has been extended thus far for a long while now, and many different attempts have been made to apply it. However, the doctrine of nature relating to the organic structures of the plant and animal kingdoms was carefully distinguished from the mathematical doctrine of nature, for the evolution of inorganic matter to orgnic was regarded as unintelligible and incapable of explanation in terms of universal natural forces. It was rather assumed that there were original and distinctive causes operating between organic phenomena, and organic structures were explained in terms of purposeful laws. There was a frequent unwillingness to deny that mind had an immediate effect upon the physical.

We have, however, learned to realise that mind, and, consequently, purposeful laws, must be wholly excluded from explanations of physical interaction, for it belongs to an entirely different class of phenomena. On the other hand, we must subsume the whole natural theory of organic structures under the laws of the mathematical doctrine of nature.

Organic nature, namely, is not to be explained in terms of the constitution of certain organic materials. It is rather subject to a universal law of nature. The nature of an organism consists of a form of reciprocal effects, such that, by its means, a series of motions necessarily repeats itself cyclically, thus maintaining itself and generating itself afresh. Such reciprocal effects are, however, necessarily determined by the law of universal gravitational attraction at a distance. Physical structures appear only the more organically formed, the more we see the cycle of reciprocal effects securely enclosed in such self-perpetuating motions. Thus, everything from the highest cyclic course of the planets, to the cycle of the water on the earth illuminated by the sun, to the succession of life and death in the structures of plants and animals — everything is subsumed under the supreme principle of explanation in the mathematical doctrine of nature. And if, hitherto, we have been able to make so little progress in the explanations of plant and animal phenomena, then the reason for this failure is to be found in the simple fact that the immeasurable diversity of these phenomena still, to such a great degree, surpasses the art of our explanations.

I am giving you these suggestions simply in order to make clear to you how all this knowledge of the physical world, from the simplest phenomenon of a falling body to the most complex motions of organic structures, is subject to the laws of the strictest knowledge, and, therefore, as task, to *knowing* with complete understanding.

Theone: Father, this remark pleases me! I tried to follow you, and now I am pleased that you once more show us open country. Even if we do not so exactly remember your laws of gravitation, chemistry, electricity, and whatever the rest of them may be called, we can still follow you, if we only remember that this doctrine of nature belongs entirely to the realm of knowing, and has nothing in common with faith or intuitive awareness.

Philanthes: Correct, dear Theone! Just pursue the matter in your own way.

It is true, our mathematics and our limited experience frequently do not enable us to achieve very much in the way of real explanation. We often have to be satisfied with probabilities and unstable conjectures. We frequently find ourselves forced to abandon the path of theories which are all too general, and to engage in merely empirical enquiries, where we seek to construe the unity of experience as a consequence of laws which are not themselves known to us.

And yet all these probabilities and conjectures belong to the realm of knowledge. The slenderest probability in our opinions about nature is simply a lower degree of the same type of conviction, which, in its completeness, is the paradigm of knowledge. These probabilities never point in the direction of faith or intuitive awareness, because for them there is no *degree of certainty* at all. No matter, therefore, how many facts in nature remain unknown to us, no matter how many events seem inexplicable to us, everything here takes place according to the laws of nature, everything happens, therefore, in a natural fashion. There is nothing here which is absolutely inexplicable, nothing miraculous, nothing mysterious — in short, everything here is, as task, an object of science.

Otto: We should not allow ourselves to be confused by those who understand by faith a mere selection of uncertain opinions, and who then proceed to confuse this play of opinions with faith and the intuitive awareness of the eternal truth. This play of opinions belongs exclusively to our knowledge of what is finite. It never, therefore, touches the eternal truth or its religious mysteries.

Philanthes: Right! But let us now look at the matter from the other point of view, and examine the limits of this scientific realm. And, in this connection, there are three propositions which I should like to explain.

(1) Explanatory knowledge of the physical world never shows us the totality of the world.

(2) By no means everything in the physical world is explained. It is only the course of events within it which is subject to explanation. The *original relationship of beings to each other* is, in respect of the laws of nature, absolutely contingent. There can be no question of explanation here.

(3) The change of the relations between bodies is capable of explanation, but none of these explanations touch those characteristics of bodies, in which they appear to the spirit.

Otto: The meaning of your first proposition is clear to me. The doctrine of nature shows us that all cosmogonies, that is to say, all attempts to explain the origin of the universe in terms of an initial state or anything else, are chimaera. We find ourselves in boundless space and in the midst of time which has no beginning. We can, for example, I suppose, venture conjectures about the origin of the solar system in terms of the transformations of its masses from earlier states. We can, to speak in general terms, give or seek information about the transformations in some limited system of bodies, whether it be large or small. But we can never arrive at the totality of the universe in incompletable time and incompletable space. We thus see that, in virtue of this incompletability, science itself, in its securest realm, is not self-sufficient. As a result, we can see that it can only lay claim to present a human view of things, not their essence.

Also clear to me is the purpose of your third assertion that we are able to explain the change of form and motion, but that there can be no question of our explaining those characteristics of bodies, such as colours and sounds, in which bodies appear to the spirit. This observation makes clear in the simplest possible way to how great a degree our knowledge is patchwork, and how small the extent of knowledge is within the living whole of our convictions. Again, if a so-called materialist were to assert that the true being of things only existed in the physical world, we could not reveal the absurdity of this opinion more simply than by referring to our proposition. The doctrine of nature, it is true, can explain under what conditions colour and sound will appear at a given time. But colours and sounds are not, themselves, forms or motions. It is not possible to express, by means of an explanatory formula, what colours or sounds are. Independently of the mind, they are nothing. It is in them alone that the physical appears to the spirit. Even our sensible knowledge thus displays many types of being, which are quite different from form and motion.

Philanthes: You will see most clearly at a later stage of what service this view of the world, which is based on the laws of motion, is to man. It simply serves the sensible mind to order its sensations and to connect them into a whole. Internally, spiritual life, and externally, colour, sound, smell, and so on, appear to us as characteristics of things themselves. None of these characteristics really enters the world of motions. Our knowledge of form and motion confers upon them, though only for the mind, their location in space and time.

These characteristics themselves only become objects of our judgement in the aesthetic judgement of the beauty and sublimity to be found in the life of nature.

Otto: There now remains your second proposition. It is only the course of events, you say, not the original relation of beings to each other, which is capable of explanation in terms of the laws of nature. My request is that you should explain this to me in greater detail.

Philanthes: It seems to me that this proposition is of great importance in the dispute between the rationalists and the supernaturalists. Not everything in the world which is subject to the laws of nature is capable of explanation in terms of those same laws. Just as the existence of individual things is only known to man contingently, by means of his senses, and is not capable of determination by the laws of nature alone, so also, even in our complete view of the physical world, the coincidence of individual things with each other is absolutely contingent.

To begin with, I should like to show that this is so in the world of motions.

Consider for a moment the following question. What do we need to know in order to calculate the course of the planets in the solar system?

Otto: The answer of the astronomers is that we must first know the laws of motion, and that we must then know the mass of each heavenly body, and the elements of its orbit.

Philanthes: So if I am to calculate the course of some planet, it is not sufficient that I know the universal laws of motion. I must, in addition, also know the magnitude of the mass of each planet in the system. Furthermore, I must also know, for a particular given moment, the position of each planet and the nature of its projectile motion. If I am given the state of things for a particular moment, I am then in a position to explain, according to the laws of nature, what the location of each particular planet was prior to any particular moment, and what the location of each particular planet will be subsequently to any particular moment. All explanation in terms of the laws of nature is limited to the course of events, which is constituted of elements which are given. On the other hand, the independent constitution of these elements itself is determined, with respect to human knowledge, by *blind fate*.

If I ask why does the earth move so much more rapidly than Jupiter and so much more slowly than Mercury, or if I ask why is the earth so much smaller than Jupiter and so much larger than Mercury, or if I ask why is the earth so much closer to the sun than Jupiter, or so much further away from it than Mercury — I could answer if I knew how the present order of the solar system had evolved from an earlier order. But to know this, the elements of this earlier order must, in their turn, be given. There is a certain original relationship, for example, of the sun to its planets and to the moons of the system; and this system is known to us, as soon as the state of things is given for some particular moment. And *then* the course of events for all time is necessarily determined in accordance with the laws of nature. But the original relations themselves cannot be known from universal laws, but only through observation. They seem to us to be implanted by blind fate in time, which has no beginning.

This inexplicable contingency in the coincidence of the beings in the world is incomparably more influential in that knowledge which is only imperfectly scientific, and especially in the history of mankind. The development of the human spirit and man's understanding unfolds according to distinctive laws of nature. Here, we can predict the course of history in general terms. We can show what stages the spirit, in the process of its development, must have passed through, and what stages it has yet to traverse, if it is to attain a certain maturity. Here, all development takes place in a natural fashion according to necessary laws. But here, under these laws, it is not, as it was with the solar system, that the elements of human history at some particular moment need to be given to enable us to determine, forwards and backwards, the place and the time of every spiritual event in the course of history. Relatively to the universal laws of the development of the spirit, it is a matter of absolute contingency at what time and in what place, that is to say, in what nation and what individual, the development of the spirit attains a given level. For this depends not only on the natural laws of the development of the spirit, it also depends on something quite different, which cannot be determined by these laws at all. It depends, namely, on the vitality of the spirit, on the strength of the stimulus it gives to science, art, the state or religion, both in particular nations and in individuals. History's happy advances are determined by the emergence of particular nations, and, still more decisively, by the emergence of individual heroes, rulers, prophets, poets and teachers. But, relatively to the laws of nature in accordance with which the human spirit develops, it is a matter of contingency when and where that exceptional energy of the spirit appears. Consider the effect of Moses on the Jews, of Lykurgus on Sparta, of Epaminondas on Thebes, Charlemagne on Europe, Henry the Fowler on Germany, Peter the Great on Russia, Penn on Pennsylvania. You cannot maintain that, without their influence, these nations would have displayed a similar development of the spirit. This development is determined not only by the laws of nature; it is also determined by the contingency of individual events. You will not say that the fresh vitality of the Reformation would have occurred at that time, even if Luther, with his spiritual energy, quiet determination and fiery enthusiasm, had not made his entry into history at that period.

From such examples as these you will easily recognise how these views influence the presentation of the doctrine of a positive revelation of God in history, or of miraculous interventions by Providence in nature, then the rationalists will certainly readily reply that nature nowhere shows any immediate interventions by God; in history, as in the physical world, every course of events is necessarily produced by what went before, and is necessarily determined by the original order of nature. But this last proposition would only have a definite and clear application to the present dispute, if everything in the world subject to natural laws depended upon the necessity of the law, and if there were no additional contingency in the coincidence of individual beings.

Of course, a blind necessity rules over this coincidence of the individual *at a particular time*, for each present emerges out of its past, in accordance with natural laws. But the original relation of individual things to one another belongs neither to this nor to that moment of time. It must be absolutely co-ordinated with time in general, must be absolutely co-ordinated with the totality of the universe. So, relatively to time in general, it is absolutely contingent. It appears to be implanted in time, which has no beginning, not according to laws but according to blind Fate.

Now, if we wished, as is usual in religious teaching, to judge the course of events in nature and history according to determinate concepts of natural purposes, no one could prevent us from referring that contingency in the coincidence of events to a specific moment, and, accordingly, speaking of particular arrangements and dispensations of Providence made for the benefit of this or that person, and speaking of prayers' being answered, for it depends on me alone in which moment I wish thankfully to accept the gift as something received immediately from the hand of Him who orders the world.

Admittedly, if we subject these human judgements to closer scrutiny, we shall always find that they are wretched and contradictory. For example, one person approves of certain changes effected in the religious views of nations by some great man in history. For that reason, he calls him a saint and a messenger of God. Others, by contrast, who dislike those same changes, call him a false prophet.

There is, however, no way in which such a view could be scientifically established. But the rationalists will only be able to show this clearly and coherently if they heed my warning, and adhere strictly to the principle that we human beings can never interpret the course of events in terms of natural purposes which are intelligible to us.

The ideas of world-purposes belong to eternal truth alone. We can only know appearances as subject to them in the feeling of beauty, never in terms of scientific concepts.

Now, with this established, if we are to be able to be loyal to our faith in the holy origin of things and the divine governance of the universe, the above-mentioned contingency in the coincidence of individual things affords us this great advantage: any explanatory subjection of appearances to natural laws is inadequate, and we are therefore permitted the religious and intuitive subjection of appearances in feeling.

It is on account of this last point that we find the recognition of the above contingency so supremely important for all man's convictions, although it seems not to have been noticed by earlier teachers.

If the necessary unity of the laws of nature could completely explain the relations of appearances, then the scientific judgement would be closed within itself, and there would be no room for aesthetic judgement. However, this contingent coincidence of appearances under rules permits the aesthetic impression to take the place of scientific explanation. This happens when our feeling is surprised with the appearance of the beautiful, where appearances harmonise in law-abidingness without a concept of this rule itself being given to us. Here lies the riddle of the combination of that which accords with a rule and that which is beautiful, where the two are entirely different in kind.

The possibility of aesthetic judgement in feeling, by means of which we know the appearance as subject to the ideas of eternal truth — this possibility is founded upon the limited character of our scientific knowledge, which itself arises from the contingency in the coincidence of individual beings.

Otto: Your observation still has its obscurities. But I realise that, if the matter is to become clearer to me, we must first discuss faith and intuitive awareness more precisely. Let us, therefore, pursue our main theme further. You said that everything which lies beyond the mathematical doctrine of nature lies beyond knowledge. How does that claim harmonise with the natural philosophy of the human spirit, with moral philosophy, jurisprudence, the theory of the history of mankind? Do we not find in inner experience, as we do with the laws of motion, that it is with necessity that thought issues from thought, decision from decision, just as motion follows with necessity from motion?

Philanthes: Certainly! But this realm is unlike the world of motions for we cannot here intuitively represent the simultaneous activities of the mind alongside each other. We merely *think* them as united in one self-consciousness. We know the mental life only according to characteristics which are not derivable, in an explanatory fashion, from anything else. The fundamental assumptions of mental self-knowledge are to be found in representation, pleasure, desire and will, and these phenomena lie outside the realm of explanations.

Consider the conditions of the development of this self-knowledge. Man knows himself only in the alterations of his inner activities, and he attributes all these changes to one and the same I. But what sort of existence does this I possess from the point of view of appearance? Is it not just like the existence of the flame of a candle? As long as combustion continues to take place in the wick of the candle, the flame continues to burn. Withdraw the heat or the supply of combustibles from the wick and the flame vanishes. In the same way, the inner appearance of knowledge, pleasure, and the activity of the will, is bound to the vital motions of our bodies. As long as they continue in wakeful play, the appearance of the vital play of the mind continues, as well. Suppress the wakefulness of the body, and you also suppress the vital play of the mind. Destroy the vital drive of the body, and the I also vanishes.

Inner experience thus does not establish the existence of the I in an immutable being; it rather subjects the transient appearance of the mind or spirit wholly to the conditions of the vital motions in our bodies — motions with which the phenomenon of our life begins, in which our life develops, and with the cessation of which our life disappears again. The mind finds itself in this particular place at this particular time only in virtue of the dependency of its appearance upon the body. It is, accordingly, not only the spatial determinations of mental life which depend upon the body; its temporal determinations are also dependent upon it. These spatial and temporal determinations of the mind, accordingly, belong only to appearance, not to the true being of things.

In this, each individual stands wondrously alone within himself, as within a closed world. And it is only within this inner world that life appears immediately to the spirit within it; it can only transfer that inner world from out of itself on to nature outside it.

You will readily appreciate that, in the discovery of minds external to ourselves, we have to rely entirely on the analogies of the reciprocal relation of the inner life of our mind and our bodies. We have no concept at all of community between mind and mind other than that which is mediated by bodies. Where I find life in the bodies outside myself, I also find mind outside me; where I descry a human figure external to myself, I also find the appearance of a rational mind outside myself. Eventually, we come to have an intuitive awareness of the mental or spiritual behind, so to speak, the appearance of bodies, through colour, sound, smell and in the beauty of forms.

On the analogy of my own body, I come to recognise representation, pleasure and will as being connected with other organised bodies, as well. But it is language alone, that is to say, the communication of ideas by means of motions of designation, which above all introduces me to the reciprocal spiritual causality which operates between reason and reason. A new world thus makes its appearance to me, a world which is physically mediated and within which, with I and you, reason enters into its own community with reason. This new world almost makes us forget the physical world, which now only has the status of a mere means to knowing the mental or spiritual world, the laws of which each person carries within himself. The spirit now sets up personal dignity and spiritual beauty as the law of the rational society of human beings. The necessity of nature, which rules all being external to myself and my own inner appearance, is, in idea, so to speak, cancelled for the society of human beings.

As a result of man's sociability there arises a world of its own. Its reciprocal causality is determined by reason and will alone. But the will acts according to purposes. In this world, therefore, it is value and purpose which give the law. This world is a *kingdom of purposes or ends*. Here, it is the value of things, as specified by individual human reason at the various stages of its development, which determines how a thing is treated. The criteria which initially hold, therefore, are the criteria of sensuous pleasure, but the criteria which hold in the end are the commands of morality. This world is the *world of the good and the beautiful*.

Civilised man thus eventually finds himself part of the *spiritual history of mankind*, part of the gradual development of the understanding; here all activity is guided by concepts of purpose and, in the end, subjected to the *ideals of the true, the good, and the beautiful*.

Now, cast your eye over all our knowledge of this world of the human spirit and tell me in what its essential feature consists.

Otto: In the world of the good and beautiful.

Philanthes: But in what does its character as knowledge consist?

Otto: In this connection, you have already drawn my attention to the fact that it is completely dependent on the physical. I appreciate that most of our knowledge of sensible stimulation, of the preservation of the individual, of our union in civil life and the state, and of the whole history of mankind, is only a part of the external doctrine of nature, where we recognise the physical as the condition of the appearance of the spiritual.

But, in addition, there continues to exist real anthropology, which is spiritual in nature. In it we come to know the laws regulating the sensible stimulation of our life, the laws regulating the succession of our memories, imaginations, emotions and passions, and, finally, the laws in accordance with which the understanding, with the help of habit, can become the master of our lives. This branch of knowledge, in its most distinctive part, is not only not dependent on the doctrine of bodies, it is actually opposed to it.

Philanthes: It is opposed, it is true, to the doctrines of bodies, but it is not opposed to the mathematical doctrine of nature. This is a more subtle matter, and I merely wish to offer it to you for consideration. I maintain, namely, that you will on closer examination find that all the knowledge and all the possibility of explanation in this spiritual anthropology is based on the law of magnitude with which it operates, the law of degree. All the effects in it which we can understand, the manner in which the play of memories, emotions and passions are given or guided, receive their explicability from the successive degrees of their liveliness alone, in respect of which they are sometimes stronger, and sometimes weaker.

Otto: I appreciate the truth of what you say at a general level. But I shall not forget to consider the matter in greater detail later.

Philanthes: You will have far less difficulty understanding the only point which is really necessary for our discussion. I am referring, namely, to the fact that, here too, knowledge is, as we have already established, only of service to man's skill, in enabling him to pursue the purposes which have been given to him. It cannot determine the purposes themselves.

The world of the spirit, which makes its appearance, is the world of human society, subject to the moral laws of virtue, justice and all beauty of soul. But there is no branch of knowledge which can, of itself, establish what is spiritually beautiful and just. That is something which announces itself to feeling alone. Knowledge serves these requirements of morality simply by indicating the cases of wise application and the means of prudent execution.

Otto: Certainly! I can see that, with this knowledge of the world of the good and the beautiful, we find ourselves standing on the foundation of eternal truth, no longer assessing things according to the laws of nature, but according to ideas.

Philanthes: We human beings do not *know* a world of the good and beautiful; we *believe* in it. And in that you will discover the complete meaning of our spiritual self-knowledge. *Spiritual self-knowledge wishes to put itself completely at the service of the subjection of things to the ideas of faith.* You will notice its superiority to knowledge and finite truth in two, previously mentioned respects.

Firstly: we know nothing of the independence of the spirit; we believe in it. In this faith, conscience awakens to the demands of justice and spiritual beauty. In these demands we feel ourselves already in the enjoyment of eternal life, and in them we make eternal truth valid for the finite appearance of temporal life.

Secondly: feeling, animated by these moral ideas of eternal life, extends its intuitive awareness over the beauty and sublimity of the whole of nature, thereby inspiring itself with the enthusiasm which leads to the recognition of the world dominion of love.

All human knowledge humbles itself before and surrenders itself to the service of faith.

DIALOGUE X

Of Faith and the World of the Good and Beautiful

Otto: Today I should like to discuss with you the fundamental ideas of faith as we recently discussed scientific knowledge.
Philanthes: With great pleasure! Recently, when we were discussing the nature of religious practice, you spoke with such clarity about the fundamental ideas of faith that I should like you to give me a brief summary of what you said.
Otto: In the first expressions of faith, we oppose the ideas of the eternally true essence of things to the limited way in which things appear to us. And we do so by thinking the true essence of things as freed from those limits in the ideas of eternity, freedom and God. But faith itself is not concerned with the empty opposition to finite knowledge. Faith is rather the confidence of the spirit that, in human modes of knowledge, we perceive eternal truth in a limited fashion.

With the help of the ideas of eternity, freedom and God, therefore, faith, through the independence of the spiritual world and through the eternal life of all spirits, expresses the eternal truth which announces itself in man's finite views of things. But this faith manifests itself in life as well. It does so by love, that is to say, the moral life, becoming the witness of faith, and by the fundamental moods of religious feeling awakening enthusiasm, resignation and devotion, which are most intimately connected with the feelings of the beautiful and the sublime.
Philanthes: Man's talk of our convictions in faith has, therefore, as its fundamental ideas, eternity, freedom and God. By their means we express the independence of the spiritual world. Shall we not have to examine this idea more closely, before we consider anything else?
Otto: Yes, I agree. And the first thing we should have to discuss would be the idea of the immortality of the soul, or the idea of eternal life. Show me the correct way of talking about this idea.
Philanthes: You know that the incompletability of our representations of magnitude forces us to reject all determinations of magnitude as

without meaning for eternal truth. In what relation to space and time will you, therefore, find the idea of immortality?

Otto: The laws of space and time only apply to man's empirical mode of representation. Our eternal being, freed from all the limitations of space and time, thus stands secure in the belief in the immortality of the soul, giving to the independent being of our spirit a place in the eternal order of the spiritual world.

Philanthes: You will not, therefore, seek the location of your eternal home in the sun, or the stars, or beyond the stars. Only pious thought can reach it, and it only employs such expressions as these as images. Nor will you associate the immortality of the soul with unstable assumptions about life before birth or life after death. The immortality of the soul indicates belief in the eternity of our being, freed from all the limitations of space and time, which we can only call being with God. The spirit of God is everywhere present through space and time, though his invisible and intangible being cannot be construed as being at any time or in any space. Likewise, our eternal life cannot be understood by attaching it to its temporal appearances. The appearance of our life in nature, both physical and spiritual, is, like the appearance of a flower, a blossoming, a fading and a dying. We cannot mention eternal meaning in connection with a flower. But with respect to our own spirit, we, in our consciousness of our own personal dignity, believe in our own eternity. Only the childish embarrassment of an imperfectly developed reason, which feels itself bounded, in the way that its own knowledge is bounded, by space and time, and which supposes that the whole being of things is likewise bounded by those same limitations — only such an imperfectly developed mind finds itself forced to resort to thinking about our eternity in the sensible terms of a future life, in order to retain a firm grasp on the idea of eternal life. We, however, know that this mode of representation is metaphorical, though we appreciate that man's understanding will always be bound to this image, if it is to form a clearer idea of the relation between the eternal and the finite life.

Otto: It is certainly true that we can distinguish non-spatio-temporal location from temporal only by means of spatio-temporal similes. This doctrine is now clear to me. But there is something else I should like you to explain. The usual, the simple view of the immortality of the soul is that this true, immutable and essential characteristic, this eternal life, belongs to our personality, belongs to each individual human spirit. And there are many who make this view more intuitive for themselves by believing in the resurrection of the body. On the other hand, there are some philosophical teachers who find this whole outlook petty and egoistic, declaring that our individual personalities are merely finite phenomena, and maintaining that man's spirit flows back into the universe, so to speak. How are we to decide between these two positions?

Philanthes: Tell me, do you take the trees and flowers in space and time to be immortal beings?

Otto: No! I see them coming to be and passing away.

Philanthes: When a flower fades away, or a tree is destroyed by fire, then, of course, the form disappears. But the essence in them is an immutable mass, and it does not disappear; it flows back into the universe. This immortality which flows back into the universe, therefore, presumably does belong to the flowers and the trees?

Otto: I do not fully understand you yet. It is only the specific forms which pass away which we call flowers and trees. The mass in them may afterwards be what it will, it is no longer a flower or a tree.

Philanthes: That is my opinion, too. You will, therefore, find that those who talk about the flowing away of our spirit into the universe, or the return of our spirit to the divine being, or who employ similar expressions for immortality, are simply making a false comparison with what is immutable in the physical world, in order to render the idea of eternal life more intuitive.

According to the richer view of bodies which we recently discussed, we call those bodies which have form, such as flowers and trees, entities. We also speak of those mortal and transient things which are not entities; they are merely generated and destroyed by the changing relations of entities to each other. If, adopting this distinction, we wished to judge the spirit relatively to the eternal being of things, we should declare that it was mortal. We should go on to assert of it that it was not itself an entity, but merely a transient thing, formed by other entities which, with the disappearance of the spirit, flow back again into the universe. This doctrine, therefore, really denies the immortality of the soul. The belief in immortality, on the contrary, asserts that our soul is not the mortal thing it appears to be. It rather maintains that the spirit, as individual person in the independent world of the spirit, is a simple entity which lasts for ever. For the eternal truth, there does not exist a mass which is merely capable of receiving form, of receiving any form. Personal spirits are the independent entities themselves within that mass.

Once the idea of eternal life is clear to us, the second fundamental idea of faith, the idea of the unconditioned freedom of the will results with great ease, in spite of the many difficulties its application may involve. Freedom here means independence of the conditions of the laws of nature. Now, it was precisely these conditions of the laws of nature which we were forced, from the finite scientific view of things, to reject as without validity for eternal truth. From the point of view of eternal truth, the power of the spirit in the independent world of the spirit, that is to say, the will, must be unconditionally free; for the entire eternal being of things is free.

Every moral consciousness thus has its being in the belief in the unconditionally free will. The expression "you ought", with which the commands of duty announce themselves, is meaningless in the absence of this belief. If I say, "you ought" (for example, "you ought to keep your promise") I am assuming that the demand on my will in the decision made by the idea of a promise shall absolutely decide the action, no matter what other motive may operate against it. The necessity of this demand can, therefore, only have meaning for a will which, even if it can be sensibly stimulated, gives the determination of every decision to itself alone. Such a will must, therefore, act in unconditioned freedom with unconditioned control over itself, so that it cannot be brought to its decision by any sensible motive, no matter how strong it may be.

You will, therefore, easily see that this idea must be presupposed for eternal truth. But you will also readily appreciate that it only has meaning for eternal truth and has no application in finite knowledge.

Otto: With respect to eternal truth, the independence of the spirit absolutely presupposes freedom of the will and unconditioned self-control. And this is because the belief is completely identical with the belief that the laws of nature have no meaning for eternal truth. But the laws of nature control man's finite scientific knowledge. If one wished to apply the idea of the freedom of the will to nature, one would be contradicting oneself. In nature, every force is finite and can be overcome by a stronger force. Accordingly, in the appearance of human life, the finite forces of the different drives struggle with each other in the making of the decision. No matter how strong the moral drive to virtue may be in a person's character, it is still possible to imagine an even stronger sensible drive capable of overcoming it.

Philanthes: Consider now what sort of view of the independent spiritual world we have arrived at through the ideas of the immortal soul and the freedom of the will.

Otto: We believe in the eternal truth of the spiritual world, in which independent rational persons are the entities: they freely stand in community with each other under a higher order of things.

In this connection, I recall your father's teaching that the idea, which completes and perfects the expression of belief in the independence of the spirit, is the idea of God. I should like you to explain this in greater detail to me.

Philanthes: If you consider the way in which scientific knowledge contradicted eternal truth, you will easily realise that we must expressly state this completion by expressing belief in God, the only Origin of all things.

Otto: In the world which is subject to natural laws, neither the contingency of the coincidence of individual things, nor their subjection to natural laws, can be thought of as existing in itself or as something independent. Beings in their contingent multiplicity are subject to laws; but the laws in themselves are nothing: they have no being in themselves, no independence.

The order of the universe and the subjection of things to it must, therefore, from the point of view of eternal truth, be thought of as determined by a higher cause. I thus find our thoughts led to higher spirits ordering the universe. But why is it that the eye of man's belief, instead of being focused on the spirits of rivers and mountains, earths and suns, with certainty only finds the one Lord of the universe?

I realise that this belief in one God, the Father of all creatures, is bound to be very important for the development of man, for it is only in accordance with this idea that all people feel themselves linked together by the common bond of the fatherhood of God. I realise that, without this idea, the idea of the unity of the universe could not be perfected. But I would raise the following question: How do we arrive at this idea of perfection? How small man is, compared with the nation of which he is a part! How small a nation is, compared with mankind as a whole and all earth's life! How small the earth itself is, compared with the solar system to which it belongs — and the solar system itself, compared with the star-studded heavens! And so on! How is it that the subordinate gods have always, from time immemorial, belonged to the poetic imagination, whereas, seriously philosophical reason has always immediately raised itself to belief in one Lord and Creator of the universe?

Philanthes: You know, of course, that if, in the world of space, we were to add region to region so as to constitute ever greater wholes, we should never, in incompletable space, arrive at the completed whole of the universe, could never arrive at the unity of all things. If we adopted that method we should be more likely to find ourselves subject to a god of the earth, or a god of the sun. We could, according to our whims, mark off areas in seas and rivers, valleys and mountains, and even among the stars, making them the realms of higher spirits. And even if all these regions were added together so as to form a single system, we should still never arrive at the all-embracing kingdom of God.

But all these projects are merely the dreams of poetry, which each may paint for himself as he feels inclined. For it is only on the analogy with our body that outer appearance permits us to discern voluntary motion in human and animal life, the will of a spirit, as moving in nature. All other larger phenomena obey necessary natural laws, without referring science to the voluntary motions of a spirit.

On the other hand, consider for a moment the following question: in what does science recognise the necessary unity of all things in the totality of the universe?

Otto: In the universality and necessity of the laws of nature alone, for, no matter how little such a law may actually order, its power extends throughout the entire universe, which is subject to natural laws.

Philanthes: What do we call the dominion of the laws of nature over the transformations of nature in the phenomenal world?

Otto: Fate.

Philanthes: If we now proclaim Fate to be the master of the universe, then, as far as eternal truth is concerned, we can stop at that idea.

Otto: I disagree. This idea is not suitable for the perfecting of eternal truth. The laws of nature are in themselves insubstantial, and the things which are subject to them are lacking in independence. We cannot think of nature, constituted of things, as existing in its own right. We have to assume that, relatively to eternal truth, it is founded in something else.

Philanthes: But the necessity of the laws of nature is a *single* necessity which holds for the entire universe. The *one* master of the laws of nature is the master of Fate and the master of the universe. He has subjected all things, from the point of view of appearances, to their fate. Man's belief in his perfection is thus expressed as the belief in God, the one Creator of all things. And since, relatively to eternal truth, only the spiritual world continues to exist, we must think of God as the Creator and Legislator of that spiritual world.

We thus believe in the eternal truth of the spiritual world. God is its Creator, and its inhabitants are personal and free beings, who are united together under the divine legislation. What do we have in this expression of faith, do you suppose?

Otto: As far as I can see, nothing but the lifeless foundation of the idea. Life first enters with the divine legislation itself. The word here is:

reverence and love are the witnesses of faith. The world of faith is the world of the good and the beautiful. But show me in greater detail how we are to arrive at knowledge of that world.

Philanthes: Reverence and love are the witnesses of faith. But how do we introduce them into the world of the good and the beautiful?

Otto: In feeling they give us the ideals of beauty and sublimity of soul. In duty and virtue, they tell man what is good and beautiful in the life of action.

Philanthes: For man there thus issues from this love of beauty of soul the laws regulating the purposes of his will. The spiritual sociability of man is here subject to the laws of a kingdom of purposes or ends.

The will acts according to purposes, and this kingdom of purposes or ends is the realm of the human will, where we strive to order the things around us according to the laws of their value.

Now, you know how this value is measured for us according to the levels of the pleasant, the useful, the noble and the just.

Otto: The pleasant is what affords us pleasure. The value of pleasure lies wholly in the needs of the sensible stimulation of our vital activities. The useful is that which serves us as a means to the achievement of our ends. The value of that which is useful lies, therefore, merely in the mediating of ends which are already otherwise given to us in comforts and amenities or in that which is good in itself. The pleasant and the useful have, therefore, both of them, merely mediate value — the pleasant in so far as it serves the stimulation of our life, the useful in that it serves some other purpose which is known in some other way. All *immediate* value lies for us in the rational spirit and the healthy appearance of that spirit in our life. And here we find the good in itself partly as the noble and partly as the just.

We find the development of the rational spirit in all parts noble and beautiful, and the more we bear within ourselves of this inner value, the more we seek self-contentment therein. Strength and vitality, health of spirit, talent and genius, understanding, imagination, pleasantness of temperament, readiness and skill of every kind — all these things can be sought or desired because they are regarded as useful. But it is not usefulness alone which determines their value. Quite apart from usefulness, the healthy spirit attributes to even the least significant skill an inner value, no matter how slight it may be, on account of which, we should rather possess it than not. This attitude arises from the comparison of one's life with the idea of a perfect human being. This is an ideal which we cannot, it is true, attain. But we do regard the increasing approximation to that ideal as important. We attach an immediate inner value to it.

In this ideal, what outshines everything else which could be called good is the pure good will, the morality of man. The pure good will consists in the disposition to follow the commands of duty for the sake of the sacredness of the command itself, and not for the sake of some other purpose. This morality is the only thing in human life which can be called incomparably good. It is the supreme condition, under which alone we may call something else truly good. Every gift of fortune, even every other kind of spiritual advantage, only possesses true value in man if it is conjoined with this morality or purity of heart.

The supreme requirement of the will of man is, therefore, that it should submit itself to the command of duty, the necessary demands of which announce themselves to the rational spirit. The pure good will, therefore, places the command of duty above itself and submits itself to it. Indeed, it is already involved in the concept of the good that, that which we call good cannot really itself determine the supreme immediate value. Something is good if it corresponds to its end; the end itself is not really good. Everything which is good is judged according to its end, which is, so to speak, above it. It is thus that the will itself submits itself to the command of duty and finds its pure goodness in obedience to the command of duty. We must, therefore, seek supreme value in the object of the command of duty itself. We shall then find that we shall absolutely attribute to the rational spirit itself an unconditioned value, *personal dignity*, and recognise it as end in itself.

This idea of personal dignity is the single fundamental idea of the necessary legislation of purposes or ends.

Philanthes: I am looking back at what you have been showing us. Pleasure only has a contingent and conditioned value. Every individual virtue of the development of the spirit has a value of determinate magnitude, which may be larger or smaller. By contrast, the rational spirit itself has an infinite value which is attributed to it with necessity. It is through this idea alone that we arrive at the necessity of the demands made upon the will. That is to say, it is only in the command of duty that we arrive at the necessary legislation of purposes or ends.

Every rational community lives under laws which regulate purposes ends. Now, if we only had the ends of pleasure and spiritual development without duty, then there would be no necessary community of rational beings: each rational will would, in social life, be abandoned to its own inclination and whims. By contrast, the necessary legislation of duties issues from the idea of the dignity of the person. The world of rational beings becomes for us a kingdom of ends which is constituted by the necessary law of personal dignity which is peculiar to it.

Now, dear Otto, let us raise the question: where is the kingdom of ends? And where is the world of the good and the beautiful?

The idea of personal dignity does not belong to finite truth, but to eternal truth. The appearance of human life in nature vanishes away like every other. The idea of personal dignity is the idea of our eternal life become a living idea. We do not have knowledge of it. We possess it in faith.

In this faith in our personal dignity, reverence subjects us to the commands of duty, and pure love in conscience causes the emergence, in addition to the commands of duty, of all the requirements of beauty of soul as the fundamental idea of man's kingdom of ends.

This kingdom of ends, with its mediating interventions in human life, belongs to finite truth. But for us it is a task set for man's earthly life, the task of making eternal truth manifest in this earthly existence.

Man here consciously subordinates his earthly existence to faith. For do not forget, man is not good in virtue of the fact that he possesses within himself personal dignity. Every rational spirit, whether it be good or bad, possesses that dignity. Personal dignity is the *sublime* fundamental idea of faith in our eternal destiny.

Man first becomes good in his temporal existence when, in justice, honour and friendship, he subjects his life to the idea of his personal dignity, and remains loyal to that idea.

From faith in the eternal truth of the world of the good and the beautiful there awaken within us reverence and love and, in them, the ideas of the moral life. But they are merely a task for man, the task of learning to feel the eternal truth in his earthly existence. But where are the ideas of the world of the good and the beautiful itself? How is the world-dominion of the good and the beautiful recognised as belonging to man?

Otto: In the living faith in God. All things are created by holy Omnipotence, and Eternal Love rules the universe.

Philanthes: That is how man ought to express his faith. For his moral consciousness tells him the *necessary* fundamental ideas of the good and the beautiful. We must, therefore, call the Lord of the spiritual world, which is subordinated to the moral order of things, the *holy* Author of the universe, and we must recognise His world as the ideal of eternal goodness. Looked at from the perspective of eternal truth, the world is the world of the good and the beautiful. That which is eternally true appears to us, however, in the transformations of nature. Now, in what do we recognise the eternal significance of natural phenomena?

Otto: In the sublime and beautiful.

Philanthes: You have entered the realm of intuitive awareness. Holy Omnipotence, so we believe, is the Lord of the universe, and the true world is the world of the good and the beautiful. But the fundamental idea cannot be scientifically apprehended in nature. It can only be apprehended in those intuitive feelings of beauty. No human concept can securely capture such feelings. No man can teach them, even though the formed spirit lives in them.

Our observation thus leads us closer to your first question.

Otto: We believe in the personal dignity of our eternal, free and rational spirit, and with this we find ourselves in the community of the independent spiritual world, in the world of the good and the beautiful, in the kingdom of God, which is subject to the holy Omnipotence and Eternal Love of God.

The question which I asked was: why, with respect to the acknowledgement of eternal truth, do you unite the two modes of human conviction in faith and intuitive awareness, whereas for finite truth you only posit one conviction of knowing.

Philanthes: Our knowledge in the case of finite truth is scientific knowledge, in which we are able to judge everything according to concepts which are distinct and capable of intuitive clarity. Individual facts are here connected with each other under the necessity of the laws of nature. The intermediate concept in the inference leads me in the explanation from the universal law to the nexus of individual facts. We grasp finite truth with one scientific type of knowledge, in which the sequence of appearances is subjected to the principles.

But this is not the case with our awareness of eternal truth. Faith shows us the fundamental ideas of eternal truth in an entirely idiosyncratic fashion: it shows us these ideas in the infinite concepts of progression towards that which is supreme, unconditioned and perfect.

But how is their truth to be acknowledged in natural phenomena? How is the phenomenal world to be subordinated to these fundamental ideas?

Here, no inference will safely lead you from an article of faith to an appearance. The significance of eternal truth for appearances is only manifest to us in the truth of beauty alone, about the rights of which you have heard my father speak. It is, so to speak, only through an inexpressible intermediate concept that beauty and sublimity can subsume appearances under the ideas of faith, only thus that they permit us to feel — to have an intuitive awareness of — eternal truth in appearances. No concept will enable us to translate this combination of ideas into inferences.

Religious feeling combines living aesthetic judgements with faith. If we examine more closely the nature of these religious-aesthetic judgements, which express the intuitive awareness of the eternal truth, we shall easily find that the fundamental ideas of faith contained in specific articles of faith constitute a type of conviction which is wholly different from the feelings of intuitive awareness.

To clarify this, let us first observe that we cannot subordinate appearances to the ideas of faith either according to concepts or scientifically. The world of faith is the kingdom of ends. I now maintain that we cannot understand the nature of things under the legislation of purposes or ends.

In this connection, let us compare the idea of the legislation of purposes or ends with the course of nature in general.

The necessary course of natural events according to the universal law of nature is in no wise incompatible with the assumption of the purposefulness of natural phenomena, or with the subordination of those natural phenomena under the legislation of purposes or ends. The legislation of ends could happily co-exist with the complete, self-sufficient course of events in accordance with the laws of nature. Suppose that a will ordered the laws of nature and, at every moment, intended precisely that state of affairs which the laws of nature produced. It would follow that the whole realm of the laws of nature would also be a kingdom of purposes or ends. To assume the purposefulness of the course of nature does not, therefore, require any disruptive interventions in the laws of nature. The idea of the legislation of purposes or ends can rather be conceived as set above the whole legislation of nature. The course of events in nature would, so to speak, be the instrument of the will which organised the whole, just as human beings in their artificial productions make use of a part of the forces of nature in order to make them realise their ends.

But as for the application of this idea to real natural phenomena: observe well that the idea of the legislation of purposes or ends for the world is peculiar to the world of the good and the beautiful, that is to say, to the eternal truth in which we have faith but about which we have no knowledge. With respect to our understanding of phenomena, this faith can only express itself in the intuitive feelings of a religious-aesthetic judgement of things. Scientifically or conceptually, we are absolutely incapable of recognising that the world, subject to natural laws, is a kingdom of purposes or ends.

Otto: In general terms this is clear to me. The intelligent will acts according to purposes or ends. A kingdom of purposes or ends can only make its appearance where things are ordered by an intelligent will. Voluntary action, however, only manifests itself to us in the life of animals, and intelligent will only in the life of man. We shall, therefore, only be able to apply teleological concepts to the explanation of appearances within the sphere of human skill. The phenomenal kingdom of purposes or ends is, as we have just found, the achievement of man himself.

Philanthes: The occurrence of species of plants and animals on earth is, according to the natural laws of the formative drives, a natural product, not an intention or a purpose. If the conditions of their generation had not been present, they would not have come into existence. If the conditions of their survival had been absent, they would have disappeared. Here, interpreting the inner conditions of self-preservation or the external conditions favourable to life in terms of intention and purpose in nature is merely an arbitrary play of the human imagination. It is only what we find pleasing in the dispositions of nature that we praise as purposeful or describe as the intentional gifts of nature. Nonetheless, nature leads us inevitably to this view when she helpfully caters to man's inescapable spiritual needs, not by the necessity of her laws, but by means which are for us entirely contingent. Independently of the physical conditions of self-preservation, nature orders the eye so that we can see, the ear so that we can hear, and the arm so that we can seize, grasp and move things. In terms of natural laws, we shall never understand how nature has here favoured our purpose to enter the world of light and sound, or our purpose to intervene by movement in the world. We can only arrange these contingent harmonies according to purposes. And, once we have secured an entry into the world for these concepts, we shall not be able to resist their further employment.

Otto: Now for the first time, I fail to understand you. You are accepting a scientific theory of natural purpose!

Philanthes: But no! Just listen to me a little longer. It is true, we inevitably began to toy with these concepts of the purposes of nature. But this toying with teleological concepts yields no definite results capable of expression in distinct concepts. It affords us no satisfaction. It merely leads to an aesthetic judgement, in which alone it has its true existence.

If we wanted to retain a scientific hold on this view, we should not be led to natural or divine purposes. What would happen would be that our imaginations would, in humbler spheres, praise nature only where she charmed us with her blandishments, and just as readily condemn her where she presented an hostile face to us.

The simplest poetic vision would then always be that of Zoroaster. God, according to this vision, has set up two lords of the world alongside each other: Ormuzd, the lord of light, the friend of man, the creator of good spirits, of life, and all good gifts; and fighting against him, Ahriman, the lord of darkness, the enemy of man, the creator of evil spirits, sickness and death, and of all evil and vermin.

We could never take such a view seriously. We cannot scientifically conceive a purpose of the universe.

One impediment to such a conception is the fact that we cannot grasp the universe as a whole at all. On the contrary, if we look for intelligible natural purposes we shall never see more than the life of this world and mankind — a tiny fraction of the incompletable totality.

More specifically: we shall only have concepts for a system of purposes, where the purpose is thought of as something to be arrived at indirectly. It is thus that man's skill involves instrumental activity; man achieves his objectives by strenuous effort and by means of implements and machines. In a like manner, man's skill also involves development to maturity. It is thus, for example, that the spirit of the child is developed. But neither instrumental action nor development to maturity occur if a purpose, as something temporally later, is not presupposed.

A finite will, such as man's, may, in its temporal strivings, pursue its purposes by instrumental means and by processes of development. But to attribute such an art to either God or nature is demeaning to them both. As far as the world and its natural or divine purpose is concerned, each thing must contain its purpose, its value, its meaningfulness, immediately within itself. Each thing must be satisfied with itself independently of any comparison. What name, do you suppose, shall we give to that which we describe as natural purpose?

Otto: For us, the only thing which could count as a purpose of nature is the beautiful. It bears its meaning within itself, independently of any comparison. Only the sense of beauty can judge here, for, sunk in the present, it grasps the momentary appearance wholly in itself, not allowing its comparative gaze to range through time.

Philanthes: With all questions about purpose and intention one must, therefore, clearly distinguish moral requirements from questions about natural purposes. Questions of the first kind can always be answered in the most definite manner. Questions of the second kind, however, are concerned with what will always be a mystery for us. If we raise a moral question about purpose and intention, all we are ever asking to know is what we ought to do, and that can always be specified exactly. If, on the other hand, we ask: what is the meaning of our existence in the world? Or if we ask: What is the intention and final purpose of the universe itself? — then these questions relate to God's purposes in the universe, and here all human knowledge falls silent.

If, therefore, one asks about the destiny of man, wishing to know what the practical destiny of his life is, wishing to know what he ought to do, wishing to know what ought to be done in the history of mankind — if that is the question, then the answer is to be found in the teachings of practical wisdom. Virtue and justice are given to us as two sublime ideas for realisation. The true value of life consists for man in asserting the validity of those ideas in nature.

There is, as you say, to be found in the inner life of the individual the pure good will to be true to duty. And this loyalty to the convictions of one's innermost character is, beyond all comparison, worthy of praise.

Health, riches, power, honour, or sickness, poverty, weakness, oppression — the value of all these things is limited to the moment in which they are experienced. Once life is over, it is a matter of indifference to man whether he looks back on happiness or misery, for the only thing which continues to be important for him is virtue. Many a misfortune can make virtue seem all the more beautiful. Indeed, for the impartial observer, happiness has so little value of its own, that the virtue of the individual is the condition under which alone he can find pleasure in someone's uninterrupted prosperity. The happiness of a vicious man is a source of displeasure to him.

The possession of wit and talents, the appearance of charm in society, courage and resolution in danger, even the possession of self-control over the emotions and passions — all these things are praiseworthy, and they may be of great importance to man, both in society and in private life. But, before the inner judge who delivers the final verdict on our own value, none of this, unless it be subject to the laws of virtue, will be of any importance alongside the pure disposition to virtue.

It can be a source of prestige to an individual if he carries out great plans in the state, or if he tirelessly works for the advancement of the well-being of society, or if he devotes his life to the advance of some branch of knowledge, or if he pursues some art with success, or if, in the quiet retirement of domestic life, he devotes himself to his family. But the pure, selfless sacrifice in the smallest circumstances of the most constricted of lives is of greater value before the supreme court of morality than the most comprehensive activity of self-interested skill, or art, or learning. It will be the cause of virtue alone which is decisive both in matters large and in matters small. It is in virtue alone that the spirit raises itself to the height of its eternal destiny.

We are likewise certain of the answer when our question relates to the purposes which are given to man as a task in the history of mankind. The natural outcome of mankind is the gradual development of the understanding. Once a certain level has been reached, progress can only be guaranteed if the understanding itself takes over the guidance of this development. From the standpoint of human wisdom it is clear that there are two purposes: external prosperity and inner spiritual development. But it will also be clear that all other purposes are outshone by the effort to develop public justice, both in the nation and between nations, and the effort to educate the nation to virtue. And yet, here too, it is not the attainment of the end but the striving to attain it which is intrinsically valuable. And of this no man can be deprived.

The destiny of man is thus perfectly clear to us, if our questions relate only to the purpose of human action. But if we wish to know more than what we ought to do, if we wish to solve the riddle of the final destiny of an individual, of of mankind in history, or of the entire course of nature — if that is our wish, then we are venturing on the penetration of mysteries which must always be inaccessible to human knowledge.

Only the feelings of intuitive awareness which issue from the ideas of the beautiful and the sublime will enable us, in an aesthetic judgement wholly abandoned to feeling, to recognise the purposefulness of nature and, with it, the spirit of the eternal which holds sway throughout nature. It is not, however, nature herself which presses this intuitive awareness of the eternal upon us, as it manifests its finite being to human knowledge. This intuitive awareness is rather the possession of the man of cultivation. The cultivated spirit is alone receptive to it, for it seeks the traces of the eternal in nature. The man of cultivation brings faith to the contemplation of nature, and it is only by means of this faith that the contemplation of forms and life in nature is aroused to intuitive awareness of the eternal. Then, for the first time, the ever mobile beauty of the changing forms of nature stirs and rises to immutable youth. It is with that beauty that the divine in nature manifests itself to the man of cultivation.

The wildest image of destruction moves him by its sublimity. Life presents itself to him with forms of beauty — beauty in the wondrous play of the moving waters, greater beauty in the delicate forms of the flowers, and yet greater beauty still in the living eye itself. But the supreme beauty manifests itself to him in the spiritual appearance of virtue in the power, the life, the beauty of the soul, which we admire or love in the actions of the world outside.

Otto: I understand you. The world of the good and the beautiful is the world of faith, the world of eternal truth. Man is an inhabitant of that world in so far as he submits the appearance of his life to moral ideas. Reverence and love here lead him. The ideas of the spiritually sublime and beautiful go hand in hand with the concepts of the good in itself, are for him one and the same. But if he wishes to interpret the law of the good and beautiful as the law of the universe, then his finite concepts abandon him. Not according to the concepts of the good, but only in the feelings of the beautiful, can he apprehend the world as subordinate to the eternal good.

Thus, for man, the acknowledgement of faith lives in the intuitive awareness of eternal truth alone.

Adelheid: Allow me to make a remark by way of objection to what you have said. You here derive reverence and love, the whole of the moral life, from faith. In addition to that, you locate feeling at the centre of the spiritual life, raising it above the concepts of knowledge, and saying that they only serve a mediating function in life. It is feeling, you say, which tells the will its supreme purposes. It seems to me that all virtue flows from religious feelings, virtue subordinating itself, so to speak, to religious feeling. Now, how does this harmonise with the other view, which I have heard you defending with such eagerness, the view, namely, that the doctrine of virtue ought not to be founded on the doctrine of religion, and that it ought not to elevate religion above morality.

Philanthes: There are several things which could be said in reply to your question. But, first of all, let the Apostle Paul be my authority. He says: "And though I have all faith, so that I could remove mountains, and have no charity, I am nothing." The highest development of the feelings counts for nothing unless they manifest themselves in practical life. Piety is virtue in feeling and, at the same time, it is religious feeling in the moral life. Here, none is earlier, none later. Consciousness of not having any obligations to virtue is to lack the faith and the intuitive awareness of religion. Religion acquires all its life from consciousness of the obligation to virtue. Religion in itself only lives in feeling. But every virtue, too, only emerges into life from feeling. But no matter how high the ideals of feeling may rise in devotion and love, every human feeling only acquires its meaning from its influence on the life of action. A man is worth no more than his action. Feeling only has value to the extent to which it affects life by action. All proud feeling enclosed within itself, the sublimest religiosity would count for nothing, unless it emerged from itself to confront the commonest effects which life and action spread around themselves. Without action, energy and struggle, the most magnificent and the most complete achievement would be cold and lifeless. Even the infinite and immobile joy of the millennial realm would be for us but a lifeless form. As Lessing said, the existence of a God contemplating his perfect creation for eternity would be endless boredom. Aristotle likewise says: "Without friends, who would wish to live — even if he had the enjoyment of all other goods?" The healthy moral feeling has no wish to be enclosed within itself. Its wish is to live for others, to care for others, to achieve things for others, for friends. The person imprisoned in his own feeling ought not to vaunt his finely developed taste or the fervour of his devotion. He has little reason to feel superior to the pleasure of the man who only wallows in sensual pleasure — for he has not charity.

I accordingly find it important for life that religion should be subordinated to morality, in order to protect sound feeling from sentimentalism and pious canting fanaticism. The scientific interest, with its simpler clarity, then comes to the assistance of sound feeling.

Alongside moral feeling and conscience, so to speak, religious feeling also involves the emotions of submission to God and devotion, the elevation of thought to God. But, for man, reverence and love are the witnesses of faith. It is in honour, justice and love that man first perceives eternal truth. And it is only when he is morally animated that he is able to raise above them the ideas of divine perfection, holiness and eternal love.

Without this awakening in the moral life, you cannot humanly understand the language of the divine ideas at all. The science of the theory of virtue must, therefore, come before the teaching of religion.

It is also certain that a mere emotion, like the religious emotion, cannot prescribe any new duties. The only thing it can do is encourage us to practise the duties we already have from other sources. For us, therefore, all obligation issues from the moral consciousness of the value of virtue, and religion derives its whole interest from this consciousness.

Adelheid: That is clear to me. Our consciousness must rise from the human to the divine. Our consciousness can only become aware of the divine through human love, for no man has seen God. But tell me now more clearly what you mean by resistance to sentimentalism and sanctimoniousness.

Philanthes: We must take the value of religion independent of that of morality in life as well, for religion is merely an emotional mood and ought to serve virtuous action. To it are opposed fanaticism and sentimentalism. With antipathy towards the power of deeds, they glorify a treasure of the emotions.

The weak man deludes himself with the sublimity of his feelings, if he lacks the courage or the energy to act. The feeling of devotion is for many people the most important thing in the world. But if the result is that the person becomes a prisoner within himself and neglects the life of action, in which alone true value lies, then, no matter how much he may regard himself as the special darling of God or an initiate of higher mysteries, he is still a fanatic. His whole life and outlook is but the pathetic delusion of his imagination, for he merely delights in the pleasant titillation of a few curious dreams. In fact, the most desiccated, the coldest moral or judicial mode of behaviour is worth more than all the fire of these fanatical and sanctimonious feelings which shrink from action.

If someone were unreceptive to religious emotion — the purest emotion of all — it would be indicative of a lack of life, and a breach of beauty of soul. But these emotions only possess value in so far as they serve action and, therewith, communicate vitality to the strength of the moral will. In devotion there is also to be found the surest means of restraining the sensuous desires and restricting the turbulence of the lower emotions. And yet, the more a person needs enthusiasm to sustain his interest in duty and justice, the more it is a sign of weakness. The true and healthy power of the moral life is to be found in the firm quietness of loyalty to one's convictions. Nor is there any pure enthusiasm without it.

But the most essential thing for man is that he should learn to acknowledge the holiness of the command above him, that he should learn obedience to the moral law, that he should be moved towards it with quiet reverence and awe. For it is far more necessary for man that he learn to obey than that he should learn to command.

Moral sentimentalism and a certain sweet and flattering talk of love is thus distasteful to us. Let no one deceive himself into thinking that he has transcended the law by love. Every healthy human being will need to exert an effort to comply with duty when it solemnly and coldly opposes his favourite inclinations and wishes. Indeed, even the quiet habit of loyalty to duty is, in the case of man, not the work of love but the result of awe. Love, it is true, sounds more pleasant and attractive, for it is always the object of choice. But it above all beseems man to learn to *submit* to duty. Only reverence and awe give sound moral strength to the will.

Moral strength of will, purity of soul, the pure good will, or that loyalty to conviction by which man continues faithful to the command of duty for the sake of duty itself — it is in virtue of this that man himself is good. Every religious feeling, too, is only of value in so far as it issues from this innermost moral disposition.

Religion is the life of intuitive awareness; in other words, religion is the faith which has become a living faith. But faith only becomes a truly living faith through awe and love.

Adelheid: I too understand you now. Let me go further. At the beginning, when you were drawing the distinction between intuitive awareness and faith, you said that faith could be expressed in certain articles of faith. There can only be a few such articles because the whole connection between faith and human life is to be found in the feelings of intuitive awareness alone. How, do you suppose, would you give a brief but comprehensive summary of those articles of faith?

Philanthes: All we should need to do to produce such a summary would be to collect our ideas from what has been discussed so far.

From the speculative point of view, the fundamental ideas of faith are contained in the following articles: faith in God as the *one* Creator of all things, faith in the eternity of the human spirit, and faith in the freedom of the will. But this faith only comes alive in the belief in the *holiness* of the Creator of the world.

It is through the self-confidence of our rational spirit that we come to possess belief in the personal dignity of our being. Reverence and love for the moral life awaken in that belief, and with it there awakens belief in the eternal destiny of man in the divine world of the good and the beautiful.

In that divine world, we feel ourselves to be the subjects of God, and we believe in the providence of God, in the divine direction of all our fates by Eternal Love.

But in this earthly life we feel inadequate, relatively to the purity of moral ideas. As a result, belief in Eternal Love becomes for us faith in the All-merciful, who will prepare an eternal purification and sanctification for our wills.

These will be the sum of our ideas of faith.

Otto: We, therefore, believe in Providence, in the eternal destiny of man and in the eternal purification of our wills.

I thus appreciate that the eternal destiny of man is acknowledged in the aesthetic view of life through the religious emotions of enthusiasm. But I also realise that, notwithstanding, we must, with our sense of our own moral inadequacy, humbly submit to the higher dispensations of Providence, with feelings of submissiveness to God. Finally, I recognise that it is only in the feelings of devotion and recognition of holy Omnipotence that the deepest peace of faith is to be found.

DIALOGUE XI

Man's Sense of Guilt

Philanthes: We recently agreed that it was only possible to make eternal truth intuitive for man by animating his moral feeling and his sense of beauty. You have also explained to me with such clarity how the truth of man's convictions is based for him on the self-reliance of the rational spirit alone, the source of all truth being for man that *of which he is certain in himself*. From this it followed that the eternal truths belong to the first truths, for which there can be no question of proof or derivation, and of which we are immediately certain in ourselves, just in the form in which the healthy cultivated spirit announces them to us.

This final idea must be examined more closely. We say, for example, that man believes in God, the one almighty Creator of all things, because the contingency of the coincidence of entities under insubstantial laws indicates a lack of independence, the completion of which can only be thought in a higher cause of the order of nature and of the things subsumed under this order.

This argument displays the greatest similarity to that which earlier teachers, in particular, Leibniz, called the proof of the existence of God from the contingency of the world, and which later teachers, especially Kant, so emphatically rejected as inadequate. We shall adhere to the latter view and say that belief in God belongs to the first fundamental truths of our spirit which transcend all proof and of which the spirit is certain in itself.

Otto: And yet you gave a derivation of the expression of our ideas of God.

Philanthes: Yes, but only for our, for man's idea of God, and for the way in which man has to express it. We live in faith, and the self-confidence of our spirit in faith says: there is eternal truth in the appearances of things as you see them, but you must grasp the phenomenal beings of things under the ideas of perfection, if you are to think that phenomenal being from the point of view of its eternal truth.

What has just been said would be a straightforward contradiction if our intention had been to establish faith on experience and natural law, and to prove it by reference to them. Indeed, what we said began with the words: in experience and under natural laws we do not come to know things in accordance with eternal truth. Now, if that were our only conviction, if our only knowledge was of appearances, then our convictions would be unstable and it would be impossible to establish any connection between them and eternal truth.

No, the situation is precisely the reverse! Faith is the first thing of which we are certain in ourselves. Upon it we found the truth of appearances, and from it there issues the intuitive awareness of eternal truth in appearances.

However, if we expressed faith in the ideas of perfection in this way, we also saw that an inexpressible idea clearly manifested itself to man in those ideas of perfection, an idea which could not be compared with any branch of knowledge, an idea upon which we could in no wise retain a scientific hold without reducing it to contradictions and destroying it.

Human beings have to think of God, the holy and ultimate Foundation of all things, as the omnipotent Architect of the laws of nature. But this only imparts to us, in faith, the idea which is fundamental to all pious feelings and all sublime aesthetic ideas.

Taken scientifically, it turns into an empty contradiction. The knowledge of our reason is so constituted that, in it, we can only know unity and necessity through and under natural laws. If we in some way wish to conceive how God established and maintained the universe, we should have to think of the divine Being as also subject to a law, in accordance with which the foundation and maintenance of the universe took place, and we should not be able to raise God above the law.

Indeed, there is yet more. Our whole conscious acknowledgement of the moral order of things makes it a requirement for us to subject every free will to the law of morality, and to make the sacredness of the law supreme, to make it independent of any will. As Plato says: "That which is sacred is loved by the gods because it is sacred; but that which is sacred is not sacred because the gods love it." Our concepts only evolve under the law, they can never rise above it. The idea of the sacred creator of the universe is, therefore, simply an idea of faith which cannot be captured conceptually at all.

Faith thus eludes any intellectual development of its ideas. Its only wish is that its eternal truth for man should be acknowledged in feeling.

In this distinction between faith and knowledge, and in the elevation of eternal truth above all knowledge, there are three fundamental ideas of eternal truth which are valid for us.

Firstly, we believe in the truthfulness of our reason and in the personal dignity of our eternal and free spirit.

Secondly, we believe in God, the holy Creator of all things, and in the universal dominion of his Eternal Love.

Thirdly, in faith, we have the feeling of the moral inadequacy of each person, but, at the same time and on account of Eternal Love, we also have the assurance of the eternal purification and purgation of the will.

Otto: Yes, that is what we recently established.

Philanthes: Now, attend for a moment to the following question. What is the supreme principle of this view of the world held by faith?

Otto: The holiness of God and belief in the universal dominion of Eternal Love.

Philanthes: With respect to the universe, this is quite certainly the supreme and dominant idea which is the foundation of everything. But what about its status subjectively for us, for man's view of the world?

Otto: Here I see two, so to speak, conflicting ideas. On the one hand, I see the ideas of the self-confidence and independence of the spirit, and of the freedom of the will. On the other hand, I see consciousness of our moral inadequacy, the consciousness of guilt within our own heart, or however we are to express the matter.

Philanthes: What I would say to you is this: subjectively, for man, consciousness of moral inadequacy is indeed to be designated the fundamental idea, without which we could not introduce any agreement into our convictions.

Otto: I fully appreciate that, as things stand, this idea must be included among the ideas of faith. And yet it has frequently seemed to us as if the whole doctrine would be purer and simpler if, with respect to the moral life, we started out from the ideas of self-reliance within us, and, with respect to religion, from the idea of eternal love alone. We are, indeed, convinced of the inadequacy of our knowledge, and we do not expect to be able to understand or explain everything. But, in the moral life, the ideas of self-reliance are the only sure guides of the healthy spirit. We appreciate that all the visissitudes of happiness and misery, like any natural lack, are without meaning for eternal truth. All that is left, therefore, is the moral inadequacy of man, for, beyond the limits of human life, we are willing to forgo judging the goodness or badness of the dispositions of the universe.

Man's moral imperfection is itself, indeed, merely the consequence of natural defects. If we could attain the ideal of education and the guidance of youth, everybody would, from youth onwards, acknowledge in duty and love the only value of life, and would, as a matter of habit, be loyal to duty and love.

If we then go on to imagine the course of the universe as subsumed under the idea of eternal love, then all intelligibility disappears: the only thing which the aesthetic judgement leaves us is the luminous splendour of the world of the sublime and the beautiful.

Philanthes: What you are really asking is where the mistake lies in supposing that the view of the universe and life which you portrayed was sufficient. My answer is this: you have made a mistake in two respects. Firstly, in order to remove the difficulties, you made everything depend on the inadequacy of our knowledge. But can you really be absolutely satisfied with that? Secondly, you say — correctly, it is true — that in our moral life the only sure guides are the ideas of self-reliance. However, in your judgement of our moral inadequacy you were disloyal to the eternal ideas, for you only attended to the temporal development of the appearance of our life, instead of attending to the freedom of the will.

Must it not be a source of sadness to us that we are tied to this finite knowledge, that we are imprisoned in these bodies and that we only find bodies external to ourselves instead of intuiting, from spirit to spirit, to use Plato's words, the eternal truth, health of soul and justice itself? Must it not be a source of sadness to us to see ourselves restricted in our knowledge of the moral purposes of our life, to see ourselves likewise restricted in our power to pursue those moral ends? Must it not be a source of sadness to us to find ourselves forced, in this temporal existence, to care so much more for the satisfaction of physical needs than to live in the ideas of sublimity and beauty of soul?

No matter that natural defects have no meaning for the eternal. Our gaze, focused on the eternally true, is still clouded by the finite truth, and our eternally true life itself is still, so to speak, limited thereby.

And whom shall we hold responsible for this sad state of affairs? Must we not humbly accept it from the hand of the creator of the universe, while attributing to ourselves the guilt itself of all defects?

Otto: Right! Now I understand. We believe in the freedom of the will, and as a consequence we must regard ourselves as the authors of our temporal existence. The moral inadequacy of our lives is, therefore, of eternal significance. If the spirit of man did not bear this lack within itself, it would not manifest itself in such an imperfect temporal existence.

Philanthes: You will now understand that this consciousness of our moral inadequacy is the fundamental idea, in terms of which we must interpret the entire human mode of knowledge.

But, of necessity, we pronounce this moral condemnation of each person, even the best. And we do so simply because each person's free will manifests itself in this temporal existence in an only limited power of self-control. A cultivated person may be confident that, in the ordinary circumstances of life, he will be master of his own decisions. And the more noble the social development around him, the greater the culture of his nation, the more true this will be. But, in general, everybody must admit that his self-mastery could, contrary to the admonitions of conscience, be misled into yielding to the turbulence of his sensual desires and the force of an emotion. For, in this temporal existence, it is not the thought of the necessity of the moral command which itself determines our decisions. We must first, through self-control, confer a vital power on reverence for duty and the love for beauty of soul. This vital power will then enable us to oppose the desires which spring from our sensual drives. Finally, the power of man's sentiments are, like self-control itself, limited. Each can be overcome by a stronger. Thus, the nature of our will fails to meet the moral demands made upon the free will. Each must be the judge of his own moral inadequacy.

Otto: Instruct me further. What is the practical significance of this idea of our own inadequacy? How is that idea to be correctly expressed?

Philanthes: The healthy fundamental idea of the moral life is independence of the spirit, self-reliance. Of course, the person who is sensibly aroused, above all needs reverence and awe for duty, and, under its command alone, love. But duty commands reverence and respect for human dignity, and in this way duty itself lives in the ideas of self-reliance. The moral consciousness of guilt and the humiliation therein involved, are, on the other hand, only of religious significance. They are supposed to awaken in man the feelings of submission to God. It is unbecoming for anybody, out of mere consideration for personal worth, to humble his spirit before anyone else, no matter whom. On the other hand, it is by no means weakness but true strength of character, an attitude which purifies and cleanses, to humble oneself before the law, before the sublime idea of the holy will, in humility acknowledging the higher though inaccessible dignity of this pure will.

This humility ought not to detract from the feeling of our own power to practise virtue, for it issues from our consciousness of freedom, and it imputes to man the guilt of disloyalty to duty, even though we are capable of freely following duty. This humility is the deepest fundamental consciousness of the religious view of our life. It reconciles man in friendship to death, for death leads us along the path to eternal purification and cleansing. This humility ought to protect us from being befooled by the brilliance of happiness and success, and from being thereby led into vanity and being induced to forget the eternal in favour of the terrestrial. It ought, on the contrary, to elevate us above unhappiness and failure, by showing us that the loveliest objective in human life is the sacrifice of what is temporal for eternal ideas. This humility ought to induce us, even in the bitterest misfortune, loyally and humbly to submit to Providence, and in the bitterest suffering to learn to descry the hand of the All-merciful above us.

You will also find that, in the absence of these perfecting ideas, even our aesthetic view of the world is incapable of resolving its disharmonies.

Otto: You convince me. I mistakenly appealed to the unclouded brilliancy of the world of the sublime and the beautiful. But this corresponds only to the epic and lyric aesthetic outlook, and among them there are also to be found the dramatic aesthetic ideas. They only acquire their life through these feelings of sacrifice, and permit the beauty and sublimity of the rejection of the finite appearance in favour of the eternal to emerge. In this way alone do love and eternal hope issue in beautiful form from the feelings of grief. In this way alone does conciousness of one's spiritual power emerge victorious over finite oppression and misfortune in the ideas of tragedy and all that is dynamically sublime. Indeed, even in the images of the distorted and perverted, the spirit, employing comic ideas, is able to play, so to speak, with the vanity of that which is finite.

Philanthes: Correct. We must now, in the service of these elegiac and tragic ideas, express the idea of our own guilt in images, like all the ideas of intuitive awareness. And in this we must take care not to base the image on any idea which conflicts with moral ideas.

In God's eye, man is of value only because of the reverence and the love which he bears within his heart for the holy, the beautiful and the good. Consciousness bestows upon each person the feeling of moral inadequacy. This feeling generates religious humility, which submissively accepts from the higher hand of Providence every turn of fate in this earthly existence. But at the same time the heart is filled with yearning to return to eternal purity. To this yearning there corresponds the consolation which arises from eternal expectations. Just as it is true that eternal love established the world and maintains it, so also does it guide man and enable him to achieve the purification of his will.

As you know, these ideas have been expressed by means of the images of man's fall away from God, and in the doctrines of eternal reward and punishment. It was natural that these latter ideas should have been borrowed from civil life where we work for reward, and then transferred metaphorically to religious ideas. But it is manifest that they have no meaning here. There can be no question of reward and punishment where man's value is to be found within himself in beauty of soul, where virtue is its own reward and where vice is its own punishment. And if the talk of fear as a motive to the good life were really seriously intended, we should then destroy all morality, instead of awakening it.

Adelheid: Do you, then, entirely reject the fear of eternal punishment? What means of reform would you adopt instead, at least for the common masses?

Philanthes: If we are to awaken the moral life, then we must certainly entirely banish fear, and, along with it, we must banish all those views of bad conscience which are lit by the flames of hell alone.

Let us, in this matter, simply follow Aristotle: "It is only those youths who have enjoyed a free education who can be won for virtue by instruction. For what makes youth receptive to virtue are noble customs, customs which truly love the beautiful. The common masses, on the other hand, have not been accustomed to the sense of honour; they have been habituated to obedience through fear alone. They avoid what is unjust, not because it is disgraceful, but only from fear of punishment."

How effective is this fear of punishment in the well ordered life?

The peaceful citizen will be obedient to the positive laws in the state, if not from patriotism then at least from habit and the love of order. He will also be kept from breaking the laws from a sense of honour, to avoid being found worthy of punishment. Only in a few unfortunate cases, where the motive to break the law is very strong, will fear of punishment be necessary to restrain the potential transgressor. But where this fear alone decides, one always finds barbarity and lack of culture. Motivation from fear is entirely opposed to morality, and an action has no moral value at all if it is the product of constraint resulting from fear alone.

And in this connection it is a matter of complete indifference whether we are talking about temporal or eternal punishment. Fear is always the decisive factor. Certainly, it would be highly unjust to speak in this pejorative fashion of anybody who, in his religious opinions, adopted, along with other ideas, the idea of eternal retribution; for this idea, whether it is connected to a greater or a lesser degree with superstition, is nonetheless an image of the holiness of the law and of reverence for that law. The situation here is as before: in most cases, habituation to a moral order of life, along with reverence and love, are sufficient to keep the educated man on the path of virtue. It is only in exceptional cases that the fear of eternal punishment is necessary as well.

But, in fact, all these fantasies belong to the ancient criminal justice of priestly states, where a ceremonial service, or the whole order of life governed by the form of that service, was imposed upon the common masses through fear of punishment. It is, indeed, possible to achieve a great deal with the common masses in this way, but the real result is slavish submission to superstition, not a free moral existence. As I have already said to you: true power over primitive minds is to be won, not through fear, but by serene tranquillity of soul and the peace of God, which the missionaries employed against the fury of sensual desire and reluctance of disposition.

The educator of the people ought, above all things, to know how to work upon this inner moral pacification of the dispositions. But once moral education has begun, then the feeling of human dignity will awaken self-respect and the sense of honour, and they will be the soundest and the surest guide in the moral life. Only when a man would be ashamed to do what was immoral, only when a man esteems himself too highly to do what was wrong, only then will success be quite certain. This moral feeling of self-respect is the tranquil guide which does not need to raise the emotional temperature in order to guarantee loyal adherence to the moral law.

Closer observation will reveal to you that the good ordering of existence in social life can only be secured to the extent that habituation is protected for everybody by the sense of honour.

The secure establishing of the moral life needs no false assistance.

Adelheid: Your view of life, free from fear, is, in any case, more cheerful and more pure.

Otto: With respect to the hope of faith, we thus adhere to the simple dictum that the divine all-merciful Love will help our inadequacy and lead us back to the purity of our will in the life eternal. And it will do so, by drawing back for us the veil which cloaks the eternal truth from our eyes, thus affording us an unimpeded view of our own independent and free will, in which we are able to submit ourselves in purity to the holy one.

But what if we compare these same ideas with the holiness of God and the divine governance of the universe? In all the imperfection of this earthly existence man fails to match his eternal destiny. Indeed, in his moral inadequacy, he manifestly contradicts it. How could the impure have emerged from the eternally pure? How could God have been willing to establish the possibility of evil in the world? How could he have permitted evil?

Philanthes: These questions will show you most clearly that the only way in which harmony can be introduced into our convictions is by the free elevation of faith above man's finite and imperfect knowledge.

In consciousness of the freedom of our will, we must say to ourselves that it is through our own fault that the appearance of our earthly existence contradicts the ideas of the perfectly good and beautiful. Free though our will may be, the view of eternal truth is veiled for us through our own fault. All we know is what we ought to do in this earthly existence. Our knowledge does not embrace the divine purpose of the universe, nor does it embrace our own eternal destiny.

We bear within our own moral consciousness the contradiction of our earthly existence with the holiness of God, and we shall not be able to resolve this contradiction during this earthly existence. In our knowledge, the idea that God permits evil likewise contains a contradiction which we shall not resolve, and, indeed, are not supposed to resolve, in this earthly existence. Here, we merely say to ourselves: man does not understand the purpose of the universe, nor does he know how the temporal phenomenon harmonises with the eternal truth. From the fact that there is a contradiction between things and the eternal ideas of the good and the beautiful, it does not follow that a similar contradiction exists in the eternally true essence of things. It is merely human knowledge which is unable to grasp the harmony of appearance with eternal truth.

On the other hand, *in virtue of the necessity of the command of morality*, love is to be found in the deepest recesses of every human spirit, love the witness of faith, faith in the universal dominion of the good and the beautiful, faith in the universal dominion of eternal love. And faith in God, the holy creator of all things, is for us the triumphant idea of eternal truth.

You will, therefore, readily appreciate that in reply to your question about the permitting of evil we may only reply *with our ignorance*, for it is, indeed, only in aesthetic judgement that we can compare the appearance with the external purposes. This aesthetic comparison is made in three different ways. In the epic ideas of the phenomenal triumph of the good we have an intuitive awareness of eternal beauty. In comic, elegiac and tragic ideas, the appearance of that triumph is dismissed as vain, relatively to eternal truth. Finally, in the highest lyrical ideas of devotion we entirely lose ourselves in our belief in the holy.

Take care, therefore, not to involve yourselves in any intellectual theodicy (as this type of reflection has very naively been called).

Earlier philosophers, it is true, tried to show that evil was the necessary condition of the possibility of the emergence of goodness, and that it could not be otherwise in the created world. But what is the force of this argument when it is confronted with the idea of an almighty Creator? Before the Omnipotent, everything which fails to correspond to the perfectly good, can and ought to be otherwise. These teachings of Leibniz, and all related teachings, are the mere product of confusing human knowledge with eternal truth: the contradictions of knowledge and the laws of nature are taken to be eternally true, and even the Almighty is subjected to the Fate of the laws of nature.

The situation is even worse with the teaching of those who wish to assert of appearances that evil is not to be taken so seriously, that in appearances everything is good in its own fashion. This teaching wholly misunderstands the nature of moral judgement.

No! The energetic and sound understanding is more excellent than barbarity, error and stupidity. Friendship is noble, conflict is base. Peacefulness and loyalty are absolutely good. Arrogance and treachery are absolutely bad. Only in these moral convictions does the consciousness of man establish connection with the eternal truth. The person who cancels these moral oppositions destroys the whole higher significance of human life. And only someone who is ignorant of the limits of human knowledge could wish to equate the eternally true with appearances.

That which is eternally true, divine and holy cannot be rationally explored by us. And no matter under what image we may worship God, every image will display the powerlessness of our spirit to grasp his holy being. The relations of the eternal are only wholly clear to us in the ideas of virtue and justice. We can only understand the eternal order of things in our knowledge of how people ought to behave towards each other. For that reason the only worthy worship of God consists in our striving, in humble acknowledgement of our own weakness, to practise virtue and to work for the spread of holy justice. Apart from the morality of our actions, all worship of God is merely the feeling of devotion in prayer and pure love. We are also aware of the dominion of the holy spirit in the sublimity with which the magnitude of nature addresses us. The imperishable beauty of the life which is constantly being generated anew in a thousand diverse forms, affords an intuitive awareness of the creative Love, whose hand rules our fate, too, and to whom we loyally and humbly submit.

DIALOGUE XII

Intuitive Awareness

Adelheid: Why is it, dear Philanthes, that our friends so readily incline to the views of your father, while almost everybody adopts Clarissa's side in his dispute with her about our belief in Providence, indeed, accusing her of having surrendered too early.

Philanthes: I should have thought the answer was this: everybody is interested in this belief in God's providential concern for us, and, as a result, everybody thinks that his own opinion is the correct one. And do not forget, my father did discuss the matter in a provocative and polemical fashion.

You remember, I suppose, how indulgently my father judged any superstitious belief which contained sincere and honest piety, and did not serve corrupt self-interest. Only when he was dealing with an intellectually educated person or with some judgement which laid pretentious claim to be scientific in character, did he oppose superstition with bitterness. It was his opinion that under such circumstances we ought to see clearly, and that all mystery-mongering was dishonest and fraudulent. Let us, therefore, in this dispute ignore corrupt superstition. You will then certainly be mistaken if you do not find that Clarissa is ultimately in agreement with my father. What else is belief in Providence than the confidence that, no matter what may happen to us in this earthly existence, we are under the protection of the Love Eternal. Now, tell me yourself: is the confidence of this faith in eternal truth to be accepted as valid? Or do you wish to subject the dispensations of Divine Love to the sophistry of men, with a view to either praising or blaming them?

Adelheid: We do not pray for God's sake, but for our own. It is not our intention to tell Providence what ought to happen. We say: not my will but thine be done. We only make our requests in our belief in eternal truth, modestly and humbly acknowledging that we do not always know what is good for us.

Philanthes: Let us see if we are not in agreement. Every prayer, even for temporal assistance, belongs to the pious heart alone. All boastfulness about divine assistance is here alien to the true opinion of the heart. Here, the wish of each one of us is simply that of daily keeping the feeling alive that the sacred hand of Eternal Love rules over us.

Whether the individual, like Alcibiades on the advice of Socrates, withdraws from the temple, not presuming to pray for the fulfilment of temporal wishes, or whether he happily presents every petty care to the divine Friend of his heart — this is simply a difference of temperament, the one more serene, the other more anxious.

You remember how our friend replied to us: "Am I no longer to pray for you?" — And our reply was: "But no, dear friend, continue to pray for us! Not on account of the granting of the prayer, for that lies in God's hand anyway, but for our own sake." Certainly, the best friendship is the friendship which an honest mind is happy to recall, even before God himself.

Otto: On this issue, I no longer have any scruples. Obviously, the feelings of religion and of submission to God have no firm foundation unless, in belief in Eternal Love, we can rise above all the vicissitudes of good fortune and adversity in this earthly existence. And on this ruling thought we are all agreed.

Adelheid: I can see that I am faring even worse than Clarissa, who did succeed in defending herself for a good while. I have nothing to object to what you say, for you are letting us have our own way.

Philanthes: The naive belief in higher beings who have, according to the nature of their desires, chosen this or that in nature and given form to it, is an almost inevitable and natural presupposition of the human spirit when the understanding is less developed. Man compares the strenuous efforts he has to make to secure his own comforts with the magnitude and artifice of nature. How much more energy must it not require to construct a mountain than to build a house, to lay rivers than to dig a well, not to mention all the beauty of the forests teeming with animals and richly plumed birds, and rich with flowers and delightful fruits. — Without wasting all too much time on finding a justification for such a view, man, with nimble imagination, invents for himself dryads and nymphs who live in the forest as he lives in his house, who lay out this thing as he lays out his garden, and who make this other thing as he makes his clothes, his bow and arrow. And his garden he populates with crowds of elves and gnomes. He thinks that his holy spirits have chosen this area, or that, around their shrine or sacred tree as their favourite haunt. He probably chooses his own protecting spirit from among the higher spirits himself. And when his poetic creation is complete, he then happily believes in the poor contrivance of his own imagination, believes in the gods he has himself created.

Adelheid: Do you hear that, Theone? What about it? Are you going to allow your protective spirit to be destroyed like that?

Theone: Do not be afraid of father! He always does all the talking, and we give in. And afterwards everything goes on as before. But this time, I am going to stand firm. You are not going to steal away my guardian angel, are you, father?

Philanthes: That would be rash of me. After all, you assured me that he likes me very much as well. I must, I suppose, give him my backing. But take care that he does not abandon you, one day.

Theone: Father, that is something which you do not understand. He abandon me? That would be impossible. My only care is that I should be loyal to him. That is what counts — that he does not find himself forced to turn away from me in sadness.

Philanthes: My child, do not confuse me. I was talking about certain uneducated people who invent their gods for themselves and then, consoled by their invention, proceed to believe in the images of their own imaginations. Frequently, all goes well for a long time. Whole nations lead tranquil lives, dreaming the same dream.

But when the understanding begins to develop and a freer reflection awakens, it tries to impose unity and completeness on this belief, as it does on every belief with which it is familiar. It forms the idea of a totality of nature, and attempts to construe this totality as the work of an omnipotent formative understanding, which executes it like a work of art. But, with the awakening of reflection, understanding looses the innocence of its first poetic creation, while not yet having made the acquaintance of truth, the sure-footed guide. Its efforts are frustrated as a result of the blunder of taking over from those childish poetic inventions the idea of an artistic wisdom ruling throughout nature, without first examining whether it is even possible for human concepts to be acquainted with such a being.

If it eventually institutes such an examination, it finds that it can only think the purpose of the universe in the eternal ideas of faith, and in the moral order of things. On the other hand, it comes to recognise that, if it is to acknowledge the existence of purposes in nature, it will be constrained, so to speak, to return to those poetic inventions, which it will no longer, of course, take for conceptual truth.

Theone: That is very agreeable to us. Mother and I would like to linger over these poetic visions. We do not want instruction and understanding. Continue your argument with your learned companions, who do not understand the matter as well as you.

Philanthes: Very well. I shall not disturb you with learning. But how do matters stand with your taste?

Theone: With our taste? I have heard that there is no disputing about taste.

Philanthes: Yes, that is what the ladies like to hear. Nor do I have any intention of quarrelling with your taste. But you must be prepared to tolerate rivalry to it. Suppose that you were lovingly absorbed in the contemplation of something, and a friend were to exclaim to you: "Look at this, for a moment. I should like to show you something even greater, something even more impressive, even more beautiful!" Would you then stubbornly avert your gaze from her, and not even make the trial?

Theone: Oh, no! I should happily do her the favour, and then decide according to my taste.

Philanthes: More than that I do not ask of you. We must, therefore, first establish ourselves firmly on the foundation of taste, and keep all false learning from ourselves.

I recently showed Otto that we were constrained to judge the order of nature in terms of concepts of purposes, at any rate where nature corresponds to the needs of the human spirit in a fashion which is not further explicable to us. I pointed out to him that, from this starting point, our judgement is also led to the entire order of nature and to all the dispensations of history, but that, notwithstanding, we can never succeed in investing this view with the character of real knowledge. The purposefulness of the phenomena of nature only has its existence for us in aesthetic ideas. True feeling, which is produced by the pious contemplation of nature alone, only exists in the admiration of the beauty and sublimity of the phenomena of nature.

Of course, where all the forces of nature operate together in great complexity there will emerge effects of a character more complex than could be produced by the artifice of man. The whole wisdom of the grotesque claim to understand nature's art reduces to the innocuous remark that a will, to which the whole of nature was subject, would be able to achieve a great deal more than the will of man — or it consists in the naive amusement of imagining all that Omnipotence can do and Omniscience know.

There are people who oppose to this glorification of the wisdom and goodness of God the transitory and destructive features of nature and history. They point out that Providence either manifestly operates against all the purposes which we attribute to it, even the progress and advancement of the human spirit itself, or unconcernedly ignores them, without exploiting the advantage. They argue that Providence, with feckless indifference, destroys its supposedly most successful achievements, often before they can even have an effect. There are also those who allow themselves to be annoyed by this way of arguing. But the source of the annoyance or indignation is not so much the menace that God's wisdom will be converted into foolishness, as the threat that their own wisdom will be reduced to stupidity. Who gave us the task of cannily excogitating the plans of God in his governance of the universe? The only reward we can expect from our efforts must be the eventual recognition of our own short-sightedness! Let us take care that the pride and presumption of our own wisdom does not lead us astray into anger — an anger which we shall subsequently and ridiculously ascribe to the eagerness of our commitment to the cause of God! What makes us think that God needs *our* help?

So, once more: all understanding and comprehension must be set aside if we wish to recognise the kingdom of ends, the world of the good and the beautiful in the appearances of nature, and, in addition, the moral life of man in this earthly existence. This eternal truth only exists for us in the feelings of intuitive awareness in the religious-aesthetic judgement of the beautiful and the sublime.

Otto: We believe in the eternal truth of a world of the good and beautiful. I now see that we are unable to apprehend the harmony of the appearances of nature with this belief, using our concepts of the good. If we are to judge something as good, we must already possess the concepts of a purpose, for which the thing in question is suited, or to which the thing in itself should correspond. But we can only apply this to the finite knowledge of human strivings. We are not told of such purposes for the world. In the ideal of the eternal or supreme good we simply imagine, with respect to eternal truth, the cancelling of the limits of the limited good, which makes its appearance in human life. We are not, however, able to set up the positive idea of the eternal good opposite the limited idea. On the other hand, the situation is quite different in the case of the acknowledgement of beauty and sublimity by feeling. Feeling invests what is contemplated with a value and a meaningfulness in itself. To be recognised, this value needs no comparisons from other sources, and least of all does it need a purpose to be given, with which the object in question is required to harmonise.

The intuitive awareness of the eternal truth of the good and the beautiful thus has its existence for us in the feelings of the beautiful and the sublime. And here I was primarily thinking of natural beauty, not of beauty in art. But you go further than this, and attribute the acknowledgement of purposefulness in nature even to the voluntary play of poetic invention. What do you mean by this claim?

Philanthes: Think first of what my father said about the truth of beauty. You will easily recall what he said.

Otto: Certainly. In the ideas of beauty there exists for us, apart from the conceptual view of things, another, higher, transfigured view of the world, which has a wholly individual right of its own to eternal truth. This truth we recognise in enthusiasm, submission to God and devotion. When the affairs of man are to be ordered in accordance with concepts, the understanding soberly speaks its own language with nature and receives nature's answer in return. But feeling and taste listen in silence to nature's own living language, the language of the gods, the language with which the unfolding of every flower in the light, and all the splendour of the beauty of nature perceptibly speaks to us.

Philanthes: And does not all serious poetic invention enter into this higher truth? Is not every serious poetic invention thereby religious in character? In every poetic invention there is, of course, an arbitrary adoption of images; but this is not intended merely to entertain. It bears within itself the sacred seriousness of beauty.

Otto: That is clear to me, of course. But there seems to be more than this in what you are saying. The way in which you require poetic invention for the acknowledgement of purposefulness in nature is such that it not only seems to contain a memory of living beauty in nature; the images of poetic invention themselves acquire, so to speak, a share in the eternal truth. The person who lives in such poetic invention also believes, as it were, in its images, ranging from Theone's protecting spirit to all the saints, heroes and gods.

Philanthes: Behold! You have now put your finger on the whole mystery of intuitive awareness. No religious view of man will be able to escape from the metaphorical, figurative character of poetic invention.

Otto: And why not?

Philanthes: I recently showed you that, with respect to the finite knowledge of appearances, we have only one mode of conviction: the explanation of the connection of appearances according to the laws of nature. But, with respect to the acknowledgement of eternal truth, we have to combine two modes of conviction: faith and intuitive awareness. Our faith in the fundamental ideas of eternal truth we express in the infinite concepts of the ideas of faith. But no concept is capable of subsuming appearances under these ideas. The recognition of eternal truth in appearances exists only in aesthetic judgements, which belong to feeling alone. Let us examine the meaning of this claim more closely.

Intuitive awareness, I maintain, is always the recognition of *religious mysteries*. Since the mode of knowledge of intuitive awareness only exists through feeling without concepts, we can say that it has this distinctive feature: what we know in intuitive awareness is always a mystery for us.

Adelheid: Something which I know but which is always a mystery? — That sounds strange to me!

Philanthes: But why? If I can speak of a mystery at all, I must have noticed that there is a mystery. There are many laws of nature which are still impenetrable to us. We understand little about the earth's organic structures. There are, accordingly effects in nature which are still mysteries to us. We notice the effect but we do not yet understand the cause in accordance with which it was produced. We can thus see that there is a mystery for us here. However, the mysteries of eternal truth have another feature as well.

Adelheid: That is my impression, as well! Explain the matter more clearly to us.

Philanthes: Every mystery in nature contains something which is only in degree and for the present inaccessible to the understanding. Explanations and elucidations have hitherto not been discovered by us, for we have not yet observed nature long enough or with sufficient exactness. But when, one day, we are able to pursue these observations, and to carry them far enough, there will be no mystery left in our knowledge of the laws of nature. The capacity of our mind is thus, in this connection, always adequate to a clear knowledge of nature. All that we have hitherto lacked has been the appropriate degree of education to explain everything.

In matters of intuitive awareness, however, we are not merely too weak in degree. The very nature of the human mind is so constituted that the solution of these mysteries is impossible for it. Man's faculty of intuition is sensible, and we are incapable of arriving at any immediately clear knowledge of the eternal, so long as our own spirit continues to be imprisoned by the shackles of its own nature, and thus remains unchanged. Eternal ideas are only clear to the cultivated *thinking* person. With respect to the real representation of eternal being, the human mind is limited to the intuitive awareness of the eternal in the finite. That is to say, it is limited to a feeling which is neither intuition nor capable of analysis into specific concepts.

The development of our knowledge can only either increase the amount we know or clarify our belief in the eternal. But if our knowledge wished to penetrate to an immediate knowledge of the eternal, it would not only have to perfect itself in degree, it would also have to break through the limits of its own being. There are of necessity, therefore, for intuitive awareness, impenetrable mysteries in the relation of the finite to the eternal — a relation which can only be thought, so to speak, in unanalysable concepts as the fundamental ideas of the beautiful and the sublime.

These religious mysteries are, therefore, necessarily mysteries for the human mind, not mysteries on the analogy with secrets. If someone invented something or discovered something in physics, he could keep it a secret for himself and his friends, and conceal it from everybody else. In this way, he could form a society of initiates for his secret. Religious mysteries, however, cannot be established in this fashion. Religous mysteries are not the kind of mystery which, while remaining concealed from the common people, could be revealed to chosen initiates. Religious mysteries are equally impenetrable to everybody. If a philosophical priest were to initiate his pupils into the mysteries of his secret teaching and opened their inner eye to its truth, they would either both of them, or at least the disciples, be deceived. The metaphysical opening of people's eyes is nothing but delusion. And, indeed, all the riddles of a religious secret teaching merely consist in the interpretation of metaphorical language, of religious poetic inventions, the images of which are customarily shown to the people, without their interpretation being given.

Man's religious teaching will always contain such poetic inventions because the expression of faith forcibly drives us in that direction. We must now subject this claim to closer scrutiny.

As soon as, in faith, we go beyond the universal ideas of the perfect, the unlimited and the unconditioned, we have to employ finite representations in order to think the eternal. Our mode of knowledge of necessity becomes metaphorical, and its value is soon only figurative. As soon as we seek to give a more detailed expression to our belief, we are constrained to think everything in merely human fashion by imagining unconditioned reason on the analogy with human reason. Our language must, therefore, make use of metaphor. But every metaphorical representation, not being the thing itself, can only to a certain extent be compared with the thing itself. Every equation of the image and the thing, which goes beyond this limit, must consequently fall into contradiction. Every representation of the eternal by means of images derived from the sphere of the finite must be incomplete, for the idea stands in contradiction to finite concepts.

Hence, as soon as we fail to recognise the metaphorical character of the representation in these expressions of faith, we inevitably become involved in irresoluble contradictions.

The dependent character of the world of appearances, with its insubstantial laws, and the contingent coincidence of the entities within it, drives us to belief in God, the Creator and Legislator of the universe. But, as far as we know, there can be nothing above the necessary law and its destiny. No entity can come into being, and everything which is produced arises in accordance with and under laws. Our knowledge so contradicts this faith that we cannot conceive the eternal truth of faith with human concepts. On the contrary, we can only pursue the ideas of faith by means of positive poetic invention.

Furthermore, this belief in the divine origin of all things is the belief in the holy origin of the universe. Our belief in the eternity of our nature and the freedom of our will is associated with the belief in the best universe and the ideal of the good and the beautiful. But what, then, is the sacred, and what is this ideal of the good and the beautiful? We cannot conceive it. This idea, as the fundamental idea of all devotion, all reverence and veneration, exists within us veiled in sacred darkness.

Eternity elevates us, in faith, above time and space. Freedom elevates us above the necessity of the laws of nature. But even this idea of elevation above space, time and nature is inconceivable for us.

Consciousness of freedom enables man to recognise within himself an original propensity to evil. But confidence in the Love Eternal at the same time awakens belief in the purifying of our will and the creation of its purity and sanctity.

None of these ideas are conceivable to the finite spirit. Consciousness of the evil within ourselves seems to us to stand in irresoluble contradiction with the ideal of the good and the beautiful. We can only pursue this idea of eternal hope with images which are temporal in character and derived from natural change.

Intuitive awareness will thus present itself in poetic creations, and holy truth will live for man in these poetic inventions. The best and the most beautiful positive religion will, therefore, be the religion which, by means of poetic creations of the greatest purity, sublimity and beauty, awakens the feelings of holy truth in the purest and most powerful fashion.

My dear Otto, take care to understand this last idea correctly. It will make clear to you the great power which the beautiful or the aesthetic view of the world has over human convictions.

In leaving the first ideal expression of the doctrine of faith, which is determined by the ideas of the perfect, our thought passes to intuitive awareness. It abandons all conceptual truth, displaying the eternal in merely temporal images. It bears within itself the truth of beauty alone, which is the stimulus of religious poetic creation.

Otto: I am now clear about the matter. The truths of faith awaken within us inexpressible concepts as the guiding ideas of intuitive awareness. But under these ideas, intuitive awareness is only able to give a poetically metaphorical expression to eternal truth. The reason is that, affirmatively, we can only put a temporal image at the side of the infinite concept contained in the idea of faith.

We believe in God's holy omnipotence, the ground of the existence of all things. But we can only conceive our relation to God by assuming that he is the Legislator of the world of the good and the beautiful. Here, the concepts of law and legislation are finite concepts. Man's poetic invention is merely led to a simile in which, employing the image of a human state, we venerate God as the Ruler and Legislator of his eternal kingdom, and desire to be the loyal subjects of his Eternal Love. We could just as well think of the world as the garden of God, in which he protects and cherishes us as his flowers.

You mentioned earlier how, in the ideas of immortality and freedom, we raised ourselves above the laws of nature, space and time, and how we were only able to retain a firm grasp on this belief by means of the temporal images of the future. This emerges most clearly here. The most important article of faith is that of the eternal creation of the purity of our will. We can only call this belief an expectation, a hope. But expectation and hope refer to the future and yield a temporal image. Let us not, therefore, portray our falling away from the holy, followed by our cleansing and purification. Let us not portray our yearning to return to our eternal home, our longing for the re-union of love and friendship. The simplest expression of eternal hope is a temporal image.

Philanthes: You see that there is no doctrine of faith, which can be treated as knowledge, beyond the pure expression, by means of which the ideas of the absolute, of the truths of faith relating to the holiness of God, the eternal destiny of man, and the creation of the purity of our will. Under the command of these ideas, it is the feeling of beauty which alone causes our thought to unfold. The poetic creations of the feeling of beauty ought to be judged, without any appeal to theoretical concepts, by taste alone.

DIALOGUE XIII

Beauty

Philanthes: Tell me, Theone, whom do you deem happy?
Theone: Ah! I have learnt the answer to that question. It is, Aristotle says, really and truly the person to whom God grants a long life filled with virtuous deeds. — If, however, you are asking how someone judges himself in himself, then it is the man who is contented with himself.
Philanthes: Now, to take your "really and truly" first of all. Aristotle has more to say. He tells us that of the virtuous the happiest are the learned, those who spend their lives in the pursuit of truth. They alone spend their lives in a pleasure which could even be ascribed to the gods themselves.
Theone: Listen, father. I do not understand that claim. And even if I did, I should not like it.
Philanthes: Well, Aristotle was a highly learned man, and perhaps for that reason a life devoted to the pursuit of truth may have pleased him. Your view is different. You will have to make a choice. One man cannot unite in his life the wealth of all virtue. Which virtue is the most important for you. Aristotle says that it is the search for truth. The man who is thirsty for power will say: my supreme pleasure is the nation, thankful at my feet! The person in love, on the other hand, will say: eighty years of a love-filled life: for the child — parental love; for the youth and the man of maturity — the love of women and the love of his bride, followed by that of his children; and for the old man — the supreme form of love: love for one's own grandchildren. — At this point, Theone broke out into violent tears and threw herself round the old man's neck with the words: "Oh, grandfather! Would that father were still with us!"
Philanthes: Gently, gently, my Theone, we want to talk quietly. . . .
I was saying that the lover of truth, the ruler and the lover, each has his own idea of what the supreme virtue is. — Crates used to be in the habit of saying that the supreme pleasure would be, not merely doing good to one's bitterest enemy, but being able to save him and his

family in such a way that they were unaware of their benefactor's sacrifice on their behalf and did not feel humiliated by his generosity, or put at his mercy.

Theone: I shall support Crates. So — love and not hate, peace and not conflict!

Philanthes: You are evading me, and you know it. No one ought to hate anybody. Do we not tell our children: we are all of us the children of God, even the most wicked of criminals? Nor shall we preach to the evil doer: be afraid! — but rather: be ashamed! God, in punishing us, will harm no one. What is important is that a man should count for something in himself. Here we have hate side by side with love! You ought to hate injustice, treachery and brutality. What you ought, therefore, to hate, is not people but types of character, views of life and modes of action.

Theone: I know that, but the matter is now becoming clearer to me. The virtuous life assumes many forms, and people should allow these many forms to blossom side by side in God's earthly garden. But they all draw their light and warmth from the sun of the Holy One alone!

Philanthes: Listen to me further. How does this strike you? Man must choose his virtue, and he will come to possess the virtue in which he takes the greatest pleasure. Does not a person's virtue correspond to his desire, his pleasure? It is not the most virtuous life, but the pleasantest life, the life which is richest in pleasure, which makes the happiest man. And we celebrate the virtue of the man striving after pleasure according to his taste, only because it affords the surest and the purest pleasure.

Theone: I do not like the sound of that! But explain the matter more clearly to me.

Philanthes: Well, that is how the matter seems to stand when our question relates to happiness really and truly. But what is the situation when we make individual opinion judge of the matter? You say: self-contentment affords happiness to the man of education. But what brings self-contentment?

With the expression "self-contentment" you are distinguishing, are you not, between a person's contentment with his own inner life and the deeds which issue from his character, and a person's contentment with his external situation, his civil prosperity, his domestic happiness, his outward social distinction, his health or sickness.

Theone: Certainly! You have instructed me thus.

Philanthes: But I do not see what is supposed to depend upon this distinction?

Theone: What do you think? What I thought was this: for the educated man, the contentment of a quiet conscience and the pure love within him is much more important than the contentment of outward fortune. It is self-contentment alone which decides the happiness of his life.

Philanthes: That may be so. But what counts here is simply a man's own judgement about himself and his own situation. Am I not right?

Theone: Certainly!

Philanthes: Then take care. Who, do you suppose, decides this? What is it that makes a person most easily *content* in general, both with himself, and with the world? Obviously his happy disposition, his temperament — in other words, a good digestion, an easy circulation of the blood, light nourishment, the love of exercise — and whatever else the physicians may prescribe.

Theone: Ah! That answer pleases me least of all!

Philanthes: Can you deny that it is as I have said?

Theone: Explain it to me!

Philanthes: No one is more readily content than the man of joyful light-heartedness, who takes everything lightly and puts the best construction on whatever happens: at the greatest misfortune he promptly finds that things could have been a great deal worse, and that the tolerable nature of what did happen was the result of his own prudence alone.

The morbid thoughtfulness of the melancholic man is, by contrast, the true source of all discontent. Or, to express the matter more precisely: there are as many ways of being happy as there are temperaments.

Easy joyfulness is the happiness of a healthy light-heartedness. Sensibility is far from finding that interesting: for it, it is insufficiently mordant. All that really deeply pleases it is sighing melancholy and tearful yearning. Delight in the feeling of unhappiness, delight in discontent itself, is what occupies the melancholic person. The distinctive joy of the impatient character is the easily achieved deed. The joy of the man of cold disposition is proud self-confidence.

Is it not true that every temperament has its own justice and its own truth?

Theone: Perhaps!

Philanthes: But even with all this, we have not yet got the most colourful picture of all. Behind these moods, some purpose, such as the good, will present itself to joyfulness, to yearning, to the feeling of unhappiness, to the impetuous or the reflective deed. And it is with the achievement of that purpose that the contented man really flatters himself.

Let me pursue my questions further. In what do people find the purpose of life. In the replies to this question you will find a true medley of truth and unstable opinion. Here, everything depends upon the views about life which are contained in feeling, and they are the play of mood *par excellence*!

The enthusiasts know how to praise the sublimity of moral ideals, how to commend the effort expended on acquiring and spreading the truth, how to praise the struggle for the victory of justice — but there are many, indeed, who hate, or despise, or mock them for it, dismissing their enthusiasm as pitiful or pernicious fanaticism. Most people adhere to the idyllic view of life, as its flowering and charm is to be found among the shepherds of Theocritus, Virgil, Florian and Gessner. A comfortable people which loves peace and serenity, and, in particular, esteems the tenderness of love, accusing the enthusiasts of even criminal sentiments, in that they culpably interfere with God's governance of the universe. And are they not, in part, right? How little can man call himself master of the results of his undertakings when he makes grandiose efforts to advance the cause of truth and justice. The battle is certain, but the victory is unsure!

There are yet others, the laughers and the mockers, for whom the right of the strong is an acceptable principle, and for whom the purpose of life is a successful day. For them the devotees of the idyllic life, the people who are comfortably tender, are weakly fanatics, while the enthusiasts are for them vain fools. But it is the latter — the fools with caps of bells — who can most easily cope with life, for any human motive can be laughed at, and the more seriously it is pursued, the more easily it can be ridiculed.

Theone: Stop, father! I know how you have snared me!
Philanthes: Well, my dear?
Theone: You have caught me in the trap of happiness. Who told me to get involved in your enquiry about the happiest man? No man is the happiest. Pleasure and happiness have almost no reliable criterion. If we seek to evaluate human life according to the criterion of pleasure, virtue will end up below even eating and drinking. The man whose whim is to seek his pleasure in the lowest things can mock even what is noblest.
Philanthes: Right! But how do you go on?
Theone: I have it! I was wrong to contradict Otto in wanting to decide everything according to the single criterion of a moral necessity in life.

The hand of God brings peace and strife, the hand of God introduces war. And it does so to enable friend to sacrifice himself for friend, to enable life to unfold all the magnificent forms of its beauty, does so that man, in the high memories of his eternal home, should learn to rise above all the vicissitudes of fortune.

Only the pure, free beauty of the life of the spirit in all its multifarious forms is of inward importance in itself, the pure free beauty as it blossoms in friendship, truth, loveliness and justice, as it flowers in tenderness and in strength of soul, in submission and devotion, in the woman's love of peace and the man's virtue of strength — Otto is right!

Philanthes: Theone, the generous spirited victor, returns to the vanquished his shield and spear! Otto — bend the knee and receive the generous spirited gift.

Theone: No! We are not that far advanced yet. Otto must first promise that he will valorously support me and not desert me again if I should, for example, have to survive another argument with you.

Otto: Since the umpire of the battle has himself declared me the loser, I must, I suppose, devote myself to your service. But before doing so, I should first like to know what new battle you have in mind.

Theone replied: "At the moment none at all." And then, addressing herself to her grandfather and mother, she continued: "The wind has dropped, the evening is so calm. Let us go for a walk in the open air." They all agreed. Jesting with the children they went up a green valley, through a beechwood and over a hill, on the other side of which they came to a green spot over which three ancient oaks spread a canopy of foliage.

Here they sat down to rest. The glade afforded them an unimpeded view westwards across the sea where the sun was declining to its rest. The waves of the sea below them beat foaming against the rocks. The wind had dropped and out at sea the waves advanced in an extended line, playing with the blue of the sky and the serene light of the evening. On their right, the view was blocked by a lofty promontory, which jutted boldly into the sea. On their left, a verdant shore extended towards the harbour and the town. The view was framed with wooded hills, and, at a greater distance, by higher mountains, which circled the sea in the blue distance. Ships and boats, with gleaming sails and coloured pennants, hastened harbourwards.

When they had settled down in this spot, Philanthes said: "Is it not true that, in the splendour before us, one becomes aware that religion and the sense of beauty are animated by a single spirit?"

BEAUTY 225

Theone thoughtfully responded: "Yes, that is certainly true here. But, surely, religious feeling and the sense of beauty are not absolutely one, are they? But today I have an ally. From him I may venture to ask for more detailed instruction on this matter."

Otto: Permit me to launch the attack. As recently as this evening, Philanthes, you led Theone to the truth, which we have so often expressed, that virtue is beauty of soul. Now, if that is the case, then it follows that, at least for the evaluation of the spiritual life of man, moral feeling and the sense of beauty must be one and the same. But the good and the beautiful are not the same. And now religious feeling and the sense of beauty are supposed to be the same as well. But what, in all the world, is pious about finding a bunch of flowers beautiful, or about judging the beauty of a human form?

Philanthes: Why so modest? Go even further. I can call any well-formed body beautiful. What is there pious about praising a beautiful knife-handle, a beautiful needle-box, a beautiful fruit-basket?

Otto: All right, then. That is even better. You also recently maintained that every judgement of beauty was, so to speak, based upon an inexpressible concept. Now, I do not at all find that confirmed in the case of judgements about the beauty of human forms, or about any proportioned beauty. I should have thought that in these cases handsomeness and symmetry would be determined by very clear and easily expressed concepts.

Suppose now, finally, that you were right. Moral feeling, the sense of beauty and religious feeling would then be one and the same. Goodness, beauty and piety would depend upon one and the same aesthetic judgement of things. Now, what is the position?

Philanthes: Dear Otto, you do not seem to have a very good conscience today, for you suddenly press me with this veritable storm of objections. Could it, perhaps, be that you only trust your reasons *en bloc* because, individually, they are too weak? . . . But first I must introduce some order into your crowd of attacks. Let us, accordingly, first compare the sense of beauty with religious feeling, and then with moral feeling, and let us then, finally, see how they are related to the aesthetic judgement of things.

Otto: We shall allow you that. First show us, therefore, how the sense of beauty is the same as piety.

Philanthes: You two can help each other, so I shall seek outside help as well. In Wilhelm Meister's diary the nameless one has this to say: "In beauty the divine speaks in an image. In beauty the divine has arrayed itself like the human spirit, and assumed form as the thought takes on the form of a word. Those who are thoughtful perceive the eternal in beauty and venerate it, like religion in human form."

Our old friend Kant says:

Now I willingly admit that the interest in the *beautiful of art* . . . gives no evidence at all of a habit of mind attached to the morally good, or even inclined that way. But, on the other hand, I do maintain that to take an *immediate interest* in the beauty of *nature* (not merely to have taste in estimating it) is always the mark of a good soul; and that, where this interest is habitual, it is at least indicative of a temper of mind favourable to the moral feeling that it should readily associate itself with the *contemplation of nature*. It must, however, be borne in mind that I mean to refer strictly to the beautiful *forms* of nature, and to put to one side the *charms* which she is wont so lavishly to combine with them; because, though the interest in these is no doubt immediate, it is nevertheless empirical.

One who alone regards the beautiful form of a wild flower, a bird, an insect, or the like, out of admiration and love of them, and being loath to let them escape him in nature, takes an immediate, and in fact intellectual, interest in the beauty of nature. This means that he is not alone pleased with nature's product in respect of its form, but is also pleased at its existence, and is so without any charm of sense having a share in the matter, or without his associating with it any end whatsoever.

In this connection, however, it is of note that were we to play a trick on our lover of the beautiful, and plant in the ground artificial flowers and perch artfully carved birds on the branches of trees, and he were to find out how he had been taken in, the immediate interest which these things previously had for him would at once vanish — though, perhaps, a different interest might intervene in its stead, that, namely, of vanity in decorating his room with them for the eyes of others. The fact is that our intuition and reflection must have as their concomitant the thought that the beauty in question is nature's handiwork; and this is the sole basis of the immediate interest that is taken in it. Failing this we are either left with a bare judgement of taste void of all interest whatever, or else only with one that is combined with an interest that is mediate, involving, namely, a reference to society: which latter affords no reliable indication of morally good habits of thought.

The superiority which natural beauty has over that of art, even where it is excelled by the latter in point of form, in yet being alone able to awaken an immediate interest, accords with the refined and well-grounded habits of thought of all men who have cultivated their moral feeling. If a man with taste enough to judge works of fine art with the greatest correctness and refinement readily quits the room in which he meets with those beauties that minister to vanity or, at least, social joys, and betakes himself to the beautiful in nature, so that he may there find as it were a feast for his soul in a train of thought which he can never completely evolve, we will then regard this his choice even with veneration, and give him credit for a beautiful soul, to which no connoisseur or art collector can lay claim on the score of the interest which his objects have for him. — Here, now, are two kinds of objects which in the judgement of mere taste could scarcely contend with one another for a superiority. What then, is the distinction that makes us hold them in such different esteem?

But, now, reason is further interested in ideas (for which in our moral feeling it brings about an immediate interest) having also objective reality. That is to say, it is of interest to reason that nature should at least show a trace or give a hint that it contains in itself some ground or other for assuming a uniform accordance of its products with our wholly disinterested delight. That being so, reason must take an interest in every manifestation on the part of nature of some such accordance. Hence the mind cannot reflect on the beauty of *nature* without at the same time finding its interest engaged. But this interest is akin to the moral. One, then, who takes such an interest in the beautiful in nature can only do so in so far as he has previously set his interest deep in the foundation of the morally good.

It will be said that this interpretation of aesthetic judgements on the basis of kinship with our moral feeling has far too studied an appearance to be accepted as the true construction of the cypher in which nature speaks to us figuratively in its beautiful forms. But, first of all, this immediate interest in the beauty of nature is not in fact common. It is peculiar to those whose habits of thought are already trained to the good or else are eminently susceptible of such training; under these circumstances the analogy in which the pure judgement of taste that, without relying upon any interest, gives us a feeling of delight, and at the same time, represents it as proper to mankind in general, stands to the moral judgement that does just the same from concepts, is one which, without any clear, subtle, and deliberate reflection, conduces to a like immediate interest being taken in the objects of the former judgement as in those of the latter — with this one difference, that the interest in the first case is free, while in the latter it is one founded on objective laws.

What do you think, Otto? The old man is always right, is he not? How excellently he proves with his immediate interest in natural beauty the connection of religious feeling with the judgement of taste in the feeling of beauty, and its relatedness to the moral feeling!

Otto: I have the task of opposition today. Permit me, therefore, with all my respect for the old Kant, to raise an objection against him. I am well aware that the religious feeling is most clearly and purely present, so to speak, in the sense of beauty in the case of the simple recognition of natural beauty. But is not Kant mistaken in respect of art when he limits its interest to vanity and social entertainment? Life does not agree with this view. Can we not awaken religious feeling, in a fashion which moves the spirit more powerfully, by means of artistically beautiful ideas, than is possible through natural beauty? It seems to me that architecture, music and historical painting are cases in point.

Philanthes: I agree with you. But you are not really contradicting what Kant says at all. Kant is speaking of the immediate interest in the naturally beautiful, and I add that this is the religious feeling.

Now, you will concede that religious feeling is the immediate acknowledgement of faith in life?

Otto: Certainly!

Philanthes: But in that case it only exists in the many emotions of piety in the inner life of the mind. Devotion and the peace of piety belong to one's own inner life. Their animation by natural sublimity and art will only ever permit the beautiful and the sublime to operate figuratively or in some other symbolic fashion. Such is the case with the sublime impression of architecture and the deeply penetrating power of music on the emotions. It is only in the emotions of enthusiasm that the thought goes beyond one's own moral life to the life of man in general, and to the contemplation of the whole of nature.

This is the location of what Kant calls immediate interest in the beautiful of nature. It is here that intuitive awareness will recognise the eternal truth of the world of the good and the beautiful in natural phenomena as well. This can only occur in so far as we recognise the beautiful as the reflection of the eternally true in nature itself and therefore have an intuitive awareness of the formative spirit of the whole in the beautiful forms of nature. This interest essentially belongs to the naturally beautiful, and in art it can only be borrowed, indirectly, from this source.

Accordingly, as long as art is concerned only to capture and imitate common beauty in form and play, this interest is not to be found in it, for the creative and formative spirit is absent from it. But the higher, ideal, spiritual beauty in the energy, life and purity of the beautiful soul is our own achievement in the moral life. In artistic presentation what interests us is the possibility of given form. Free delight in that form unites with religious interest.

Finally, with respect to the sublime, this distinction occurs less frequently. The sublime is immediately closer to the idea, and in the sublime of art we always contemplate, so to speak, something sublime from nature as well. For this reason, every sublime representation, particularly if it is combined with beauty, is receptive to and worthy of religious interest. It can even be said that every representation of natural beauty, in so far as it interests in a religious fashion, is connected with a representation of the sublime of nature.

Otto: In this I now fully understand you.
Philanthes: But so far I have only dealt with your objection. I repeated Kant's observation to you, however, in order to show you the union of taste and religious feeling in the sense of beauty. Is it not the case that the contemplation of the beautiful affords us an aesthetic impression which moves and delights the mind. The life and warmth of the feeling of beauty is really to be found in this aesthetic impression. In the absence of that impression the feeling of beauty is cold and indifferent. But what else is this impression than that immediate interest in the beautiful, so well described by Kant — in other words, the religious feeling in the sense of beauty. The sense of beauty at all times involves a judgement of taste, where we recognise the beauty of that which is contemplated; it also involves the impression of the religious feeling, where we sense the significance of the beautiful appearance relatively to eternal truth.

You will, therefore, also easily understand how judgements of the beautiful may occur in a cold form, without this religious feeling. This happens when we get lost in the critique of taste, and thus fail to proceed beyond the mere judgement of taste. One is then not living in the contemplation of the beautiful or in the sense of beauty. One is simply entrapped in a comparative judgement relating, say, to the formation of taste or the making of something beautiful.

Theone: Grandfather, we are grateful to you for your instructions. But you have not yet repelled our first attack. How do matters stand with respect to the beautiful knife-handle, and the beautiful needle-box?

Philanthes: It seems that you think that there are many beautiful objects which are too trivial to be related to the eternal ideas.

Theone: Yes, that does seem to be the case to me.

Philanthes: Do you perhaps know of a better expression for designating what we judge according to the ideas of the eternal?

Theone: The good, perhaps?

Philanthes: Recently, I was speaking to an ordnance blacksmith, and he said to me that he had not seen such good sword-blades as those which I had had made in his workshop for a long while. Now, how is it with the eternal truth of sword-blades? I also think that you women-folk would like good knife-blades for your beautiful knife-handles, and good needles to put in your beautiful needle-boxes.

Theone: But then, what are you really calling good, and what beautiful?

Philanthes: A thing is beautiful if, as Aristotle says, it is pleasing on its own account, and if it is praised because it is thus pleasing. A thing is good if it corresponds to its purpose. Now, the intelligent will acts according to purposes. If something is judged as good, therefore, it is always referred to a will, and to the laws in accordance with which that will operates. With respect to our will, that happens in two radically different ways. We call everything good which is advantageous and useful, everything which, as a means, corresponds to the purposes of our wills. All these means will be referred to a purpose beyond themselves. But above these means there must be that which is good in and for itself, that which is a purpose in itself, that which is a final purpose which bears its value immediately within itself.

Otto: This good in itself is the virtue and healthy appearance of the life of the spirit.

Philanthes: But since this good in itself has all its value, independently of all comparison, within itself, it is also, at the same time, beautiful. You can see that for man virtue is at the same time the good in itself and the spiritually beautiful.

And with that we have arrived at the centre of this whole observation. The spiritually beautiful and the good in itself are one and the same. Since virtue is pleasing to us on its own account, without any comparisons and, so to speak, simply as a natural phenomenon, and since the appearance in virtue corresponds to the value of things absolutely, corresponds to the purposes of the universe — because this is so, we call virtue beautiful. But, because it is also commanded or prescribed to our will as a final purpose, we call it good in itself.

From this central point of the spiritually beautiful as the good in itself, our judgements now extend in two directions.

In one direction, using distinct concepts, we follow the strivings and achievements of our will, and evaluate purpose and purposefulness relatively to it. Our judgement concerning the good thus extends over everything which can be used for any purpose, even down to the smallest and remotest things.

In the other direction, feeling is led by the representation of inner value, by the representation of a thing's own significance, once more to a judgement of the smallest and remotest things, for fairness of form, symmetry and harmony appear beautiful even in the most trivial of things. And just as that immediate interest in the naturally beautiful, as characterised by Kant, enables us to love beauty even in the smallest product of nature, so too, for the man of cultivation, an artistic taste will also assert itself, a taste which will ascribe value to beautiful form even in the most trivial feature of our environment, and avoid that which is unbeautiful.

In this connection, you will now find the following to be true. The judgement of the good, as far as living feeling is concerned, loses all meaning and becomes an arid matter of concepts as soon as we leave the spiritually beautiful and speak only of what is instrumentally useful. On the other hand, the beautiful, even in the smallest of things, is beautiful in itself, and it thus makes a claim, small as it may be, upon feeling. We find in the arteries of our spirit, even in their finest ramifications, religious feeling, albeit ever so gently stimulated, united with the contemplation of the beautiful.

Adelheid: I think I understand you. Your teaching that the feeling of beauty moves so constantly and so continuously in our spirit, both on a large scale and on a small, is a source of delight to me. For me, this observation rightly distinguishes the truth of beauty, which we daily and continuously recognise in ourselves and which prescribes to life all value and every purpose, from the truth of concepts, which always strides along beside the truth of beauty, and which is on the look out for what is useful, and orders all the instrumental work of life. I now see how we daily live with an all-embracing aesthetic judgement of things.

To this aesthetic judgement there now manifestly belongs religion and piety as well, for it is this, indeed, which is the supreme thing, the most important thing, in the world of the spirit. However, if you now go on to say that the feeling of beauty is completely identical with pious feeling, then I am unable to agree with you. If I look into the great, cheerful, laughing life of nature here before me, then my whole spirit is joyfully moved by the beauty of nature. But this feeling of beauty does not harmonise with what I call religious feeling. For me it is not an immediate stimulus to piety.

Philanthes: I have no difficulty in understanding you. Two reasons condition your judgement: one of them I accept, but the other I wish, in part, to dispute. If you look out upon the laughing, cheerful life of nature, there is much, apart from the beauty of the forms of nature, which affords you entertainment. You are affected by a wealth of charms, which the old Kant forbad, in respect of their effect upon the feeling of beauty. Such a wealth of charms belongs only to sense, to sensation, not to beauty. I was not referring to these charms either.

With reference to your second reason, however, my opinion is that your feeling is too scrupulous. Unless you wish to find devotion in the dull numbing of feeling where no thought is to be found, then you must admit that every pious feeling is animated by an aesthetic idea.

Adelheid: I have no objection to that.

Philanthes: Now, see if you do not underestimate the cheerful ideas of enthusiasm which extend the breast and joyfully drive us out of ourselves into the active life. See if you are not being biassed and only allowing validity to the aesthetic ideas of submission, humility and devotion, ideas which force the spirit back upon itself, and which are of service to the quiet collection of thought.

I do not see what justifies you in esteeming these lyrical and elegiac ideas more highly than the ideas which fill us with joyful enthusiasm.

Theone: This is another case where one surrenders to you in a dispute, and then, when one meets again, one finds one still has the old opinion.

Philanthes: May be! But look! The sun has already sunk into the waves, dusk covers land and sea, the stars are beginning to shine — is it not true, Theone, nature too is growing pious for you?

Theone smiled and replied: Come, father, do not get cold. Let us return home before it gets dark.

Philanthes: But I have not yet reached my conclusion. I must, I suppose, summon your defender myself.

Otto: Very well! Then I declare your dispute with mother a dispute of words! Mother admitted, straightaway, that every pious feeling was moved by an aesthetic idea. But you have only spoken about the feeling of beauty, and shown the religious interest within that feeling, to adopt your way of speaking. But in addition to the beautiful there is the sublime. The feeling for the beautiful inclines ever more towards the intelligible and the earthly, whereas the sublime awakens, with greater immediacy and intimacy, the ideas of eternal truth. The sublime is most firmly joined to faith. What objection can you have to our calling the impression made by the sublime as the symbol of faith the religious feeling *par excellence*. Let the whole wealth of aesthetic ideas pass before your eyes. In the presence of the beautiful, you will, in your joy, combine sensible charms together in a variety of ways, and in your sorrow you will combine sensible emotions in the same way. But now let the mind, in its relation to the sublime, withdraw itself into itself. Outward splendour and sound shall no longer be of assistance to it here. The mind, now most fully in control of itself, and least dependent on outward help, will find within itself the quiet idea of God, the holy idea of peace.

Can you refuse to ascribe this to religious feeling *par excellence*?

Philanthes: How should I wish to do so? The ladies shall today, for once, carry off the victory.

They rose to return. Otto walked dreaming at Theone's side. He had already begun to descry in each of her words, in each of her movements, a significance of its own. And so now, in particular, as she offered him her hand in farewell, and said to him: "Do not forget, we have not yet concluded our common battle against grandfather."

Otto, therefore, hastened to Philanthes' house at the first opportunity, and led the conversation back to the theme of their previous discussion. "Noble Philanthes," he said to the old man, "the dispute of Theone and myself with you is not yet ended. You will, I think, have to give an account of yourself once more."

Philanthes: Renew your attack.

Otto: You recently showed us the relation of the feeling of beauty to religious feeling. But you also promised to make the relation of the feeling of beauty to moral feeling more clear. If you are agreed, let us now pursue this idea. What you have already taught us has prepared the ground for the comparison. The good in itself, you told us, was at the same time the spiritually beautiful. Accordingly, moral feeling is also presumably the taste which judges the beauty of the spiritual life; and the feeling which lives in piety is, so to speak, the religious feeling, which accompanies these judgements of taste about spiritual beauty.

Philanthes: Well, I have no objection to that. If you wish to regard moral feeling as the feeling of beauty, Adelheid will cease to contradict me, too. But you ought to have resisted me, and you could reasonably have done so. Now you have left a bastion, upon the firmness of which you recently seemed to insist, wholly unoccupied. How was it with the inexpressibility of the rules of the beautiful?

Otto: Ah! I have already taken possession of that bastion again! You say: all judgement about beauty is based, so to speak, on inexpressible concepts. I do not, however, find that at all confirmed in proportioned beauty. I should have thought that easily expressible concepts lay at the foundation of the judgement of the beauty of human forms, at the foundation of the judgement of symmetry and other beautiful relations in architecture. With respect to the whole of music, how simple are the numerical relations which underlie harmony and, thus, every musical system. It is this which makes the measurement of melodic scales possible.

Philanthes: I have to confess, I am no musician. But I have heard about the hated fifth. I never knew that the combination of the tonic with the octave and the fifth, without the third, yielded a pleasant chord; I never knew that the sequence of notes in a scale, whether ascending or descending, yielded a capital tune.

Otto: Certainly, all these relations are far too monotonous.

Philanthes: I never heard anyone praise the cube or the sphere as beautiful forms. Painters and sculptors also say that a face which is properly symmetrical in all respects is not for that reason beautiful.
Otto: Certainly! The excessively regular is not beautiful.
Philanthes: I should have thought that the monotonic and the regular are never, in and for themselves, beautiful. No regularity of form or motion would be called beautiful if we could immediately understand the rule of that regularity at first sight.

If form or motion are to be found beautiful, then regularity must be present in them. But this regularity is not understood; it announces itself mysteriously, so to speak, to feeling.

Proportionality in music and in form will make an aesthetic impression upon us, as soon as, upon the apprehension of the music or the form, we feel the proportionality. But we shall not be able to reduce it immediately to concepts, we shall not be able, in other words, to express it.
Otto: I agree with that.
Philanthes: In life, however, conceptual judgement is everywhere combined with aesthetic judgement. We shall, accordingly, have to divide beauty into free beauty, which is not bound to any concept of what a thing is supposed to be, and into such beauty as is based upon a rule of what a thing is supposed to be.

In the first case, for example, in the case of the song of the nightingale or of free natural beauty, there is no talk of regularity or play of form. In other cases, however, the beauty is always based upon regularity. This regularity does not in itself render form or play beautiful; but it does contain a condition to which that regularity must correspond, if we are to be able to call it beautiful.

Rhythm is not itself music. But we do demand of beautiful music that it be based upon a regular measure of time. A tree which has been clipped into the form of a vase or even a human figure, and no matter how exactly it has been done, we find grotesque, not beautiful. We here bring to our judgement the requirement as to how a tree ought to look. We thus demand, still more specifically, of a beautiful human face that the drawing of it should be based upon a certain regularity, though this alone does not make it beautiful.

In the case of everything which is beautiful and which admits a rule or even an ideal, there is, therefore, an underlying condition of regularity which is to be specified conceptually. In the absence of this condition, beauty cannot make its appearance here, though beauty never consists in this regularity alone, but in something else which is only captured in feeling, independently of concepts.

Otto: I cannot contradict what you say.
Philanthes: Let us now apply this to the moral feeling.
 To what kind of the beautiful do you reckon the morally beautiful, spiritual beauty?
Otto: To that which admits an ideal.
Philanthes: We shall, therefore, have to examine in what the regularity of the moral life consists relatively to that ideal. We shall also have to examine in what, in the appearance of the moral life, beauty consists, over and above this regularity.
Otto: You have given me some light. I think I can answer myself. The regularity of the moral life consists in dutifulness; its beauty consists in dutifulness; its beauty consists in character or morality. Dutifulness is the condition to which the moral life must be subject and in the absence of which it cannot be beautiful. But the spirit lives in the character. If, therefore, the character from which the life of a person issues does not make its appearance as well, if the person's life does not manifest itself in its morality and love, but only in dutiful exactitude, all that then appears is a dead regularity. If someone only displays the conformity to law of a respectable, honourable and just life, I do not, on that basis, yet know whether he is motivated by the ideas of duty or merely by a love of order, or whatever other insignificant sentiment you please. The contemplation of such a life cannot, therefore, operate upon the feeling. It can only be praised conceptually, on account of its regularity.
 The painting is not animated until the spirit of the love of honour, justice, valour, love, or of whatever other beautiful sentiment, presents itself to contemplation.
Philanthes: Excellent! Now, where does this aesthetic moral judgement belong? Am I to judge life or art in accordance with it?
Otto: I should think both — life and art.
Philanthes: Very well. Let us take life first of all. Here, I can partly judge my own life in conscience, and partly the life of someone else. What, do you suppose, is the situation in respect of one's own life?
Otto: That is peculiar. No one may judge his own life aesthetically; that would be affected. In one's own case, one is bound to the rule.
Philanthes: Why, do you suppose?
Otto: I cannot say, straightaway.
Philanthes: Consider. To which mode of representation is an object given to you, if you have yourself been able to find it beautiful?
Otto: To contemplation.
Philanthes: Well?
Otto: I can see my way now. For me, my life is not an object of con-

templation but of action. It is a task for my will. Its value or lack of value are represented to me as a purpose of my will. I must, therefore, judge my own life, construed as my own achievement, in accordance with the concepts of the good, and not according to the ideas of the beautiful. I must see that I act with prudence and wisdom — with wisdom, however, both in acting dutifully and in acting nobly. I am also aware of my dispositions and, hence, I demand of myself that I should pursue good ones and be loyal to their rule.

Philanthes: I think you are right. In so far as we regard our own life as a task for our will, and, in so far as we strive to realise that task, we must judge it wholly according to the rules of the good. Do you not, however, also find in addition to this an aesthetic judgement about yourself in your conscience?

Otto: Yes, indeed! Certainly! My future action and the bringing about of my actions — this I must judge according to concepts. But when the performed deed really presents itself to me, it is offered to me for contemplation. It thus excites the religiously attributive and evaluative judgement of conscience; and here my action is, so to speak, praised as beautiful, or censured as ugly, for I evaluate the action immediately, in and for itself, without entering into the history of its cause or genesis.

Philanthes: To pursue our question further: how is it with the moral judgement of the life of another person?

Otto: Here I become aware of a peculiar conflict between the judgement of rule-conformity and the aesthetic judgement. I should prefer to ask you for enlightenment about it. This peculiar conflict particularly occurs with a certain judgement of criminals who are declared worthy of punishment; and yet, on occasion, such a criminal is not only pardoned; he must live according to his view of life.

Philanthes: You will readily admit that I only have a regular judgement about the life of another person in respect of the conformity to law of his external actions, that is to say, whether they conform, or do not conform, with our laws of justice, propriety, and other popular moral practices. I shall, therefore, be able to judge regularly whether someone, whose situation I know, has, in an action, acted justly or unjustly, morally or immorally. The judgement will also be the same if I put myself, with my conviction, in his position, and then ask how I ought to have acted.

But, in doing this, the other person's conviction has not yet been taken into account, nor has the action yet been related to his sentiments. Now, here it will frequently be very difficult to adopt the other person's way of thinking. It will, for example, be very difficult for me to adopt, in imagination, Jewish, or Mohammedan, or Chinese convictions with all their subleties — and so on in a thousand other cases. But I can never know the character of another person according to rules; I can never get beyond an evaluation according to feeling.

We shall, accordingly, never lay claim to more than an aesthetic judgement about the inner life of someone else, always focusing our gaze on the spiritually beautiful or ugly appearance of that life. Indeed, since, in the last analysis, our whole life in its subtler form and concordantly with the requirements of reverence and pure love is moved and guided by feeling alone, all living moral judgement merges into the aesthetic evaluation of an ideal beauty.

Otto: There now remains the famous and much disputed question: How do the moral and aesthetic judgements coincide in the judgement of the artistic presentations of human life?

It seems to me that the whole difference here is a difference of the conditions of presentation, and that the genuine judgement about spiritual beauty must, for art, be taken from life, so that what is found praiseworthy here must be exactly the same both in life and in art.

Philanthes: Now, in what do you find the different conditions of presentation?

Otto: In the case of poetry, a very large number of secondary determining factors operate upon our judgement. They are, in part, factors which do not occur in life at all, and, in part, factors which can be easily excluded.

Above all, the conditions of presentation. As little as verse distinguishes poetry from prose, so little shall we want to call any story a work of art. If someone is unable to present things intuitively, then he must not expect an aesthetic judgement of his stories at all. For this reason, we must banish the majority of our entertaining storybooks from the realm of pure taste altogether.

But let us suppose that we are dealing with stories which really do offer themselves to contemplation. The creative writer has a thousand means at his disposal, apart from beauty of soul, for arousing the interest of his reader and affording him entertainment. He has at his disposal, for example, so many descriptions of the charming and the moving, of the mysterious and the thrilling; there is also suspense, as well as innumerable fantastic descriptions. By these means the writer can attract his reader without touching the supreme tasks of presenting beauty of soul, though he can combine the above means with that supreme undertaking.

Now, if we isolate the real representations of spiritual beauty, there is but one estimation valid for them, both in art and in life.

Philanthes: But I have frequently heard it said that the poets and creative writers are not bound to the manuals of morality.

Otto: I find the proposition repugnant. It has primarily gained currency in order to protect that foppish and lascivious literature which has chosen as its Muse the Indian dancing girl, the Bajadere. Lasciviousness is as little lovely in literature as it is in life. Imagination's flights of lascivious fancy — they can titillate the senses of youth — have been confused with literature. That this has happened seems to me to be nothing but evidence of the impoverishment of the feelings of the nations which allow themselves to be pleased by such productions.

Philanthes: But that does not exhaust the matter.

Otto: Far from it. The error could also lie with the composers of the manuals of morality, or even with the writers of novels. When the composers of the moral handbooks are not themselves acquainted with beauty of soul, and can do no more than lay down prescriptions about the external forms of a just, honourable and respectable life, then, of course, no judgement of taste is involved at all. On the other hand, we often hear the portrayal of all too great heroes of virtue subjected to censure — and this for the same reason! The mere description of the regularity of a law-governed process does not affect the aesthetic feeling at all. It is the soul of the moral life which is supposed to make its appeal through the portrayal. Without spiritual depth, the painting has no poetic significance. There is, therefore, for art no greater task than the portrayal of an invincible hero of virtue. But the artist must possess the power of breathing life and soul into his picture. He must not operate merely according to a cold rule.

Philanthes: I should like to add something to what you have said. The creative writer has a one-sided power over our attention, and this is something which cannot happen in life itself. The writer is, accordingly, able to introduce a feature of moral beauty into a life which is otherwise squalid, corrupt and criminal, and in so doing he is able to complete a beautiful picture.

Otto: Certainly! And in this way, literature comes to have a great variety of tasks when it comes to attractive portrayals.

Philanthes: But what is your opinion about the view maintained by some that it is only the quite exceptional and magnificent work of art which is to be esteemed worthy?

Otto: It seems to me that this opinion is mistaken. As far as the area of aesthetic ideas extend in nature and in life, thus far do the claims on art extend as well. The true world of art should be animated by all the forms of the beautiful, from the small to the great, from the tenderest to the most powerful and the most magnificent. Certainly, the value of artistic tasks is very diverse, the portrayal of the most sublime spiritual greatness outshining every other task. But among these tasks, even the humblest is of importance to taste, provided that it pays hommage to an aesthetic idea.

Theone: When Ruisdael paints a view of a mere beech-grove, or Gerhard Dow simply shows us a peasant girl opening the shutters of her room with the first rays of the morning sun, the result may be a beautiful painting as well, may it not?

Otto: That is my opinion. And the same thing occurs with the portrayal of character, too. Even in the smallest portrait, innocence, contentment, love, loyalty and every other beauty of spirit, will achieve its objective, if the poet knows how to paint with warmth and life.

In every type of epic and dramatic poetry, the tasks ascend, by a thousand gradations, from the idyllic, the humorous, the comic, or the elegiac to the heroic epos and true tragedy. And none of these realms should be missing from the world of beauty.

But any work of art is to be dismissed as unworthy, no matter how much representational energy has been expended upon it, if it does not serve beauty, but has betrayed itself to primitive sensuality, lasciviousness, malice, mockery, delight in what is ugly or like the ugly.

Philanthes: We have traversed the circle of our observations. You will now appreciate how religious feeling lives in our whole aesthetic view of the world, as that view manifests itself both in life and in art. You will also understand how the whole aesthetic view of the world has its focus and unique source of vitality in the moral life, in reverence and in love.

Noble greatness of soul, as it animates the highest ideals of epic and dramatic poetry, is the dominating ideal of this world. Every beauty of soul, including the tenderest form of spiritual life, attaches itself to that noble greatness of soul. And from here, it is only the comparison with the spiritual which leads us further; it is this alone which causes the play and the form of the phenomena of nature to appear beautiful to us. On the analogy with how we find the spirit by means of the human form, beauty leads us into the world of forms as well, for it is beauty which animates the form. Even motion is animated by increases and decreases of the pulsebeat and muscular movement, for it is by means of the latter that the living spirit feels that it is in the world of motions. Dance and music are only beautiful in virtue of the measurements of time which repeat the rhythms of our vital motions.

Otto: You are now leading us to the last of the things which you recently promised to discuss, namely, the question: what is the significance in general of the aesthetic view of the world?

Philanthes: Wilhelm Meister's journal tells us this:

> The beautiful makes the thoughts of the soul like a harmony of colours, makes its feelings like an accord of sounds, makes its life like a melodic song, which soothes away all tears, assuages all seeking, lends a flush to every palid fear, garlands all love, fills every void, heals every wound — or makes the thoughts of the soul like a noble and charming picture created by God, when he wished to make an image of himself, and took the elements of the human world for that purpose. — There is nothing more beautiful than a soul which, without writing any works, forms itself poetically within and creates the beautiful in itself.
>
> The beautiful combines all opposites. The person of purity with fervid patriotism wishes to die the plain death of self-sacrifice; and he wishes to sit quietly by the lotos flowers with Sakontata at the side of the Ganges — he wishes both, because each is beautiful. He wishes to wander in freedom far afield through the whispering forests of the Alps, through the dawn-pink Orient, through all the lovely places of the earth; and, like a child, he also wishes not to stir from all the beloved places within the narrow limits of his home — he wishes both, once more because each is beautiful. The truly reflective man thus always chooses — boldly or modestly, powerfully or gently, with hope or full of reminiscences, flourishing or declining — the truly reflective man thus always chooses *one* ideal, which, like Brahma, manifests itself in a hundred forms as *one*, the *divine in the image of the beautiful*.

Let this, dear Otto, be our text. I should prefer to have it explained by my father.

He called Theone, got her to bring him a book of manuscripts, found one of the speeches of Evagoras, and got her to read it aloud. It was as follows.

Evagoras: Three rulers rule in the human spirit: wisdom, piety and valour. Three leaders guide us under their dominion: the spirit of truth, the spirit of beauty, the spirit of glory.

But no jealously guarded borders separate the realms of these rulers in the sphere of the human spirit. United together in the manner of a trinity, each rules over the whole life of the spirit, each acknowledges complete obedience where the service of the one is united with that of the other. For the highest command of wisdom is justice, that it should acknowledge the valour and independent power of the spirit. The highest command of piety is surrender to the Eternal Love which created the world, and enthusiasm for the moral will and the ideals of spiritual beauty, where homage to valour is required. But the supreme command of valour is purity of soul. And in that purity of soul, valour, furthering dignity and grace, subjects life to the power of the spirit of beauty.

In this unity of life we now wish to contemplate the *realm of beauty*. To that realm there belongs, we know, the religious and aesthetic view of the world. The fundamental ideas of that view are the ideas of religious conviction: the elevation of faith to the divine and the eternal above all the vicissitudes of finite appearances, and faith's elevation of the perfect and the eternal above the imperfectibility of all scientific knowledge. But we experience this truth of faith in intuitive awareness of the aesthetic view of the world.

Alongside the realm of the insight of our cognitive spirit with its ideal of truth, there lies the realm of the active life with its ideals of goodness, and the realm of the contemplative inner life with its ideals of beauty.

Now, what is the objective of this inner life, which exists alongside understanding and will, for the life of man? Our reply is that it serves religion. Its objective is the animation of the supreme idea of spiritual peace and self-understanding. And it aims to realise that objective by reconciling the mind of man to his dread of his eternal destiny. This reconciliation allows the solemn and serene faith in Eternal Love — a faith which belongs to eternal hope — to prevail in the healthy feeling of man.

But this solemn sublimity of devotion and sacrifice, and the serious power of enthusiasm, are nothing but the fundamental ideas which are to be found in the deepest recesses of our spirit. It is by their means that the contemplative inner life is stirred. And we can even follow its stirrings in the light and cheerful, in the gentle and sad moods which belong to the quickly changing play of our amusements.

In this way, we subject the aesthetic world, the inner life, to the truth of beauty which illuminates our spirit with a pure unclouded brilliancy. It is darkened by and exposed to no error. On the contrary, the truth of beauty is served by everything which it invites into its service.

We find life so wonderfully multifarious in form in the aesthetic ideas that, whatever form life may assume, it only serves to make the transformations of eternal beauty manifest.

The splendour of the sun or the mildness of the moon, the lightness of the day or the darkness of the night, meadows full of flowers or the Milky Way glowing in the sky, the babbling of children or the sacrifice of heroic death — all will be the living appearance of beauty, beauty eternally youthful.

Light and joy lead the enthusiastic gaze to the eternally pure origin of all things — and even when the old man mournfully laments that the flower-decked dreams of youth have not ripened to fruition, the spirit of beauty again replies: why do you seek the interpretation and the fulfillment of the dream while you are still dreaming the dream? Does not every flower-decked dream of youth point to the eternal morning, the dawn of which presents itself unclouded to your soul? Is not every flower-decked dream its own fulfilment in the light of this eternal morning, where only the inner beauty of life is important?

What, then, should all this inner life and all its tranquil contemplation, from the solemnity of religion to the light play of lovely dreams — what should all this be for the life of man, alongside the realm of power and deed?

The pure splendour of the light which we see immutably streaming from the archetypal source of the sun also radiates from the fleeting evanescence of the golden mists of morning. So too, it is the same light of the spirit of the high eternal destiny of man contained in the feeling of the immortal independence of our spirit — it is that same light which manifests itself immutably to us in the splendour of the ideas of moral power, and which also plays past us in the lightest gleam of beautiful dreams.

And this aesthetic development of the spirit is deeply significant for the whole person, *for the impulses to action issue in their highest purity from the spirit, and the true purposes of spiritual activity are first named in the contemplative life*.

Knowledge and the insight of knowledge has validity for the understanding; its wish is to order and guide the business of man and its machine-like being. Its truth is of service to the instrumental interventions of the active life. But in respect of the first recognition of the true purposes of human life, only feeling can purely instruct him. Aesthetic truth, the truth of beauty, is here the proper guide.

Here is to be found the power of religion. But here there is also to be found the power of that vital freedom which is the distinctive mark of the play of aesthetic ideas.

This vital freedom, in contrast to the constraint of everyday affairs, is the precious possession both of aesthetic development and the distinctive world of the feelings — for the individual in respect of the world of thought which cheerfully ranges, wide and free, and for the nation in respect of the life which cheerfully manifests itself in festivities and celebrations.

With this thought we ought to escape from the painful preoccupation with possessions and power characteristic of the everyday life of affairs to the free movement of thought — even if it merely dwells in the misty metamorphoses of dreams. And the life of the nation ought also, on occasion, to emerge from its everyday effort, from the sweat and dust of labour into the world of festive decorations and cheerful festivity, so that life may, once in a while, be a source of refreshment for each person.

Our wish, therefore, is that the aesthetic life of the nation should be guided towards religious solemnity in public devotion and enthusiasm. But, to begin with, we shall have to kindle that devotion and enthusiasm in patriotic fashion, by seeking to make the festivals once more the objects of veneration, not in the gloomy sense of sinfulness, or in musing introspectiveness, but in cheerful joyfulness. Festivals and celebrations ought, once more, to lead us to a free and cheerful national life, so that the thought of the nation may, in freedom and dignity, escape from its everyday preoccupation with common toil, so that life may, with its own power, give form to itself.

But what is the national spirit other than the unity of spiritual communication arising from the life of the individuals? The energy and life of the individuals produces the energy and life of the whole. That is why the following wise counsel applies to each person: in order to keep the spirit youthfully free in the midst of the life of business, each person should, in festive mood, give way to enthusiastic rapture in resonant and richly coloured dreams, fortifying and vitalizing himself with the great achievements of genius from all periods of history, but especially of the genius of his own country.

This is no mere implement for the individual, no mere plaything for the child, no mere trifle of whim — it is part of the great service of patriotism, part of the spirit of our nation.

Theone had come to an end.

Otto: See how Evagoras' dreams have come to fruition. He was able to unite our nation around the newly revived festivities, and his spirit will continue to lead us.

It is now clear to me how the public life of the nation acquires, and ought to acquire, this aesthetic-religious view of the world in the powerful uniting of its whole life around festivals which are regarded as sacred. It is also clear to me how the really positive aspect of religion is an independent and living force in the nation, free from all conflict with superstition and error. Finally, it it clear to me that such religion belongs, not to any individual official department of the state, nor to any one part of civil life, but to the fullness of the entire life of the nation, as beauty belongs to the flower.

Index

action, and contemplation, 12–13, 30–1
Aeschylus, 76, 123
Almighty, the, 10, 92, 207
Aristotle, 103, 194, 204, 220, 229
art, of a nation, 122f.
beauty, 77–9, 106–7, 175, 178–98, 203, 206–7, 214, 220–46
    artistic, 227
    contemplation of, 231
    development of sense of, 132f.
    heavenly origins of, 15
    and religious feeling, 112, 119–20, 126–8; (distinction between) 225
    of soul, 14–32, 35, 38–41, 184, 193, 201, 204, 237, 240
    sublime, 11, 50, 54, 72, 74f., 101, 153, 184, 187, 192, 203
    varieties of, 225f., 229
    and the world, 81, 133
Bible, the, 111
Buddha, 111

cause, and effect, 59–60
certainty, 54, 55
    and probability, 167
    and proof, 198
    and self-evidence, 58, 64
    and the senses, 56
character, 30
Christianity, 108
    essence of, 107
class distinction, 113
community of saints, 107
conscience, 5, 100, 132, 200
contentment, inner, 131, 221–2
conviction, 6, 8, 199
    immediate, 59, 64
    moral and religious, 65–6, 100, 125
    and proof, 128
Creator, the, 162, 183, 198, 200, 207, 217
    and creation of, 162
culture, and religious ideas, 98f.

dance, 239
death, dread of, 9
    love of, 8
    and purification, 203
    tranquillity in face of, 9, 12
deception, 61
dependence, feeling of, 100
destiny, of man, 191–2
Divine, the,
    contemplation of, 12
    education, 95
    ideas of, 53
    symbolic significance of, 53, 92
duty, 185
    and beauty of soul, 3–5, 38–41

education, 44, 109, 115
    of children, 39
    divine, 95
    and enlightenment, 159
egoism, 27–9, 180
eleatics, 157

eternal, 207, 215, 229
   destiny, 10—11, 219, 242
   goodness, 68, 85
   life, 178
   love, 196, 200—9, 217—18, 241; (and vicissitudes of fortune) 210
   no immediate knowledge of, 216
   reward and punishment, 48—50, 106, 204—5
   truth, 103, 105, 125—57, 172, 178—9, 181, 183, 186—7, 197—9, 201
eternity, 47, 51, 65, 178, 192, 217
   and nature, 75
evil, problem of, 206—7
evolution, 166
experience, inner, 174

faith, 46, 53—4, 100, 103, 168 178—99, 205, 232
   and feeling, 46f., 158, 160, 163
   and intellectual development, 199
   and knowledge, 60, 137—40, 153, 157—8, 177, 200—1, 218
   and moral self-reliance, 68
   and negative limitations, 140
   and reflection, 60
   and trust, 60, 67
   and virtue, 159—60
fantasies, 133f.
fate, 10—11, 44, 50, 76, 92, 106, 170, 183, 207
feeling, 53, 134f., 178, 184, 243
   and faith, 46f., 158, 160, 163
   moral, 198, 233, 235
   for the world, 80—1, 85, 95, 212, 214
   religious, 233
   and religious beauty, 112, 119—20, 126—8, 193, 219, 233
   serious life of, 140
   what belongs to, 91
Florian, 223
freedom, 178, 218
   from vicissitudes of life, 7f.
   and virtue, 159—60
   of the will, 141, 180, 199, 201, 206, 217

Genghis Khan, 29
Gessner, S., 223
ghosts, 62, 134
glory, 240
God, 3, 11, 30, 34—6, 39, 47—8, 50—1, 60—6, 70—2, 76—87, 89—92, 94, 99—100, 111, 115, 117, 129, 134, 151—5, 162—3, 172, 178—9, 181, 183, 186—7, 193, 198—9, 203—9, 213, 220—4, 232, 240
   God-fearing spirit, 12
   in history, 171
   holy will of, 203
   idea of not derivative, 67
   and negative limitations, 141
   proofs for existence of, 55, 66, 126, 198
   purposes of, 87f.
Goethe, J. W., 77
good, functional use of, 229—30
good, the, 175, 178—97, 213
Greek Orthodoxy, 116
guilt, 99, 198—208

habit, 25
happiness, 24—5, 51, 88—9, 220—1, 223
heaven, 48, 92
hell, 48
Hesiod, 83
higher beings, naive belief in, 210—11
history, 96
Homer, 121
human nature, and contemplation, 36
humility, 202—3

images, 82, 94, 96—7, 112, 117, 119
imagination, 61
immortality,
   physical, 180
   of the soul, 55, 141, 178—9, 218
   and truth, 121

infinity, paradoxes of, 149
intuition, 188, 192, 196
   and measurement, 147–8
   and the thing itself, 121
intuitive awareness, 197, 209–19

judgement, of others, 21–3

Kant, I., 198, 226–30
kingdom of ends, 186, 189
kingdom of God, 183
   on earth, 107
kingdom of heaven, 155
knowledge, 30, 63, 165, 169–70, 175–6, 206, 242
   and faith, 60, 137–40, 153, 157–8, 177
   and knowing, 157–77
   of other minds, 151, 174
   and perception, 54–5
   and proof, 54–5
   and scepticism, 64
   and self-evidence, 54–5
   and the senses, 137–46
   and testimony, 54
Koran, the, 111

language, 46, 69, 102, 174
   physical and mental, 143
Leibniz, G. W., 198, 207
Lessing, G. E., 194
life,
   aesthetic judgement of, 235
   contemplation of, 236
literature, 98
love, 178, 220
   divine, 84
Lutherans, 116

means–ends relations, and the world, 91
metaphor, 69, 101, 105–6, 117, 179, 216
   and the thing itself, 69
mind, power over body, 52
miracles, 51

moral demands, 181, 202, 206, 223
moral development, 99, 132
moral ideals, 223
   and education, 134
   and the spirit, 33–45
moral inadequacy, 200–2
moral practices, 109
moral prescriptions, 201
music, 233–4, 239
mystery, 52, 121, 124, 191, 195, 237
   necessary and contingent, 215–16
   religious, 215
myth, 69, 106–7, 121–2

naturalists, 163
natural religion, 111
nature, 10, 53, 74
   aesthetic view of, 229
   contemplation of, 90, 210, 226
   and eternity, 75
   laws of, 50, 52, 101, 145, 162–6, 169–70, 173, 180, 182–3, 188–9, 199, 207
   and mathematics, 166–7
   organic, 166–7
   and the sublime, 228
   understanding of, 90, 133, 137
needs, 26
number, 138

omnipotence, 10–11, 30, 65, 85, 88, 187, 197, 199, 207
omnipresence, 65
omniscience, 135–43, 151–2

Pascal, B., 165
Paul, the Apostle, 154, 157
perception,
   causal account of, 56–7
   and certainty, 57
   and knowledge, 54–5
perfection, 182, 198–9
personality, 179
Plato, 103, 121, 133, 157, 199, 201
pleasure, 184–5, 220, 223

poetry, 79–80, 123, 214, 216, 218–19; (lyric) 176
positive ethics, 108
positive religion, 101f., 117f.
practical wisdom, 7, 146, 191
prayer, 35, 93, 208–10
primitives, 34, 37, 112
propositions, truth of, 58
Providence, 83–97, 197, 236
prudence, 132, 171–2, 203–4, 209, 213
  and wisdom, 35, 37–8
public life,
  and the individual, 35, 41–5
  and the nation, 110
purity of will, 196, 218

rationalists, 111, 164, 169, 172
rationality, 137
religion,
  and aesthetics, 188–9
  of the heart, 100
  and morality, 35–7
religious,
  consolation, 93
  convictions, 65, 68; (expression of) 69f.
  education, 125f.
  mysteries, 215
  practice, 69, 98–124
  tolerance, 116
  truth, 54, 110
resurrection, of the body, 179
Roman Catholics, 116

sacrifice, 192, 224
sanctimoniousness, 195
scepticism, 64, 128f., 132
Schiller, F., 77
science, 159
  and education, 53
  limits of, 168
  and understanding the world, 80–2, 85

self-evidence, 57–9, 158
self-interest,
  and market-place, 28
  and morality, 130f.
self-knowledge, 173
self-preservation, 189
sentimentalism, 195
Shakespeare, W., 77
Socrates, 210
Sophocles, 76, 123
soul,
  beauty of, 14–32, 35, 38–41, 184, 193, 201, 204, 237
  immortality of, 55, 141, 178–9, 218
  peace of, 2–13, 20–1; (distinguished from error) 14f., 19; (distinguished from passivity) 14f.; (and freedom from vicissitudes of life) 7f.; (how to gain it and preserve it) 6f., 15f.; (and the satisfaction of desire) 4–5; purity of, 20–1, 196, 241
space, 136–8, 142, 144–5, 148–9, 163, 179
spirit, 15, 32, 63, 158, 175, 198, 224
  God-fearing, 12
  and higher good and virtue, 15
  independence of, 16f., 20, 26–7, 29–31, 202, 242
  moral development of, 19f., 33–45, 134, 171
spiritual, 239
  anthropology, 175
  ideals of sublimity and beauty, 15f., 19
  intrinsic value of, 15
  interpretation of the world, 70, 179
  life, 151, 225, 239
state, the, 113f., 159, 244
submission, 51, 100, 194, 197, 202, 208
suffering, 93
supernaturalists, 163, 169
superstition, 33–4, 51–4, 64, 67, 106, 113–14, 117–19, 159, 205

symbolism, 69, 82, 101, 106, 109, 112–13, 117, 119–20, 124, 134
   and denominations, 116
   and the nation, 105

taste, 212
   relativity of, 21
teleological concepts, 189
Theocritus, 223
theodicy, 207
time, 136–8, 142, 144–5, 148, 163, 178
tragedy, 76, 239
truth, 175, 220, 240
   aesthetic, 242
   and error, 63
   eternal, 103, 105, 125–57, 172
   finite, 135
   holy, 218
   immediate, 111
   innate, 68
   necessary, 126f.
   and poetry, 214, 216, 218–19
   and propositions, 58
   religious, 54, 110

Vedah, the, 111
Virgil, 223

virtue, 30, 193–4, 221, 230, 238
wars of religion, 116
will, 32
   moral, 20
   purity of, 196, 218
wisdom, 236
world,
   and aesthetic judgement, 201, 203, 207
   aesthetic-religious view of, 79–80
   final purpose of, 85–7, 89, 190, 206, 213, 230
   history, 87
   mental and physical, 164
   non-being of the physical, 142
   physical interpretation of, 70, 164
   transfigured view of, 79–80
   wonder at, 89
world-views,
   astronomers, 150
   human, 144
   mathematical, 145
   moral, 152
   outer sensible, 144
worth,
   difficulty of discernment, 22–3
   and external circumstances, 16–17
   inner, 19

Zwinglians, 116

BJ
1107
.F74
1982

CANISIUS COLLEGE LIBRARY
BJ1107 .F74 1982
Dialogues on moralit

3 5084 00176 8913

CANISIUS COLLEGE LIBRARY
BUFFALO, N. Y.